Diary of a Dad

Aurora Seraph

Copyright © 2017 Aurora Seraph

Cover design © 2017 Aurora Seraph

Cover art © 2017 Aurora Seraph

All rights reserved.

No part of this publication may be reproduced or used in any matter without the express written permission of the author except for the use of brief quotations in a book review.

ISBN-10: **1999758005**
ISBN-13: **978-1999758004 (Aurora Seraph)**

This book is written of non-fiction. I have related to the best of my knowledge. All identities, other than those clearly in the public domain, have been changed or are composites. I give notice that the book is authorized- written with the help and backing of the subject, reconstructed from memory.

For my angel above

For all those times you said...
"write the book"

I did it!

prologue

There comes a time in one's life, I believe, where we say the words, "if only I knew what I know now". Some of us, probably most of us, would give anything to have a helping hand, by way of a crystal ball. To be able to see, or even have the slightest little peak at our life ahead, to know if we end up where we would like to be.

But no, that's cheating. You have a life and you must live it. Day by day, the highs and lows. If everything was so simple in life we would never know the meaning, or have the know-how, of making things better.

When situations arise that very easily push us into a corner, we only ever have two choices. Stay there - accept that we are there, have the 'oh well' attitude, spend our days and nights in that very corner wishing for that magical crystal ball, hoping life will change on its own or.... CHANGE IT ourselves!

I'm no life coach but I think we all learn, one way or another, that sometimes, life hits you and if you do not change certain negative aspects, they can spiral out of control. The things we moan about but never act on. The things we write off as nothing when they are, in fact, everything. The wrongs that happen in our lives that we do not put right.

Being pushed into a corner can be defined in so many ways. Many situations can lead you there. Majority of the time we are put there purely because of our own doing or we have allowed others the power to do so.

I was in a corner. The room was huge in my mind. A spacious room made that corner bearable but, by conditioning my brain to think like that, accepting things 'are how they are', sugar coating what put me in that spot in the first place, was in no way going to make my life better at all and I was going to learn that whether I liked it or not. If anything, my non-actions made that room get smaller and smaller to the point where I could hardly breathe, let alone move. Not only was my life not going to get better, if I didn't stand up and intervene, but it could get a whole lot worse and way out of control.

It did.

My journey ahead was going to be tough. Tougher than I ever imagined. It's not until you have been through something, that you can look back and see where you went wrong, what you SHOULD have done. I'm aware of where I went wrong.

One thing very nearly kept me in that corner. Pride. Manly pride. That 'me man, me strong' attitude and fear. Fear brought on by pure, unconditional love which, in turn, brought weakness and contradicted any manly pride I, indeed, thought I possessed. I then faced those choices. Stay in that corner or get out. I chose to get out. Eventually. I had too. For my kids' sake. For my own sake.

Later, rather than sooner, and there was to be a lot of suffering before any sight of a silver lining.

This is my story.

This was my life.

I am a parent. I am a Father.

chapter one

I've never really been one of the 'lads'. You know, out every weekend and loving every minute of it. Yes, I went out and had fun but it wasn't the routine I wanted. Having them 'beers', wasting all my wages, certainly wasn't going to get me 'that house' or 'that car'.

I always dreamt of an attractive, joyous life and I've never been afraid to work hard to get those results. This is quite an ironic statement for me to make really, which will come clear as my story unfolds. I honestly never thought I would ever end up in the situation I was in.

I always wanted more, especially when I didn't start off with very much to begin with. Being in my twenty's, I think it was a good way to be. Wanting to lay foundations. The area I was living in, where I grew up, was changing. I had been noticing it for a while. It wasn't where I wanted to be and, as I got older, it felt like it wasn't where I was supposed to be either. I wanted a better life and I was going to try, and hopefully not fail, to achieve it.

I had plans and I wanted them in motion. First things first, move away from this place. The place where everyone seemed to be standing still, not going anywhere and not caring that they weren't either. I had nothing holding me back. I had worked hard, I had done right by my savings, so I began looking for properties far away from the area. I was going. Bye-bye. Good riddance! My new life was in the process of becoming reality.

Family. That word has always meant a lot to me and always will do too. I would visit Marie, my sister, as often as I could. Seeing her meant I got to see Kaine, my nephew, too. Being an uncle is a great feeling. A first-hand experience at being a dad when you have no children of your own.

It was here I was to meet Carrie. A girl, not that much younger than me, who lived in the same complex as my sister. Carrie was a young single mum and after getting to know her, over the course of visiting, we got on quite well. Sofie, her daughter, was six months old at the time and a delight to be around. Such a funny little thing. I recall times where I would walk through the front door and immediately catch a glimpse of her. Her eyes would light up at the sight of me.

My visits became more frequent, as my relationship with Carrie grew. Over the course of time, I started to learn about her. I found myself feeling sorry for this young mum. She seemed like she was in a life that she didn't belong in. Didn't deserve. Bringing up a child on her own because the father couldn't care less about this little life that he had helped create. Or so I was lead to believe.

A first-time parent that seemed to, at times, not be coping well. Sofie came across strong-minded from a young age. She wasn't a 'sit in a bouncer, watching television' kind of kid. She needed stimulating and loved constant attention and interaction. It is only now, years later, that I see a different picture, the real picture. Sofie wanted attention because she wasn't getting it often.

I recall Carrie's technique of getting Sofie to sleep. She would cradle her in her arms, most times with Sofie crying, then Carrie would start to vigorously shake her up and down. To me, this didn't look normal. The movements were hard and Sofie's head would jolt back and forward, but I was no parent. Who was I to judge if this was right or wrong? If this was how a mother got her child to sleep, then it was none of my business. Who was I to say otherwise? Somewhat strangely bizarre, but it did get Sofie to sleep and as my relationship with her mother grew stronger, so did my feelings for Sofie. She seemed to flourish around me and it was clear that my relationship with her mother was having a tremendously positive impact on her.

Carrie very rarely spoke about her family in the beginning. I remember her nan visiting on the odd occasion but we did visit her nan once. Which is where I met Alf, Carrie's grandfather. He came across quite rude and obnoxious and ignored Carrie the whole time we were there. It was rather uncomfortable but again, who was I to be nosy.

Carrie, along with Sofie, started to stay over at mine the odd night or two. She would sometimes just pop over in the day if she wasn't staying overnight. She would offer to do my washing and bring it back when she was due to stay over, which I found sweet of her. We had fun together, we would laugh about stuff, play with Sofie, watch movies. Dating stuff, I suppose.

One time, though, our views clashed. We were watching something about war, I can't remember exactly what was said, only that, to me, it was largely trivial. Carrie didn't like my opinion and she turned it into a huge debate. I had one of those little bottles of pop in my hand and, as I was about to take a drink, she whacked it, making it catch my lip. I was amazed at what had just happened but also found it funny in a way. Perhaps I found it funny because she was being so childish, I don't know. Regardless, there was no need for Carrie to get so uptight. Her action was over the top. She had giving me a fat lip and made me bled a little. She later apologized and seemed embarrassed. We laughed it off saying it was our first fight.

As I got caught up in this new-found love affair, I had forgotten that my plans were, very much, still in motion. I was to leave this area. In months to come in fact. Leaving a new relationship would have been easy, I think. It was early days. I could have talked my way out of it by looking at the bigger picture, that was already in place before the relationship even started, but Sofie!? Walk away from Sofie too? She wasn't mine, I told myself. Probably to convince myself that it was perfectly acceptable to leave, that I would not have been the 'bad guy'. That I bared no resemblance to her real father.

Looking at Sofie, seeing Sofie looking back at me, that was not what I was feeling in my heart, at all. I loved this little girl. I had strong feelings for her mum, I don't think it was madly deeply in love but, still, I was soon to leave. It will probably sound so profound but I had this sense that leaving Sofie wasn't what I was meant to do. I had this weird feeling of 'don't leave her behind'.

Time was ticking and I needed to decide. To end this relationship and continue on the road I was making for myself or, stay and make a new road that involved two extra passengers. I knew for certain that my life was not in this place and that I now had strong positive feelings that my life was maybe meant to involve Carrie and Sofie. In all honesty, Sofie being in my life was a stronger feeling than her mothers. Her real father abandoned her, I don't think I could ever live with that on my shoulders. Biological or not. I altered my plan slightly, still set on a better life but these two people that had come into my life were now going to be on the journey with me.

Carrie and Sofie moved in and we experienced being a 'real' couple for a few months before the actual move. I had laid everything out and explained to Carrie where I was going before I met her, that I had already secured a mortgage on a property. We talked and talked some more. It seemed that we wanted the same things in life. It was also still obvious that Carrie became a mother far too early. She was one of those young mums that needed help and guidance but probably, more so, stability. She continued to rarely speak of family but when she did, the conversation had a negative feel within it. Lacking bonds and love. Again, who was I to judge, how other families behave. My family and I have a strong loving bond. Not everyone is or must be the same.

We became a little family and biological matters didn't change that. I was Sofie's Father. I chose to take on that role and would do right by her. The little girl that had entered my life, now part of my life, was now my life. Carrie's parenting skills seemed to improve slightly. She appeared more confident and Sofie, thankfully on my part, didn't need to be shaken violently to get asleep anymore. I put any silly doubts I had in the back of my mind and put them down to Carrie being young and un-experienced and that, in time, and with age, she would become the parent she was intended to be. I knew it wasn't going to happen overnight. Sofie's crying would always rattle Carrie. It's only now I can say there seemed to be a void between mother and daughter, when there should have been a connection. If any hint of motherhood dawned, it disappeared as quick as it surfaced.

Time seemed to past quickly and the moving date was getting closer. I still had to work so, every morning I was up and out by 8am. I would spend a little time with Sofie before I left, get her up and seat her in her high chair. Carrie was not a morning person at all but I tried to not hold it against her. I would probably be described as one of those annoying risers. You know, the people who whistle in the morning, full of energy, ready to start the day. Fresh as a button as soon as the sun came up, that was me!

Carrie, on the other hand, needed coaxing out of bed. Like a teenager not wanting to go to school. The 'give me five more minutes' huffing and moaning. Maybe Carrie was like that because she never really had any incentive to wake up. Of course, the biggest incentive should have been her child but her life, at one point, was to wake up, see to Sofie, maybe go to town for half an hour then come home, await bedtime and redo the whole routine over. That was her life. That was my excuse on her behalf, obviously. Still, I would ease her into morning before I left the house, making sure she was up before I left.

Off I went to work, rain or shine. I owned a food stall with my father. I've always liked the idea of working for myself. My own boss. I couldn't imagine sitting in an office 9-5, being told what to do, when to do it and how to do it. Restricted on what you can earn. The idea of just 'sitting' makes me itch. Even as a kid, I always needed to be doing something. I needed to be up and on the move. Very much like young Sofie really. Boredom was never an option for me.

My first 'I am the boss' experience came in the way of an ice-cream van in my late teens. This was the start of knowing exactly what I wanted. I wanted to work for myself. I remember giving Marie a lift to school one morning. Of course, she was grateful of the ride but strangely not so much when I pulled up right outside where her friends 'just happened' to be. Cue embarrassing big brother moment. A lift is a lift. You didn't have to walk, you're not late, that's what I thought. Though maybe turning the ice-cream music on as I waved and said goodbye was a tad too much? Having a younger sibling is fun. Us older siblings must do annoying, cringe worthy things like that. It is written in stone somewhere, I'm sure of it.

So many fond memories of that van. It gave me a taster. A taste I didn't want to let go of. It was this that instigated the food stall venture. I borrowed a few thousand from my mum to get it all up and running and gained a plot in Surrey high street. A father and son venture and we enjoyed every single minute of it. Weather is always an issue when you work outside but, regardless, every morning we were there. The business grew quite quickly, as well as the rapport with customers. Yes, it was hard work sometimes, our feet would hurt. Serving hot food to then have cold hands, then hot, then cold, was extremely sore. Yet you do it, don't you? You are always able to find that self-motivated boost. Especially when you enjoy what you're doing. Especially when you see your hard work paying off. When you see satisfied customers coming back, who then recommend you to their colleagues/friends. It's a good feeling. I loved it, and the added bonus of being able to finish every day at 2pm.

With business on the up, I booked our first family holiday. Spain for eight days. Carrie was over the moon and showed extreme excitement. There was a nice family atmosphere around us. The beaches were beautiful and Carrie took every opportunity she could to sunbathe. She was happy. I would be in the pool with Sofie splashing about, no doubt looking like a child myself. Carrie would watch us from time to time but, when sunbathing got too much for her, she would join us in the pool to cool off. It wasn't the greatest, most expensive holiday but it was a family one. The start of many more, I planned. My premade family life seemed settled and I was enjoying my surroundings. I was excited by the move and the journey ahead was a lovely thought.

Then news came. I was already a 'father' but about to become one again. Carrie was expecting my child! To me, we hadn't been together that long to maybe even contemplate starting a family but we had a family already, didn't we. Carrie was happy with it, I was happy with it. Carrie was very, very, happy with it, when I look back on it now. Maybe my approach on the matter made her feel secure and gave her trust, that I wasn't going anywhere, that I wouldn't leave her stranded. The thought of how Carrie become pregnant, when we were so careful, did enter my brain though. I was always under the impression that she was using birth control but, needless to say, I did what was traditionally right. We were soon, after finding out about the pregnancy, engaged to be married.

I get that from my grandfather, my mother's father. Sadly, no longer with us. He passed away when I was about eighteen years old. Cancer stole him, as it does so many. Such a wonderful, lovely man. A strong, by the book, gentleman. He grew up in an era where 'you did the right thing'. So, I did. The engagement seemed to spur on Carrie somewhat, she had a sparkle in her eye, as well as on her finger, as the saying goes. We had so much to prepare for. My, now our, journey involved a wedding eventually and now another child. Life seemed exciting and fast-paced. The moving date could not have come quick enough. I felt so proud! I had brought my own property. Me. On my own, through hard work and now I had others to enjoy it with.

chapter two

New home.... check. My little family happy...... check. And so it started. An empty shell that would soon be filled with memories. It was early in the day but I needed to get this house in a habitable condition by nightfall. I was full of energy and determined to get what was needed, done. The fact I had to go to work the following day aided that mindset. That's what I liked about this new area, I was still able to carry on with my business.

My routine of seeing to Sofie before heading to work didn't change. We both liked it and it was set in stone by this stage anyway. It didn't hinder, I looked forward to seeing Sofie's little face in the morning and the smile on her face showed me she felt the same. My relationship with Carrie was good, though I always had a sense of something. I didn't know what that something was, it was just 'there'. I kept all my feelings to myself because some of them made me feel quite guilty. My partner was now pregnant so of course she was going to be moody sometimes, snappy and tired. That is what I reminded myself.

I took on the house husband role to make things run smoothly. My wife-to-be was carrying my child so easing her load was right. Yet, I never felt like I was a partner easing off pressure. I felt more like a work-horse. I would come home from work, Sofie would come straight to me and very rarely left my side until bedtime. Carrie, at this point heavily pregnant, always looked like she was chewing a wasp the moment I got in. There was always an issue. Always something that she wanted to moan about. I was late home, there was no milk, silly things that, that again, I shook off and excused her for. She was pregnant. A woman. Hormones. Yes, as a man I knew I had no leg to stand on here! Any argument with a pregnant woman would lead to us men bowing our heads. That pregnant card! I laughed at this thought a lot. They want you to go to the shop, you must stop and go. They are tired so tell us we must make dinner. How on earth can us men say no?!

Work mornings were becoming tiring. I was still up though. Still whistling. Indeed, more so because my tiny new person was soon to arrive and, oh, was I ready! The pregnancy wasn't to be straight forward. Carrie was suffering with the late stages of diabetes. We had to make regular visits to the hospital for tests. She was induced a few weeks earlier than the due date and it took a few attempts for our son to arrive. Andrew, our little boy, brought into the world by way of water birth. What an experience that was! The emotions of seeing your partner give birth are so overwhelming. A beautiful, amazing experience that touches your heart and never leaves. I was in no way afraid of fatherhood. Sofie had given me the experience, the confidence, to know I can do it again. I will never forget holding Andrew in my arms for the first time. Something so tiny gives you a powerful feeling. I was so proud. Content with life, wrapped up in happiness.

Carrie was very tired the first few months. I took time off work to be around more but knew I would have to return at some point. I could have stayed at home every day though. Children give you so much joy and I didn't want to miss out on anything but money wasn't going to enter our home with me staying inside it. Money was now, even more, important. I wanted to give my family as much as I could.

I would find myself watching Carrie when she was with the children. Again, something was picking at me. Like someone would poke me on the shoulder to 'look'. For a while I put it down to my own unsurfaced feelings. Perhaps I was so scared of getting parenting from birth wrong, that I was judging everything. What was the right way, what was the wrong way. Should you feel like this, should you feel like that. I just couldn't understand, I think, why Carrie didn't seem like myself. She always gave off an obligated persona. Like she would do something with, or for, the children because she had too rather than wanting too and if given the chance, maybe she wouldn't do it at all. That she would be happy to just sit there and watch someone else do everything.

Again, I ignored myself. I focused on the good, positive feelings and gave the silly thoughts, that seemed to continuously enter my head, a second fiddle. I had too, I needed to feel at ease before I left the house. Andrew was a whingey baby. Always crying! Carrie, again, didn't seem to handle this very well. She seemed more comfortable when he required no attention, like if he was sleeping or in the hands of others. On the flip side, she would beam and be attentive if she was holding Andrew and people were cooing over him. I, on the other hand, was no way phased by the crying, or screaming for that matter. He was a baby. They do that. It is their way of being able to tell us grown-ups that something is wrong or that they want something. Though, in Andrew's case, I believe he just loved crying. He was nicknamed very early on as 'the grumpy old man'. That thought doesn't bring memories of sleepless nights and tiredness, it brings warm-hearted smiles.

I had scheduled when to return back to work, to ensure Carrie would get used to not having me around as much again. She said she would be ok, so once I felt she was ok, and once I felt ok to leave, I went back to work. The first day back was strange, I wanted to be at home. I found myself always wondering what the kids were doing, how they were doing. My routine was the same. Sofie got up with me, I would prepare her breakfast, now with the added routine of Andrew, changing him, and getting both dressed. Once I got into the swing of things at work, my nerves settled and It was nice to see the regular customers again.

One day I could not, for the life of me, get home off my brain. A feeling that I needed to be there. I waited until my father said he was ok to hold the fort and I ran to the telephone box. It was 11am, I phoned Carrie. My phone call had woken her up. As she answered, I could hear Sofie and Andrew in the background crying. It was 11am. It was 11am. That was all I kept thinking, as I listened to Carrie's voice. I could not believe it! How long had they been crying for? What had they been doing while she was asleep? I was angry, in disbelief and concerned. Was this happening every morning? I woke her up every single morning! She was up and awake when I left. Ok, sometimes only awake but still! Was she going back to sleep, back to bed once I had left? Then I did what I always seemed to do, make excuses for her. She was tired. She was allowed to be tired. She was only human. I knew, always, always knew, deep down, that I was lying to myself when I would think things like this. There should have been no excuses and if there were, Carrie should have told me about them when I would ask if all was ok,

"I've not long had a baby. Soooo I didn't wake up! It's not my fault"

Deluded-ness painted that as truth because, within reason, that statement was allowed to be true.

My routine then changed. As well as waking Carrie in the morning to let her know I was leaving, I would then ring her again to make sure she was, indeed, up. The thought of Sofie and Andrew awake for so long on their own was frightening. I was like this worrying mess of a parent. Every scenario would pop up in my brain making it hard for me to focus on work. I would talk to Carrie about it but she would make me feel like I was being pathetic and over dramatic, over a 'blip', a onetime occurrence. Or so she had me believe. Thankfully, my work allowed me to finish every day at 2pm still. Some days would go just fine, others would drag and home time seemed a lifetime away. As soon as that clock struck, that was it, straight home. I would walk in and if everything looked ok, I could relax and breathe.

Sofie, on my returns home, was always such a delight. She would stand and watch me washing all the equipment and we would giggle as I flicked her with bubbles. Andrew would be sat on the kitchen floor helping to wrap potatoes in tin foil, ready for the oven. He loved wearing my gloves, that were obviously ten sizes too big for him. He struggled to get a grip on anything but never wanted to take the gloves off. I would mess about with him,

"Come on Andrew, you've got to be quicker than that"

"Daddy, An-dew. Only. Baby"

It was the cutest thing ever. I can hear his voice right now and my smile is ginormous. Since learning to talk, he would speak about himself in 3rd person, which added to his adorableness.

As soon as work commitments were finished, it was family time. And I loved it! All this happy energy bouncing off us. Being silly, running and chasing each other. Children certainly keep you on your toes and make you feel alive. They manage to make you find energy you never knew you had. Except in Carrie's case. She would be miserable. Every time I played with the children, she would sit there with a look on her face, like I was doing something wrong. She would show happiness towards going shopping or spending money though. If me and the children were playing and making too much noise, she would pull a face, to indicate to us to turn our volume down, while she sat there with her nose in her magazine.

The only way I can describe my life at this point was feelings of separation. It was like me and the children vs Carrie. I don't mean that in a battle sense, more like we were on different sides. Having rare moments of a family unit together. Holding on to those occurrences to feel like a normal family. Life was a puzzle and we were the pieces yet I could never get that sense of 'complete'. I suppose it felt like Carrie was only part of the puzzle when she chose to be. She would be, in a sense, in and out all the time. I slowly learned to judge her moods before interacting with her and it was becoming a factor that, when she got something, when something went her way, she was happy. Don't get me wrong, as a couple we did have many warm moments and mum and dad 'alone time' but Carrie's mood swings made it difficult for things to stay warm.

My family, when visiting, would notice things. Again, there I was, making up excuse after excuse, not wanting them to have bad thoughts about her. Not wanting them to think bad about me. Not wanting to accept the truth, that my family life was showing causes for concern already. As Carrie became less involved with the children, I became more involved to make up the difference. Carrie started to want for things and showed signs of boredom. She soon wanted to learn to drive, which I took as a positive sign. It showed there was motivation, at least of some sort, present.

She got what she wanted because I wanted to see her happy and if I had a way of making that happen, of course I would try and do so. Her lessons were in the evenings so I could tend to the children. Sometimes it looked like she couldn't wait to get away from us. Excitement about learning to drive and the possibilities a license can bring, maybe. She had every lesson she could, and gave it her all. She passed her test and I was very proud of her. I brought her first car not long after.

Everything was going well for us, or at least I thought so. There were weary moments, the odd row, bicker about big things, as well as little. She was still a lazy person but I stopped questioning why Carrie was sometimes the way she was, and accepted, that was the way she was. Warts and all, as they say. Carrie maybe hadn't grown up yet. She still seemed to own that teenager selfish attitude at times, but one day she would snap out of it. I hoped that one day she would.

With work being as good as it was, money was coming into the house making life financially comfortable. We didn't worry about bills, they were always paid and we always had money for anything we wanted. It's how I always wanted life to be. It was a lifestyle like this that enabled us to plan a family holiday again.

Back to Spain but this time to a different part. I also paid for Marie and Kaine to join us. They arrived a few weeks before we were due to fly out.

Marie and Carrie got on well-ish. They had known each other for quite some time, before I even came into the picture. Carrie seemed glad of the female, adult company during the day and rightly so, perhaps. Marie had, again like everyone else, brought up things that she felt the need to say but as I am to my sister, she is to me. We take on a 'do not judge' view in each other's lives, just to be there for one another and listen. She would say the same, that Carrie was lazy. I didn't need to be told this. I was very much aware. I, as well as Marie and, soon, other members of my family, accepted Carrie was Carrie.

chapter three

It wasn't an expensive trip again and this time there were signs of it being so. One of those holidays that look eye-catching on the brochure. As we drove up to our hotel, I remember looking out of the coach window. The island seemed, somewhat, unfinished. We drove for miles, seeing construction sites and mounds of rubble then suddenly, a newly built hotel was in front of us. A very different experience to our last visit to this country. We all laughed at what we were seeing but that humour just made the start of the holiday enjoyable. Something to remember, to look back on and we were to add to this when we entered our apartment.

A fairly small sized place but adequate. Plain walls but with the most awful looking sofa bed. An off-colour orange, patterned, worn out sofa and if you stared at it for too long, there was a chance of it damaging your eyes. Some light switches were, I'm sure, just for show, as they did nothing when pressed. One worked, it turned on the main ceiling light. A misty glass dish with black swirly patterns that, from later inspection, were dead cockroaches. Slightly annoyed at this point but laughed at the thought of how they got up there and if they were put there, why would someone go to that much trouble? Surely removing them from the apartment was the simpler of options? As much as it humoured us, it was still money we had spent. We paid for cockroaches. Things like this annoy me, in the end. You should get what you pay for. Yes, the holiday was cheap but nothing in that holiday brochure said, 'artistic lighting'. Putting that aside, we were dead-set on enjoying our stay. Regardless of what it looked like inside our apartment, there was a part of this country outside that we hadn't seen before. It was Marie's and Kaine's first time out of England, not counting France as a school trip when she was younger. Marie was still high on excitement from being on a plane for the first time in her life.

We went to the town and found it amazingly different to the scenery we saw on arrival. A parade of shops, palm trees and clean streets. One market stall, in particular, brought a memory that we would bring up and laugh about many times in the future. An old-ish market guy took a shine to Marie and, once being told she was my sister, asked me if he could purchase her from me. At first, we laughed, but later learned the guy was being deadly serious. I asked him how many camels he was willing to give me for her. Marie was in no way amused. I however, seeing the mortified look on my sister's face, was. I told you, that big brother nonsense never leaves. It is our purpose!

Entertainment in the evening wasn't much to write home about. Quite bog-standard really. Ok music and ok edible food. We still had such a laugh most evenings. Local alcohol beverages were free, which Carrie loved the idea of and she certainly wanted her money's worth! I enjoyed socially drinking, on the odd occasion, but never had a drink just because it was 'there' or, indeed, free. Carrie would moan,

"You don't know how to enjoy yourself! We're on holiday, why aren't you unwinding?"

You must drink to unwind? We were out having dinner, watching entertainment with our children. The last thing on my mind was 'free booze'. I was enjoying myself, thank you, I thought. I just wasn't enjoying it like she was.

The entertainment was, a tad, cheesy. The show guy asked for people to come up and dance. Carrie thought it would be hilarious to tell him I would do it. I was then egged on by all the other guests because Carrie initiated a chant of my name. I suffer with anxiety so it wasn't really the attention I wanted. I couldn't even read out loud in class when I was a kid! It was quite nerve racking for me and I would have preferred not doing it but Carrie continued to chant my name, as did the other guests, all eyes on me, so there I was, with a few others, dancing away to Y.M.C.A up on stage.

The last few days of the holiday were spent around the swimming pool, with Carrie topping up her tan. The weather was mighty hot and, with the air conditioning not working in the apartment, it was becoming unbearable and we found ourselves reminiscing of home. I would wake up in the morning and see mosquitos swarming around Sofie where her nappy had been soiled during the night. Thank-god the holiday was coming to an end.

We took part in one excursion before leaving. One of the reps had told Carrie about it and she was adamant about us all going. A boat ride to a deserted island. We were only on the island for a few hours and it was a good job too. I have never felt sand so hot in my life! Sofie and Kaine didn't enjoy being there one bit. They had nothing to do there because there was nothing there. The island was merely a place for sunbathing or jumping off the very boat that transported us there. It was certainly impossible to make any sandcastles! We had a boat ride. That's the positive I held onto from that experience. Carrie loved every minute at this island and would have stayed there all day if she could.

Marie stayed at ours for an extra week, once we were back from holiday. It was nice having her with us. She still lived in the area I had moved away from. I would get home from work and she'd wash my pots for me. Big silver catering pots. I could tell she was helping around the house too because the tidying up looked different. The house would be polished. That was definitely Marie because I was the only other person that ever did that kind of cleaning.

If Carrie was tired, Marie would be up early with Kaine anyway, so she would take Sofie and Andrew downstairs with her. She loved being an aunty and the kids loved having her around. As did I. A little while after, Marie returned to her home and life went back to normal, with me working and doing everything I could. Carrie seemed to slowly gain her place of choice and that was where she liked staying most of the time. The sofa.

When I decided to take motorbike lessons, it didn't go down too well. There was even a magazine that came out every two weeks where, as well as an information booklet, you got a motorbike miniature. I made shelves and put them up in the front room. It was my little hobby and I found myself excited, every second Tuesday, when the next addition was due out. I liked the possibility of collecting the whole set, to then one day pass them onto Andrew. I passed my motorbike test and was looking at bikes for sale but Carrie was NOT impressed. Silly idea, she said. She would even begrudge going to the local shop for me to pick up my magazine subscription. She made me feel like I was spending money that we didn't have. We did have it, I know we had it because I was earning it all. Her reaction was ironic because she was happily spending money on our credit cards without care or concern. Carrie would ask for something and the answer was always 'of course'. Carrie would ask me to do something for her and the answer was always 'of course'. My family never wanted for anything. Carrie was on her second car since passing her test and I found her quite unfair. If I suddenly said "Ok Carrie, I've changed my mind. Here you go, you have the money, go shopping", she would have snatched it right out of my hand!

Over the next few months, she started to bring up that fact that we were still only engaged. Carrie wanted a marriage abroad. I thought this was a good option as we would get a ceremony, honeymoon and holiday all in one. A good option, more so, because we had children. We couldn't exactly swan off for two weeks without them. Well, I couldn't anyway. The destination was eventually chosen. The Caribbean. I wanted to make sure we had more than enough money, to have the best time ever, so I decided to give up smoking. Plus, it was good for my health.

We had a few guests flying out with us. From Carrie's side- her mother, aunt with her two children, along with Carrie's grandfather Alf and grandma May. Alf and Carrie had made up over time. I later learned that they rowed about something which had happened when Carrie was a teenager, which stopped Alf talking to her. I had no idea what exactly happened, though me and Grandad Alf seemed to be getting on well once that ice had broken. I was sure I would eventually find out what happened between them anyway.

From my side- my dad and his partner Linda, along with my sister Marie and my Nephew. My mum didn't feel comfortable coming due to the split between her and my dad some time ago. Not that things were bitter between them, just that they both now had new partners but I knew, deep down, it was because neither of them had 'let go' yet. Marie came down again, a few weeks prior to the wedding. Carrie and I were going to be married yet I felt more uneasy than excited. Carrie was the complete opposite.

That wedding date came around quick. One minute I was working, the next we're in a gorgeous country about to say our vows. We had about a week at the resort before the actual wedding and the holiday tied in with Sofie's birthday, which was great. We got the hotel to make a cake and they brought it out to her, while we were sat having our dinner. She was growing up so quick. Only three years old but came across a lot older. A little brainy box too.

The first few days were the norm, what you would expect being on holiday with someone like Carrie. I didn't feel like I was there to get married at all. I would still get up in the morning with the kids, she would get up whenever she chose too. If you needed me, you would find me in the pool with Sofie and Andrew. Carrie, once in the land of the living, would be somewhere sunbathing or, this time, taking part in water aerobics and talking to the male workers. She had already stated, well before we arrived, that she was having a hen night.

That night arrived and she couldn't wait to leave the hotel room. Later, down the line, a photo surfaced from this day. It showed me, sat on the bed, with Carrie. I had my wallet out, she had her hand out. The kids were in the background asleep. A picture is worth a thousand words.

Carrie, and her mother's, plan was to go to the local disco area and they invited Marie to join them. With the wedding in the morning, Carrie promised me she would be back at the hotel before 10.30pm. Coming up to midnight she still wasn't back. I half expected this anyway. I gave her a little longer then knocked on my dad's room to ask him to sit with Sofie and Andrew.

I found her dancing with one of the male workers she had been doing aerobics with, earlier that day. Nothing untoward. I hoped not anyway but the dance was provocative. They were teaching the guests to salsa dance and Carrie clearly had consumed a lot of alcohol. A typical hen night then, no doubt. Having children to get ready in the morning was the very reason why I choose to not have a stag do. I had a few drinks with my dad and Alf earlier in the day. That did me just fine.

Morning arrived. The big day. Our ceremony was held on the hotel grounds and a local resident played a guitar, while words were spoken in Spanish, which Carrie had chosen. I have, to this day, have no clue what the words translated into. They could have recited how much of a pig I was, for all I know. Carrie was happy with a capital H. Looking like the 'cat that got the cream'. I looked worn out, unhappy, nervous and stressed. The only thing that kept me going through that entire day was my children. It was right for mummy and daddy to be married.

Looking back on our wedding photos, my honesty now, allows me to say that I looked like I needed saving and that quietening my gut feelings was a stupid move. Regardless, seeing Sofie's face as she was bridesmaid was enough for me. Andrew obviously didn't know what was happening but he looked so adorable in his little outfit. We had a horse and carriage take us to the beach where we had our wedding photos taken. This was a big day yet I felt like it was 'part of a procedure'.

Beautiful white sandy beaches and picturesque wedding shots but as soon as the wedding was over, it was back to the normal holiday. Me and the children were left on our own, while Carrie spent the holiday her way. I just couldn't understand it. The last two holidays, ok fair enough, but this was the holiday that marked our wedding. A wedding she very much wanted and controlled.

I tried my hardest to enjoy it for the kids' sake because they were having such a fantastic time but I felt down. I think it was this point where all those niggling things, that entered my head in the past, came up front and were making me feel vulnerable. Every excursion that was taking place Carrie wanted to attend. Like an excited child on a school trip. I understand that to some extent but when was it going to click that she had children and sometimes she wouldn't be able to do everything she wanted. Honestly, most times it felt like I had three children.

Sofie was getting a tad bored of swimming so I took her to the park on the hotel grounds. I told Carrie I was going there and that I would leave Andrew with her as he was getting sleepy. After a while, we returned to the pool. Carrie had forgotten to re-apply his sun block and Andrew was asleep on one of the lounges, looking rather burnt. Carrie, so wrapped up in burning herself for a tan, couldn't even apply protection to her pale-skinned son! She said she had forgotten. I felt guilty for going to the park without him so I spent the rest of the holiday with both Sofie and Andrew. If Carrie was with us, she was with us. If she wasn't, she wasn't. I really wasn't bothered at this point. We were to fly home soon enough anyway.

Back home as man and wife. It felt like either a check list had been ticked or I had signed my own death sentence. As I was growing tired, Carrie was over-flowing with energy and constantly smiling. Was this a mood swing, was this to stay? Arriving home from work, evenings were a lot more enjoyable with her this way, that's for sure.

As I was preparing dinner, she came out into the kitchen and sat at the table. We chatted about many things. It was nice because most of our nights were spent in silence, unless Carrie chose otherwise. As I dished up dinner she went on to talk about wanting to go to work. She had seen part-time evening work advertised in our local supermarket and wanted to apply and It took me by surprise.

Since coming home she had changed and it was lovely and, very much, long awaited. She said she wanted to contribute to the house and have a purpose other than a stay-at-home mum. The marriage gave Carrie the stability she must have wanted or needed, I thought.

As I went to make our tea one evening, I noticed Carrie's handbag on the kitchen table. I could see a letter addressed but with no stamp on it. The address was to the area of the Caribbean we had visited. My heart started to beat fast. Why would she have a letter in her bag addressed to there? My eyes opened widely and I just stood there looking at this part of the letter hanging out.

Could this have anything to do with Carrie's behavioral change? Things were slowly making sense just by staring it. Do I open it? I didn't know what to do. The letter was certainly not addressed to me. Who was I to take it upon myself to open this letter. Yes, no, yes, no, repeatedly in my head. My heart said don't open it. My gut said why haven't you opened it yet! My gut knew what it was. My gut was right.

I opened the letter. A love letter to a guy, a worker at the hotel. The very hotel where we stayed. Maybe this was why she had been talking about working, about earning her own money. Gob smacked! Someone had smacked me right in the mouth with a fist full of truth and it hurt. Hurt because deep down I knew this act she had been putting on, since we came back off holiday, our wedding holiday, was too good to be true. Was this guy the reason she forgot to keep an eye on Andrew? I confronted her. I couldn't not.

We had a massive row. I was hurt and angry yet, so was Carrie. She was angry that I went into her handbag and made me feel 'this' was happening because of me. When angry, Carrie can be equipped with such a spiteful tongue. She gains a huge confidence boost and belittles with ease. She turned the argument on to me. My issues, my ways that, supposedly, made her 'the way she was'. How I loved the children more than her, how I was "nothing and boring". Her eyes would be cold and, as she looked me right in the eye,

"Look at you, you are nothing, you are not a man!"

Her cold stare made her words seem true. She pushed and pushed, picking at me, chiseling at any worth I thought I had. Telling her how she was, just made her worse. Defending myself showed no point.

Trying to get a grip on what we were actually rowing about, made her even more irate. The fact that she had cheated seemed quite minor now. From a raging bull to a smirk, she said she was leaving. And she did. Taking the children with her, calm as a cucumber. With Sofie crying not wanting to go with her, she walked out.

I stood there broken. I couldn't believe what had just happened. She made me feel I was the one in the wrong and her walking out with the kids was justified. I kept thinking to myself, why didn't I just leave the letter alone. What was going on? How are we here? Why are we here? My head was a mess. I sat in the empty house, confused as to why my life had got to this point. This new beginning of mine. The thought of not knowing how the kids were killed me. I rang Carrie constantly and she would answer but childishly. Like she found it funny, the situation we were in. The thought of losing my kids was hard to deal with and she knew that. She would taunt down the phone how I was,

"Never going to see them again".

I realize now that, this was the moment our relationship should have ended. It also concreted my weakness where my children are concerned and Carrie learnt that and she was to hold my weakness against me whenever she saw fit. It was this moment that Carrie learnt I would do anything, and put up with anything, for the sake of not losing my kids.

It was three nights before she would return home. She said she was sorry. She spoke of how she was drunk when she kissed 'him' and that she was never going to ever send the letter. Should I forgive her? NO! That's what I would shout at myself now, a big fat NO! The letter wasn't the only issue between us was it?! How would we move on from this anyway? How would we split? We have children,

"I'm sorry", she said, "really, really, sorry. I don't want our marriage to end, it was just a silly mistake"

I looked at our children. I cried. Carrie cried.

This was my life, my family, as abnormal as it was. If she was there in front of me telling me how things WILL work, that we can get through this, I had to match her. We hadn't been married long and here we were, broken already. I felt I had to give her a chance, a chance to prove me wrong (or right, if being the case). The idea of being a part-time dad was never an option for me.

It was after this incident I was to hear more about Carrie's childhood. I still, to this day, don't know if what I was told held any truth but hearing about her upbringing changed my perspective of her and gave Carrie a reason for her behavior. She spoke of neglect. Her mother would choose men over her children. She spoke of a time where her mum would beat her with a dog lead and any man was allowed to discipline her. Physically discipline and her mother would not batter an eyelid. A lot of marijuana use, very little food or care. I never actually got whole accounts of events, just little snippets.

Carrie was, supposedly, put into care, to then later live with her nan but, in time, her nan kicked her out. It amazed me how Carrie could be so civil to her mother with the memories she was holding. It all sort of made sense, or I made it look that way to cover the cracks. Maybe that's why she behaved like a spoilt child at times. Maybe she was still a child on the inside wanting to be loved and smothered with affection and would play up if she didn't get enough. Maybe that's why she was so hurtful to me sometimes and able to say such hurtful, vicious things because of the anger built-up inside her.

I knew deep down in my gut that me and Carrie were not to take our relationship any further. That we should have ended there and then but I also knew that my children needed me around daily and belonged with me. I talked myself round the idea of fixing things. Maybe things happened too fast. We didn't date each other for long, we just jumped straight in the deep end. Maybe that's why we started drowning so early.

We had children now, we had to make it work, or at least try. I remember my mum and dad rowing all the time. My mum left once but she soon came back. Her father told her to return home. He reminded her that she chose to get married and that marriage was not something you enter lightly or throw away, so easy, either. Regardless of the issues you are faced with, you work at it, for 'better for worse'. It was those traditions, my grandad's way of thinking, that had been installed in me as a youngster. I was willing to try, for the sake of my marriage but mainly, wholeheartedly, for the sake of my children. The way I saw it, my marriage was either going to succeed or fail.

Carrie was trying and I could tell too. She, indeed, got a job at our local supermarket and our relationship like it was getting back on track. We experienced our 'blip' and it was over and forgotten. As I would go to work, she would be getting up. As I returned home and prepared dinner, she would be getting ready for work. Our together time was when she returned. She would bring home cakes from the bakery and we'd sit and eat them while on the sofa, watching television. Ironic really, Carrie was always stressing about her weight, yet, without fail, those cakes would come home with her and there would never be any left.

It reminds me of a time Carrie was attempting sit-ups in the living-room. Sofie joined in and was mimicking her. It was lovely to see. The two of them, smiling together, at each other, doing something together. Sofie was hilarious. For a while now, I had been video recording at any opportunity I got. So many nice moments were happening, especially with the children, and I wanted to have them forever. Sofie was such a character, full of confidence. It became a nightly routine with her putting on a performance, singing into her toy microphone, her favorite song, Atomic Kittens 'tide is high but I'm holding on'. Crazily adequate, now I look back. Swaying like she was a pop star who had been preforming for years. Andrew would join in and just look like a spare part. They were both comical to watch. I wanted to continue looking forward, not back. I never, ever, wanted a broken family. Mum here, dad there, every other weekend visitation. Giving Carrie a chance was the right thing to do. Giving 'us' a chance was the right thing to do.

Carrie seemed content with her new job and showed she loved her independence. She never moaned about going to work but soon started to moan when she came home. She was starting to have rows with some of her colleagues. I'm unsure as to what about, she would just come home moaning about everyone and in such a foul mood, which me and the kids ended up taking the brunt of it. It was quite possible Carrie wasn't liking being told what to do on occasions and her temper would get the better of her. Which was valid when I received a call from her one day. She was in the middle of a row, I heard a male's voice in the background, she was with the Sofie and Andrew and I have never moved so fast. I drove to where she was and found her effing and blinding at an old gentleman. Quite a big man too. I defused the situation and told Carrie to get in the car. I spoke to the man, though on guard. He explained that he was appalled to see Sofie not in her car seat, which was visible, while Carrie was driving and that a friendly suggestion to Carrie didn't go down very well and she became rude and confrontational.

Carrie's back was soon up again after a visit from my nan, who made a remark about how untidy our house was. Carrie got defensive and when my nan left, blamed me,

"I'm working and being a mum, house cleaning shouldn't be my responsibility too"

In one ear and out the other. That's what I learnt. To let her have her hot-head moments and eventually she would cool down and everything would be pleasant again. Telling her I'm working and being a dad too AND tidying up, was said in my head rather than out loud. It was better that way.

Work was so busy and still bringing in good amount of money. I would work later than normal, especially through the festive periods when town was booming with potential customers. I felt guilty about spending less time at home than before. Carrie enjoyed the money coming in until I brought presents home for the kids. It became a routine for a while.

"Daddy's home"

Sofie and Andrew would always come running to greet me. I would give them little gifts but not the spoiling, extravagant, kind. Just little silly things but Carrie hated it. She would moan that I was wasting money on things they didn't need yet she never said the same when I would give her something.

Christmas and birthdays were unpredictable too. She never showed the same interest as I did, unless it was her present opening time. I'm like a kid myself, at Christmas, and struggle to sleep knowing how the kids are going to be in the morning. Their little faces seeing what Santa had brought them. I dressed up as him once. A realistic, old man face mask which I added a beard to. Going into Sofie and Andrew was a picture. They actually believed I was him. It was hard staying in character, without laughing. Sofie was very polite to Santa,

"Nice to meet you. I'm Sofie and I have been a very good girl"

Andrew was too cute to put into words When Santa asked how old they were, Sofie proudly announced her age. Andrew filled with excitement,

"Can I have a….a….huggle" (cuddle) and he reached out for one.

I have this on video, thankfully, as I had asked Carrie to use the video camera. Sofie and Andrew never knew of the joyous tears rolling down my face under that mask.

Me and Carrie were working a lot and life was good, with iffy moments, but a break was in order. I certainly felt like I needed a break. I was still not smoking and, through the whole process of it, I continued putting away pound coins. It really does accumulate if you just put it away and forget it's there. We booked our next holiday, America for a couple of weeks. I count this as our first family holiday as the last one didn't go very well did it!

We flew into Miami and had a couple of days there first. We next rented a car to drive to Palm Bay, where we stayed for the rest of the holiday. Life always feels better when the sun's shining. The hotel had a communal pool so we were either there or out exploring. I told Carrie to watch the kids while I nipped over to the bar, on the other side of the pool, to get us all drinks and some nibbles. Not long after being in line waiting to be served, I heard a commotion behind me. I turned around and saw a man lifting a child out of the pool, spluttering. Then I saw Carrie come out of her sun coma and head towards the man. I realized then it was Andrew. I hadn't even been gone for five minutes. I couldn't just go and get a drink without there being some sort of scene. I just kept thinking, what was wrong with her?

I thanked the man for his rapid response, while trying to hide my embarrassment and guilt. The incident went over Carrie's head. She saw it as a normal thing,

"Things like this happen to parents sometimes, it's not a big deal!"

Andrew was fine and I was over reacting and needed to "chill out", as far as she was concerned.

Rows soon started to surface again. It just didn't matter where we were or how beautiful of a place we were in. This time, determined to have a good holiday, I would argue when she showed me the need to, I'd allow her to get it out of her system then I would draw a line under it and be done. I didn't want to keep arguing all the time and didn't want Sofie and Andrew's memories tainted. I made sure the two weeks were busy and excitable. We went to Islands of Adventure, Universal Studios and Busch Gardens and I took lots of photos to cherish every moment. My kids are going to hate me when they're older, when the family albums are passed down to them. There's going to be lots of them. I hope they have a lot of storage space.

We meet a lovely British couple out there, who were in the process of immigrating. Their plans sounded so appealing. Imagine being able to have this beautiful weather and country, this sunshine state, as a home. What a great place for kids to grow up in, I thought. So many things to do and see. I often imagined while listening to them.

I couldn't get my Palm bay experience out of my head. The possibilities, the sunshine, the smiles. The happiness beaming off Sofie and Andrew's faces. Me and Carrie were back to normal once home. I just couldn't work her out. She was a mystery to me. A messed-up mystery. We would have such loving moments together but I just couldn't make her happy, or I couldn't make her happiness last.

No matter what I did, I gave her too much attention, I gave her not enough, I just couldn't win. No matter how perfect I tried to be, I would always end up in the wrong. There was love there. There must have been but I think you had to squint really hard to see it and wait a long time to feel it. I just wanted to be happy and enjoy the life my hard work was bringing. Mind, body and soul happy and, by god, did I just want Carrie to be happy. If she was, we all were.

I would often speak to my father about America on our work breaks. I just couldn't stop speaking about it. I wanted my effort in life to lead me somewhere great. Like I had this cake and I wanted the icing as the final piece. Carrie would talk positive about it too. She agreed that it would be a great place for Sofie and Andrew to grow up in. She imagined 'what if' just as much as I did. Maybe America would fix us? I was desperately trying to find the solution.

Coincidently, there was a fayre, not that far from us, not long after we were back and I took it as a sign. An immigration to the U.S.A fayre. I wanted my icing. I don't know if it was icing for Carrie but we seemed to be on the same page. Even my father was on-board. We all attended the fayre together and got talking to a company who were selling businesses. It sounded very interesting and do-able. An adventure too! We had all made up our minds within minutes.

We put an offer in on one of the businesses, on the condition of our house sales. In the meantime, we sorted the visas. All in all, it took about 12-18 months before everything was finalized. While waiting for the moving date, we did as many trips to the car boot as we could. We sold everything to make us extra money and to get rid of things we couldn't take with us. Our set up fund was £120,000. Back then it was a good bit of money. I brought the property for £62,000 and the property market gave me a nice return on the sale.

The business, going half with my dad, was £60,000. Though it was better in dollars, what with the conversion rate at the time. It never occurred to me that I was making life nice on the outside so I didn't have to confront what was really happening inside. I had become an artist. Skilled, in painting over drama with better scenes.

chapter five

We stayed with my father and his partner Linda, at first, as they secured a property before we did. It was quite hard, all of us under the same roof. Carrie and Linda clashed enormously. Both strong willed, controlling at times, women who wanted things their way, with no let up or compromise. Carrie wouldn't like being spoken down to, regardless of being in someone else's home. She didn't like being told to tidy up and she certainly didn't appreciate being woken up before she was ready to get up herself.

Linda would make comments about the mess Sofie and Andrew were making. Not that the actual mess was an issue for her, more so that, when in the company of Carrie, there wouldn't be any tidying up afterwards. Things would be scattered all over the floor, used cereal bowls would be darted about, rather than being put in the kitchen or even washed up. Linda found Carrie disrespectful and it made the hostility between them worse. In turn, my father and I would get it in the neck.

Linda was great with Sofie and Andrew and had a lovely relationship with them but Carrie took it as Linda trying to take over, rather than genuine affection for them. The more the two of them butted heads, the more stress me and my father had to endure. My father has never been one for stress. He copes like an ostrich, always retreating with his head in the sand. Something I can totally relate to because it is mighty quiet buried in that sand. In his case though, the sand is alcohol. The more he was moaned at, the more time he spent down the local bar. He probably dreaded coming home most nights, just as much as I did. I kept an eye on the kids when we were home, limiting any feuds that could arise between Carrie and Linda.

Our work was busy, on an extreme level from the get go. Made to feel more so, probably because of the heat. We ran a commercial laundry service for holiday homes and it was a good earner but, wow, hard work! Harder than I had ever experienced. There was a bar on the complex so dad was in his element. Linda and Carrie both seemed to want control over the business, more so over the other. They would have been quite happy fighting to the death. Carrie did put work and effort in though. She would go out on the rounds and collect from the homes when I couldn't but she preferred being at the desk sorting through the accounts.

I could feel pressure building up as the days went on and I couldn't stop moments of high anxiety. I was starting to feel the strain. My eyes would regularly feel like I was under water, which only made my anxiety worse. If I ever felt settled, I would be brought out of it by panic attacks. Knowing you are freaking out but lack the ability to shut the emotion down is hard. I'd try talking myself out of them,

"It's ok, it's ok, you are ok"

Like every word was a countdown to my deflation. Some days it would work and soothe me back to life.

However, it is the worse feeling in the world trying to hold back a panic attack while you are out in public. My anxiety made me walk out of a restaurant without eating or even paying for the food I had ordered. I had to leave, the room became small with all the other people in there, making me feel crowded. Their voices were amplified and it was like I could hear every single one of them. Every word of theirs, over lapping the other and spoken at rapid speed. The lights seemed to up in brightness and I felt too enclosed. Carrie drove us home while I sat trying to compose myself. Telling the kids,

"Silly daddy, I've got a sickie tummy and need fresh air"

Carrie moaned at me the whole way home, annoyed,

"You can't even take me out for something to eat!"

Reflecting on more positive memories, one of my favourite days was Sofie and Andrew's first day at school. It's so different to England. Big yellow school buses taking over the highway, though we would drop Sofie and Andrew off. They were too young for the buses. If you didn't get out in the parking lot, all cars would be in a queue and you'd await your turn, eventually pulling up outside the school where the teacher waiting would open the car door and the child jumps out.

Everyone loved Sofie and Andrew, especially their accent. Sofie walked into school like it was hers. Andrew was shy, it was his first school experience but in time, he found his confidence and enjoyed going just as much as his big sister. The only thing they both had trouble with was the afternoon naps. Class would have quiet time and the American kids would sleep. Sofie and Andrew, being in English mode, would just lay there, wide-eyed. They soon got used to the change though, what with the heat and hours upon hours of pool time on tap. They would drift off just as quick eventually, in the warm quiet classroom.

I built up friendly relationships with the clients and often found myself looking forward to our meetings. I enjoyed the solo drives in the sunshine. We brought a 4x4 and it was a dream to drive. It was nice to get away, if I'm honest. Even though it was only for a few hours. No drama, just open road. I took it all in, grabbing those free air moments, collecting them until I could have it again because, once home, free air would evaporate.

Living with Linda and dad was like a time-bomb. Carrie and Linda were not letting up and the bad vibes were coming to work with them. Here we are, in this beautiful country but the women in our lives were determined to turn it sour. Juggling a busy business and children was tough most times and I was finding myself more and more exhausted. With all the bickering added on top, it was just adding to the decreasing of my energy.

The more Linda got on dad's case, the more trips he made to the bar. The more he drank, the more Linda would be on his case. There was no let up. Even if there were no problems between dad and Linda and he just fancied a nice cold beer in the sunshine, it still became an issue. Drink was very much an issue with him. He would stay longer and longer at the bar, so then I had that added worry, concerned about his drinking volume, worrying if he would get home safely. I'd get in and Linda and Carrie would be at logger heads. My only release, my only escape, was Andrew and Sofie. Time with them. They made all problems disappear. Like we had our own little bubble and, when in our bubble, nothing or no one could pop it.

After returning home one evening, I could tell Linda was not in the greatest of moods. She asked me where dad was and I told her I had left him in the bar earlier. Just by the blank expression on her face, I knew he needed to get home pretty sharpish. It was getting late so we just went straight to our room. We had already eaten so we got Sofie and Andrew washed and ready for bed and settled down for the night while be able to hear Linda walking around the house, slamming doors.

Sofie and Andrew were fast asleep when dad eventually rolled in the door. I think they had already rowed earlier that morning and If dad was hoping the dust would have settled by the time he got in, he was very much mistaken. Linda flew into him the moment I heard the door shut. Carrie's name was also being blasted and Linda was angry. Dad had consumed enough alcohol to not want this and sounded like he wasn't in the right frame of mind to chat, let alone argue. Linda became louder and louder and continued to shout, this time about his drinking and it turned into a screaming match. Dad screaming, Linda screaming louder and there were bangs and loud noises, like they were bumping into things or things were being thrown. At this point Sofie and Andrew are up, woken by the commotion. Dad's tone changed and it didn't sound like they were just throwing loud words at each other anymore, so I got out of bed.

All the rooms were sectioned by sliding doors and the doors where dad and Linda were, were shut. I pulled across one side and dad and Linda were literally wrestling on the floor. Linda was on top and dad looked in pain, trying to cusp his crotch. I ran over and pulled her off him. I got in-between them and Linda eventually walked off, mumbling under her breath and slamming the sliding doors as she left. Before I could get to the bottom of what happened, the police had arrived from Linda calling them. After talking to Linda, they spoke to us. Linda wanted dad arrested but the officers said there was bodily harm from both sides and that if they start arresting anyone, it would be both dad and Linda and, also our visas would be affected because of it.

Linda said she didn't want us or dad there and the police advised it was for the best, instead of arresting anybody. They seemed strict but fair though Linda wasn't going to be. We had to leave there and then, in the middle of the night, with only that night to take our belongings. We rapidly filled suitcases and got the kids in the car and headed to the nearest motel. Dad and Linda's marriage was over.

We only spent one night at the motel. One of our clients, the morning after, helped us find a place to rent. A three-bed house with a separate side annex flat, which was ideal for dad and gave him his own space and front-door. We had use of a communal pool and the other residents seemed friendly.

With dad's birthday coming up, I had been arranging with Marie to come out and surprise him. I wanted to see her too. I was missing family so much recently. She flew out with Kaine, and her new addition Andre and I couldn't wait to get her from the airport. The kids were super excited seeing them all, even Carrie. Dad was reduced to happy tears at the first sight of them.

We still had to work, which Marie understood. She was looking forward to seeing the business in its awe, anyway. She came to work with me and helped with the running of things, if Andre was asleep. Folding towels and bedding and putting them in their designated cubbyholes, with the help of Kaine. Andre wouldn't sleep unless it was in this huge cardboard box we had. Yes, I have a photo, kids are so funny! Marie would join Carrie on any pick-ups and when work was over, we all spent the rest of the day by the pool. To anyone that knows about corndogs - how yummy are they?! To anyone that doesn't know - You need too!

Sofie and Andrew were becoming confident swimmers. Kaine was getting there. Within a few weeks after watching his cousins though, he was on par. The three of them would have their rubber rings round them and jump in at the same time. Andre would just float about with his armbands on and vest. Carrie would join us in the pool this time and spent less time sunbathing.

Marie wanted to take her kids to Disneyland, Carrie then decided she wanted to as well. I couldn't, I needed to be at clients houses so Carrie said she will take the kids. I was a little peeved that she didn't seem bothered that I couldn't go with them. It was like 'oh well, you've got to work, never mind, bye'.

The kids absolutely loved it but Marie wasn't as impressed. She was filled with excitement before going but she said, when she got there, it wasn't as 'magical' as she expected, and joked,

"Mum and Dad should of took me there when I was little. Going as an adult killed the magic"

Tired from work, I prepared dinner with Carrie showing no interest in helping because,

"I've spent all day in the heat, queuing for rides. I'm tired!"

I hide my feelings well. Marie always assumed I was just tired from being on the go all the time. That's what I would tell her, anyway. Her presence made me feel more whole and I could forget about certain things for a while but she wasn't going to be here forever. She would eventually leave and I was dreading the day. She couldn't stay longer than three months so when that time came, she had to go back home.

I hated it. I really didn't want her to leave, neither did Sofie and Andrew. The airport wave-off was awful, I could barely string a sentence together without wanting to burst into tears. She first hugged Sofie goodbye and Sofie began crying saying she didn't want her to leave, which then made Marie cry, then me. I was struggling to keep it together, I just wanted to tell her please don't go, I need you, I need someone. Instead, I waved her off with a fake smile.

Not long after, I couldn't shake off feeling rubbish all the time. Fatigued, and the feeling of running on empty, so I went to the doctors to put my mind at rest. Anxiety is a nightmare! I had blood tests which came back fine, apart from my cholesterol being high. There was no slowing down at work but I tried as much as I could when home. Still sorting Sofie and Andrew, cooking, cleaning but enjoying more time on the sofa with them than the pool. Playing games on the PlayStation and having yo-yo, love-hate moments from Carrie. Her unpredictable ways were the least of my worries right now. I didn't have it in me anymore. I had no energy to fight.

My anxiety just wouldn't go away. It was my shadow, a dark side of me that wouldn't let me be and it pounced on me one evening, showing it was way stronger than I was. Racing heart, worrying mind and wasn't showing signs of easing off. I was feeling the tension inside me, building up, crawling on my skin like fingers on a piano that were leading up to the chorus or the big finale.

I thought I was dying, which was scaring me more, rocketing my anxiety levels through the roof. With Sofie and Andrew at school, I asked Carrie to take me to the doctors but she was annoyed. She didn't want too. I had to beg her, before she eventually got up and took me.

Sat in the passenger seat, my toes started to cramp and the sensation started to travel. My feet began to cramp and I started to panic. Desperately trying to control my breathing, it moved up into my calves, working its way up to my thighs, stomach, chest then arms. My whole body was becoming cramped and I didn't know how to stop it or make it go away. I pleaded with Carrie to hurry, who just looked at me blankly, still annoyed that I made her drive. I couldn't move, every part of me in a rigor mortis state and all I kept thinking was, this is it, I'm going to die. The next step would be my heart. The cramp sensation, taking over my body, would soon collide with it and make it stop beating. I was frightened. I didn't want to die. I wasn't ready too.

We pulled up at the doctors and I struggled to get out of the car. Stiff all over, barely able to move. Like my muscles had been in a freezer and hadn't quite defrosted yet. One step at a time, desperately wanting to be inside where someone could help me, I moved towards the doors. Like being grabbed by quick sand, I kept moving, fighting it so I didn't sink, so it didn't get me.

I was seen straight away and instantly felt safe. If anything bad was going to happen, I would be ok because I was around people who could resuscitate me. I sat with the doctor who eased me back to normal, leveling my breathing and relaxing my state of mind. The tightness softened and I felt the life coming back into my body. My heartbeat was regular and it was over. I wasn't dying and I just wanted to burst into tears.

The doctor asked me about things and I was honest. About everything. He told me to go home and had a slight smirk on his face while he said it. Well, that's how my mind perceived it and I was irritated by his recommendation. I felt stupid! Like I was wasting his time with my 'silly anxiety' and I was sarcastic,

"I'm going home in a few minutes"

"No, your body is telling you to go home"

"NO", I said, "my body told me to come here!!"

Placing his hand on my shoulder, he leaned in closer and I was soon to understand,

"No, you are not listening to me, you need to go home, your body is telling you that you don't belong here, not yet. You need to start listening to it" and I then saw the smirk for what it really was. A sympathetic smile.

I knew what I had to do. I knew all along but kept myself so occupied that I couldn't hear my inner-self. My body had made its mind up a long time ago and now my brain was listening. Telling Carrie didn't go down well. She didn't want to leave. Neither did dad but the American weather was soon to cement my decision. We experienced three hurricanes while living there. The first was hurricane Charlie, 130mph winds and caused flooding at work but we were lucky enough to salvage our stock.

The second was hurricane Jean, 70mph winds by the time it hit land, and it just lingered for a few days. Reported the size of Texas. The last, and final weather warning, we were to endure was hurricane Francis. 128mph winds which had us seeking shelter in the bathroom with a mattress over our heads, while we rode it out. I was frantically trying to get hold of dad before it reached its peak, as he was out but I couldn't get an answer from him. You're told not to use telephone lines too. Under the mattress, I prayed that he would take refuge somewhere, that he would be safe.

Come morning, I was woken by a call from him. He was in the bar near work, when the storm was brewing, so stayed there along with others who sought shelter. He decided to sleep at work rather than chance the drive back. Come morning, he woke up to the aftermath of what hurricane Francis had left behind,

"You'd better get down here quick"

I am still amazed to this day, that he slept through it.

The weather ripped through the building, taking part of the roof with it and the whole thing collapsed and caved in, letting in gallons of rain. All the customer's laundry was a mess. Soaked and covered in debris. £5000 worth of towels and bedding ruined. It was like hurricane Francis left me a voicemail,

"GO HOME"

My mind was made up. My health was in disarray and I needed to consider my well-being for the sake of Sofie and Andrew.

Carrie still didn't want to go back to the UK, saying she was fine where she was but eventually accepted it, seeing the state of the business. Sofie and Andrew seemed happy either way. They were going to miss the friends they had made and, of course, the swimming pool but were excited about another plane ride and seeing family.

The business was sort after so we didn't need to wait long for a sale, regardless of its cosmetic condition. Dad stayed on to show the new owners the ropes then became one of their employees for a while. We sold our car back to the company we brought it from but with a $10,000 loss from the original purchase price. My cut of the business meant we were coming home with £60,000.

All that we had, came on the plane with us. I have a cabinet of my grandad's that has gone wherever I have, since receiving it. I carried it as luggage. There was no way it wasn't coming home with me. Though heartbroken that I wanted to go, that I would be leaving him, dad understood my decision. He wasn't ready to give up the American dream. It wasn't his time but it was mine.

chapter six

Now back in the UK, Carrie and I were in financial difficulty and have to stay at Marie's for a while, while we sort out somewhere to live. Even though a little gutted my immigration experience didn't work out, I was glad to be home, being on familiar ground. Money comes and goes. You can always make more money but you can't make more health and well-being is far more important.

We came back with hardly anything. Few clothes, few toys for the kids and the money we had left was for a down payment on a new home. When Marie and my mum heard that we were going through a bad patch and it was possible we would have to return, they started gathering things for us. We may have come home with barely anything but on return we had enough bits to help us restart. From kitchen utensils, bedding, even a little TV for Sofie and Andrew.

While we were still in America, my aunt was back in the UK helping us find a property. Carrie said no to a few that were our options. One wasn't "big enough" and one didn't have a bath. I didn't care. I just wanted a roof over our heads. I didn't work so hard in my life to lose everything but any home would have been fine. I would make it fine.

The house we decided on in the end wasn't fantastic, it needed a lot of work and updating but we weren't homeless. That was good enough for me. When finalizing the house, Carrie wanted to go onto the mortgage and deeds. She said she had never felt like she had been a part of anything and that now back, starting again, she wanted things done properly. So, as husband and wife usually do, we entered our new home jointly. We needed money and fast, so I started up another business. Like what we had in the States but on a smaller scale.

Like any new business, it was going to take time to build a regular income. It started well, I gained customers and regulars and money was coming in but the mortgage was quite high, and doing the math's, I couldn't see how we could be comfortable like we were before. Not to begin with anyway. Bills needed paying and we were getting by on credit cards which soon made them ran up to £15,000 so I asked Carrie if she could find a job to contribute. She really wasn't happy about this. She didn't want to go to work this time. Regardless of what she wanted, she had too. Our finances were in such a mess and I couldn't do it all on my own. She eventually found a job in banking and, while still not out of the red, we were slowly getting on top of things.

Not long after Carrie started her job, she began going out a lot with her new found friends. It became very frequent and the strain on us as a family was happening again. I was still doing all the household chores and looking after Sofie and Andrew, while trying to make my business grow. Carrie's wages went into the house, begrudgingly, on her part, but with all her 'outings' she would spend over that amount before her next wages. She couldn't understand why I felt this was wrong for her to do.

"I've paid my way!"

She couldn't understand my point. Didn't want to more like. She was basically putting bill money into the house to then take it back out in dribs and drabs for her social needs, way before the bills could be paid, so not contributing at all then.

Again, like a teenager with no care or concern. This teenager that wants to go out, get dressed up and party until all hours and it wasn't long before rowing started again. As time went on, Carrie's attitude became more cocky and aggressive. She was to do what she wanted, when she wanted. This was her and it was very clear this Carrie was staying. She began to go out more and more and was hardly ever home making contact with Andrew and Sofie minimal, close to non-existent. I was mum and dad. I knew that. I've always known that. The kids showed me that in their behaviour. Majority of the time I couldn't wait for her to go out. I was hating being around her most days.

The new business was getting busier and busier. I'd get up in the morning, get Sofie and Andrew ready for school and as soon as that was done, I'd head home and begin work. Most of the time rushing through it, to be able to pick them back up at 3pm. If I had any delivery calls to make after that time, the children would always come out in the van with me. They always wanted to and I totally understood why. I couldn't get through to Carrie that she was being unfair in her actions. All the money she was spending and the time she was spending with her friends rather than us. It just wasn't a big deal to her. Nothing ever is! I was only ever the bad guy in it all,

"You just don't want me to have a life"

Not once could her brain ever think that maybe I wanted a life too,

"Ok, I'll leave and take the kids with me then, how about that?!",

She would say this whenever the conversation got too much for her.

Feeling the strain, I spoke to Marie. She was having a hard time where she was. Like me, she hated the area that I had got out of. I asked what she thought about the possibility of moving here and helping me with the business. Like helping me would, in turn, help her. She totally agreed and to be honest it was a huge relief. Within months Marie, Kaine and Andre moved in with us, while waiting to move into their own place and my load was lessened.

Carrie appreciated Marie being there one minute but then cursed her presence the next. I was just grateful that I could slow down. Carrie continued partying at every opportunity she got. She would come home in some awful states most nights. Minor bruises and ripped tights, no doubt falling over due to being intoxicated and most times ended up vomiting.

We brought our first family pet. Sofie and Andrew were excited and it was nice, just to see their little faces beam when they got their first puppy. Marie had gone with Carrie to collect it and said the house they came from looked derelict and that, as they left with our puppy, now named 'Bushy', there was another pup left and it was hiding in the corner. Marie didn't want to leave the pup behind. So, we now had two pups in the house. Sister power, Bushy and Binty. I didn't see it as extra work. Firstly, Marie would oversee her dog but with ours, it gave us reasons to stop. We'd go for walks and Sofie and Andrew played with them in the park. It was probably a nice distraction to the bad vibes that were lingering at home.

Carrie was back in regular contact with her mother, by this point and she popped round one evening. Such a hard woman to talk too. Rude and uninviting. While Carrie was out of the room she asked Marie her thoughts on myself and Carrie's relationship. Marie was polite but truthful. She said we should break up, that the relationship seemed unhealthy and not doing either of us any good, especially the children but if there was to be a split, it needed to be done in an amicable manner so the kids aren't affected. She was right.

One night, Carrie went out but this time didn't come home until the following afternoon. Perfectly acceptable in her eyes. No explanation or apology, no interaction with the children. Just straight to bed. Come evening, she surfaced. Again, no interaction with the children, just a glare at me,

"What are YOU looking at?"

Asking her where the hell she was, why she felt it ok to not come home, we began to row and Marie took the children upstairs.

"What possible reason would warrant a mother to not come home, or even phone or text?",

Unless she was having an affair, it crossed my mind. It wouldn't be the first time, would it! I asked her and she became very defensive. Shouting and spitting as she spoke,

"So what if I am, what has it got to do with you, we are over"

I was confused. Over? I said something along the lines of 'you better not be sleeping with someone else' and she raised her finger pointing and shoving it in my face then stepped towards me and her nose was literally touching mine. Still spitting,

"Why, what u gonna do about it? U gonna hit me? Go on then...go on then. Are you going too?"

Moving closer and closer to me as she spoke, like any minute she would be in my skin. I pushed her with my hand, in her face to get her away from me, to get some distance between us and my finger caught her in the corner of her eye.

While we were rowing, Marie had already started to come down from upstairs and was leaning over the bannister. She had been watching the whole thing pan out and as my finger caught Carrie in the eye, Carrie noticed Marie was there and suddenly her whole demeanor changed. This was one of her Oscar performances. She stopped spitting and her spiteful, gritted teeth, like some snarling animal then turned into a pout. She stepped back and started crying. Stumbling back like she lost her footing, grabbing hold of the kitchen counter. Really? I thought. I didn't know whether to laugh or not but this certainly was no laughing matter!

Before I even had time to react, Marie was in the kitchen. Carrie looked at her, while crying, then started to cry at me,

"I didn't deserve that!"

Everything kicked off. Marie was outraged and her face showed it.

"Oh really Carrie? Don't even try it, I saw the whole thing from the bannister! Whatever is going on with you, needs to stop! Needs to stop right now!!"

Carrie changed, literally within seconds. She was upright, her gritted teeth were back and she started to do to Marie exactly what she had just done to me,

"Who do you think you are Marie? I know all about what you said to my mum, all about it! Telling my mum how I should leave and he should kick me out!"

Marie corrects her,

"Your arguing isn't healthy Carrie!!! and, YES, I believe the relationship should end but, between you and your mum, you've concocted your own version of my speech. All you've done is use my words and twisted them!"

She continued, telling Carrie she had only come down because everything could be heard upstairs and the kids were getting upset,

"Do you have ANY idea what your children are going through upstairs?! Sofie is crying, asking why you're so mean to her daddy!"

Carrie, not caring what was being said, directed all her anger at Marie and they were soon face to face with Carrie squaring up,

"And what are you gonna to do about it then Marie?!"

This would have ended up a blood bath, I knew I had to step in. Marie can give just as good as she gets and it would of only took one second for it to turn ugly. I tried diffusing them, getting in-between them and thankfully it worked. On Marie, anyway. She told Carrie how disgusting she was and began to walk away. Carrie then turned her anger back onto me and told me to get Marie to leave. She wanted her out of the house right away. Regardless of it being the evening, dark outside and Marie living with us.

"Carrie, calm down!"

But she was having none of it. Spitting,

"She goes or I go!"

And by 'I' she meant her and the kids. Again, there it was, Carrie grabbing me by the balls and reducing me to this quivering weak mess. I looked at Marie, she looked at me. Marie knew. Marie knew exactly what Carrie was doing and she knew it had to be herself that left. Like we were talking to each other through our eyes only. Telepathically even. She knew I was sorry for doing it, I knew she understood why I was doing it. Marie went upstairs and comforted Sofie and Andrew and told them everything's going to be ok and that adults are 'silly sometimes'. She got Kaine and Andre ready and left to go to our aunts.

Everything seemed to have calmed down but then Carrie out of the blue, again said,

"That's it, I'm taking the kids and you will never see them".

And she did. Again, but this time with both Sofie and Andrew crying, not wanting to leave. Carrie constantly turned me into this helpless mess of a man. So many times, in my life I've felt like I'm in a twilight zone. Not understanding my surroundings. Trapped and confused. Any normal person would walk out. You hear about it all the time. When dads have had enough and leave. I didn't feel like one of those dads. I felt like a mum with this feeling of needing to get out, wanting to leave but not able to take my children with me so I had to just stay stuck.

Carrie returned, we spoke and she had calmed down. We ended up having sex and for a split second, the carnage that happened, hadn't. It was here, my life of doing as I'm told, keeping the peace, was in full effect. The only choice I felt I had. The children were her weapons. I couldn't live without them. I couldn't have them live with her, not without my 24/7 presence. I was their only 24/7 parent. They were safe with me and if I had to suffer at Carrie's hands then, so be it. Carrie being on the deeds and mortgage concreted the mess I was in. It felt like this woman had the power to destroy me at any given time. In rows, she had already spouted what she would be allowed to 'take', what the 'law' says she can 'take'. She had me exactly where she wanted and she knew it. I think she always did.

chapter seven

The next few days we continued to row. Any opportunity Carrie got to penalize me or start something, she took it. I was sick of being shouted at. Constantly moaned at, put down and belittled. I began fighting back with words. I wasn't going to keep standing there, not having my say. Having someone trying to overpower my voice to make it irrelevant, but this wasn't allowed. You are not allowed to defend yourself against Carrie and if your voice got louder than hers, that wasn't allowed either, which is when her famous routine would come into play. When I'm not behaving in a manner she'd prefer, when I'm not bending over backwards or being quiet while she rules me, Carrie would pull out her card,

"I'm taking the kids"

Again, she did. It was a routine I had become familiar with. By late afternoon, early evening, she still wasn't back. I called her, in desperation, I just wanted to know Sofie and Andrew were ok. She eventually answered my call and she was with her mother. I was worried, angry and very emotional whereas Carrie was mighty yet comical. She found it funny and her childish sarcasm heightened that.

She told me she's not coming back. If there was a 'ner-ner' among her words, it would have fit nicely in with her tone. I thought, ok this is it! All the threatening she had done over the years, she's going to see it through this time. I was nervous and angry and the more she taunted me and laughed at me down the phone, the angrier I become. I could feel it. A huge adrenalin rush, a pot about to boil over.

Carrie went quiet and wouldn't answer me, I continued to shout down the phone but I was met with silence. I stayed on the phone, the line was still open, but for the next few minutes I was just talking to myself. I imagined Carrie holding the phone sniggering, as I spoke to thin air. She then broke the silence but her tone had changed drastically. Softer and formal,

"I am not coming back. I am sick of you abusing me and hurting me"

I blew up! Yelling down the phone, I told her don't start playing that card and, in all honesty I said,

"Bring my kids back or I'll f****** kill you"

She put the phone down on me. Obviously, that statement wasn't meant 'literally' but I was soon to find out that words, quick off the tongue, can get you into trouble.

Carrie eventually came home and we hardly spoke and if we did, it was short and sharp. I was just glad to see the kids. Glad, they were home. I didn't care for Carrie at this point. I didn't want an explanation from her either.

The next morning, Carrie left quite early in the day on her own. No goodbye. Not that I wanted one, I mean no goodbye to Sofie and Andrew. Sofie, now seven years old and Andrew five. Andrew was still his funny little clown self. I suppose I would call him a typical five year old. Sofie was seven going on seventeen. Grown-up for her age and had obtained an adult vocabulary. She was like a little woman and her brain was aging and advancing a lot faster than her body.

With Carrie out, I got on with work, I did some drop offs with the kids and, on returning home, I noticed a police car up in the corner of our road. Not thinking anything of it, though being a nosy neighbour trying to peek, wondering what they had been up to, we went inside. Marie had finished work and said Carrie had come back earlier and asked where I was and when was I due back. We sat in the kitchen having a cup of tea while all the kids played upstairs. About five minutes later, the door knocked. Hard and stern. It was the police.

They said they had been waiting to talk to me and had been round once already but I wasn't home. I invited them in and started to evaluate the situation. My sister was with me so I knew she was ok. I had not long spoke to my mum on the phone, so I knew she was also ok, so it couldn't have been about her. The kids were upstairs so I ticked them off the list too. That just left my dad. Oh my god, has something happened to him, I thought. I had spoken to him the night before but had something happened since then? I began to panic a little, waking up my anxiety. I didn't even think of Carrie once. My brain just went through the list of who I cared about. A list Carrie didn't deserve to be on.

The police officers face expressions didn't look like they were about to speak of a death or accident, they were official. Their faces were power officials and they began to tell me I'm being arrested. They used their 'under act' wording and asked me to go quietly with them. I froze in disbelief. Is this a joke? I thought. What had I done? They proceeded to tell me about the alleged assault on my wife and that I needed to accompany them to the station for further questioning.

Carrie had me hook, line, and sinker. What a card she was playing now! Explaining myself to the police was unsolicited. They didn't care for my side, they just wanted me down the station. The way they looked at me, I was guilty, as far as they were concerned. It seemed they immediately believed I was a guy who has been beating up his wife.

Sofie and Andrew had come down at this point and I tried composing myself so they wouldn't be alarmed. I lost all faith in the police this day. Carrie could spin whatever story she wanted too. They placed me in handcuffs and I begged them not to take me. They couldn't take me because I was the main parent. I needed to do their dinner, get them sorted for bed but, It didn't matter to them.

Sofie and Andrew were crying and I told them that everything's going to be fine and that I wouldn't be long. I was escorted out like some bad criminal AND just lied to my kids because I had no idea what was going to come next, let alone when I would return home, or if I even would.

I have never been in a police cell in my life and I was disgusted that I was in one, and annoyed! Annoyed that Carrie had the power to do this through lies! Annoyed at how easy it clearly was, for her to make this happen. I was in custody for twelve hours, taken to stand in front of the judge first thing in the morning.

I learnt of Carrie's story, how I had 'punched her in the face' and that the bruises on her arm were my doing. Of course, they were going to believe her. The marks were there and they had, personally, heard me tell Carrie I was going to kill her. Carrie was clever indeed. The taunting down the phone, getting me riled up. The silence while I'm shouting my mouth off. Giving her just enough time to pass the phone to the police at the right time that she needed. She was no doubt sat outside the station while goading me. I was her pawn and she moved me into play.

After giving my side of events, in front of the judge, I was released on bail, pending further investigation but the judge placed a condition. I wasn't allowed back home until the investigation was complete. I found this totally absurd. It was like they wanted time to find out if I was telling the truth, ok granted, but yet they accepted Carrie's without hesitation. I explained to the judge that these bail conditions weren't going to work. I worked from home and I had kids to take care of, how could I not be allowed home?!

It didn't matter what I wanted or what was right or even the truth! The only change to the conditions, after my plea, was I could enter my work office from around the back of the house but I was still not allowed in the house. Work was more important than looking after children then?! Or did they not believe that I was their main carer?

I phoned Marie the moment I was out, I needed to know how Andrew and Sofie were. She said Carrie had returned after I was taken so she left. She had to. God knows what else Carrie had up her sleeve. I told Marie I would meet her at mine. Not wanting to break my bail conditions, I walked round the back of the house, while Marie, by Carrie's mum opening the front door, entered the house. Carrie was at work. I met Marie at the back door via the kitchen. With Carrie's mum was a friend of hers who had a young son and Carrie's half-sister. The friend and young son were in the garden and the mum was swearing loudly in conversation. I was so embarrassed and worried what the neighbour's would think. The house was an absolute pig-sty. Clearly from Carrie's team mates staying over. It took me hours cleaning that kitchen!

Marie noticed her dog was limping and, angrily, asked what had happened to her leg. No one answered her. She checked Binty over and asked again. Carrie's mum and sister looked at each other and like two petulant children and said to Marie,

"We don't know, she seemed fine before you got here"

We can't say for certain but me and Marie are adamant that Binty was kicked. Most probably kicked just for being Marie's dog. As I stood by the back door, Carrie's mum stands in the middle of it, as if to block my entry. This is my house, I thought, and she's certainly not one to act all superior yet she stands there like a bouncer with an amusing look on her face. I moved and sat outside my office, adjacent. I just wanted to see my kids. I was also bewildered that Carrie would allow her mother, of all people, to babysit.

As I sat there, the son of the friend, about five years old, came over and kicked me hard in the back and found it funny to do so. I turned my head and saw Carrie's mum and friend, looking and laughing. I already felt beaten and here I was being victimized by a child and his onlookers. A child wouldn't just decide to kick a stranger for no reason, especially one they hadn't met before. He was told to, I know it! All I kept thinking was, where in the world are these types of people from.

Carrie eventually came home and the next thing I know Sofie and Andrew came running out of the back door towards me. I stood up to greet them, only to drop back down on the floor and I sobbed hugging them tight and they did me,

"I'm sorry. So, so sorry, that I was gone for long. It will never, ever happen again"

I just didn't want to let them go. I wished magic was real and I had the power to transport us somewhere. Away from here, anywhere but here. I totally forgot about the onlookers in this moment. It was just me and the kids. I really wished it was just me and the kids. I later learnt that Marie had spoken briefly to Carrie while I was in awe of them. She said Carrie came across guilty and looked lost when she asked her for an explanation. All she said to Marie was "sorry".

Carrie's team mates left and Marie stayed upstairs. I didn't know what to say to Carrie. There was mostly silence. We eventually spoke, Carrie cried, saying how sorry she was and that she wanted me to stay for the kids. Regardless of the bail conditions set, I was back in the house. It was inevitable,

"I didn't mean to take it this far. My head's a mess. I was talking to my mum and things just spiraled out of control"

"Carrie, how many times are we going to push events like this under the carpet?!"

I had a court date following up the 'pending investigation', there were no charges against me and Carrie didn't even attend court. We were now just living together. Separate lives. Separate people. I was there to sort everything, be a parent, while Carrie was just there for, nothing more than, a roof over her head.

She continued going out and also got another job, at a local hotel bar which then made her working hours full time. I would constantly try and talk to her about our situation. It had to be spoken of. Things couldn't continue as they were and the past needed to be addressed. One evening we had a heart to heart. Carrie eventually said she wanted to move out so she could 'sort her head out' and that Sofie and Andrew will stay with me. It happened so easy, so painless and quiet. She spoke to Sofie and Andrew,

"I need to leave but it doesn't mean I don't love you, I just need some space"

She left saying she was going to stay with her friends.

I made regular visits to Sofie and Andrew's school to keep the head teacher up to date on the situation and I asked her if she could keep an eye on them. After many weeks, even months, the teacher told me I was doing a fantastic job and the children were 'lucky to have me'. I was the one who was lucky, I thought. They are both such a credit to me. She even said she would have never of known their mum had walked out, given their calm, content behaviour. It was lovely, yet also sad, to hear.

They would both join in with the house cleans and our space was blissful. No loudness, just a routine of life and happiness but, as much as it was peaceful, I had this feeling of regret, that life really shouldn't have ended up like this.

Trying to hold together some sort of relationship between Carrie and the children, I arranged time together. I wanted them to see mummy and daddy not rowing, being friendly, and I hoped this was apparent, now Carrie had got the space she obviously wanted. We attempted a family ice skating day but again it turned segregated. Carrie was uninterested, spending most of the time on her phone. She would, however, come around a few times a week to have dinner with us. Shortly after, she started to pop round in the evening while the kids were in bed. We would talk and be civil and it was oddly pleasant. Sometimes it would feel like Carrie was flirting with me but I put it down to maybe she had been drinking beforehand.

She was due round one day, with Sofie and Andrew waiting for her, but she didn't turn up or even call. Protecting the kids and covering for Carrie, I told them mummy might still be working and how about we arrange a bike day instead, when she isn't busy. Still painting over drama with better scenes. Carrie finally made contact and I didn't question why she didn't come like she said. There hadn't been any rows and I didn't want that routine back again so I just ignored it.

On the bike ride, the kids were happy but Carrie didn't look very well at all. She had been drinking again, the night before. Not long after we set off, she felt too ill to continue so we had to come home and Carrie laid on the sofa while I sorted the dinner. Come evening, Carrie was worse. She had a temperature of one hundred and four and severe back pains. I called the emergency doctors and they told me she needed to go to hospital. She spent ten days in hospital with a kidney infection. Looking ill, pale and thin. As she lay in the hospital bed, I remember staring at her, looking at what she was doing to herself. This woman seemed hell bent on destroying herself. I just couldn't understand it. I had feelings of resentment, looking at the state the mother of my children was in, but also felt pity. I felt sorry for her and I was annoyed at myself because she didn't deserve any pity.

As she was on the mend, she dropped into conversation that she was considering coming home. I didn't know what to say. I wanted to hate her. I hated her for everything she had done and the way she had made me feel so I dis-acknowledged her comment and just concentrated on her being in hospital. Her phone rang and whoever she was talking to wasn't happy to hear of who was there with her. The phone-call soon ended.

I turned up at the hospital a couple of days later but this time Carrie wasn't there. She had discharged herself early but later that day phoned me and said she was going to visit her mum for a week, who at this point had moved back to London. She asked how the kids were and I told her that they were fine, though Andrew had been poorly with a high temperature. She hoped he would get better soon and repeated she will be back in a week but to ring her and let her know how Andrew is doing.

A few days later I phoned Carrie but her phone was switched off so I phoned her mum. When asking for Carrie, she had no idea why I would ask because Carrie wasn't even there and hadn't been there. Confused, I called her work. She always worked at the hotel bar on most nights but the barman told me Carrie wasn't due in work because she was on holiday. Carrie's story of visiting her mum was to cover up a holiday to Rome with her boyfriend! A guy she worked with at the hotel. No doubt the person who wasn't happy to hear of my presence at her hospital bed. I believe Carrie was with this person way before her leaving and no doubt 'going to stay with friends' was a cover up too. Why would she tell me she was considering coming home before jetting off to Rome with another guy?

I loved her, but hated who she was. More honestly, I loved what we could have been. One minute I had a wife, the next an extra kid. More times, a crazy enemy. I just wanted a wife. We had beautiful children, life wasn't crummy, if only she would just stop and look at her surroundings. I gave her everything a woman could possible want but it clearly was never enough. I think if Carrie could have my undivided attention she may have been better, calmer even. If I bowed to every whim of hers, she would have loved me more. Loved her life more. I could never give her all of me, we had children. If I devoted every second of my life to her, what time would Sofie and Andrew get?! What would most likely happen, if I behaved how Carrie wanted, is Sofie and Andrew would grow up to resemble their mother.

I always tried finding the balance yet Carrie would always tip the scales. I hoped that space away would make Carrie see sense. If Carrie went away to work out what she really wanted and decided it wasn't me, then I would have accepted it. She didn't need to get me falsely arrested. Why not just tell me she didn't want me anymore? She would constantly tell me I wasn't there for her enough, if only she opened her eyes. Regardless how mean she could be sometimes, she knew deep down I would never have shut the door on her. She had issues, underline issues that really needed addressing. Especially where the kids were concerned. Why have kids if you'd prefer to not be a mother?!

She returned from Rome and it was about a week before I would hear from her. She phoned and asked if she could pop round in the evening. She didn't say much more than that. Her tone was soft and drained. There was so much I wanted to say but she wanted to talk in person. Once Sofie and Andrew were in bed, she knocked at the door. I opened it to see this pale figure. Once a size sixteen, now a size six. Her jeans hanging off her waist and bags under her eyes. Her eyes looked defeated.

We sat and spoke for hours, most of it in tears. I spent the whole evening trying to understand her. She cried like I had never seen before, it was real. It seemed real. She begged to come home and I was torn. She reeled me in and out daily, was this her holding the rod again? She said it wasn't me, it was her and, again, how messed up she was in the head. The new boyfriend was supposedly a mistake and she reassured me that she wasn't cheating, that she got with him after she left but she had now realized he wasn't who she wanted and she didn't know what she was even thinking. She wanted me and the kids and wanted to be better. Not only did Carrie sound a mess, she looked it too. I couldn't stop myself feeling sorry for her. This was my downfall. My compassion towards Carrie always ended up being the wrong emotion to have. I should have told Carrie that we need to accept that we just don't work as a couple. Not with who she is. My presence wasn't enough, who I was wasn't enough. Sofie and Andrew didn't seem enough for her either. She needed to help herself, work on herself. She needed to delve deep into her soul and figure out why she behaves the way she does. All this drinking and partying wasn't compatible with a mother's role. Regardless of why, she became a mother early and she needed to accept that was her choice but she wasn't a single mum anymore, lonely and lost. She had got out of that life and into a new one. One that should have made her happy, content and safe. It was time to grow up. Importantly for Sofie and Andrew but she also needed to grow up for herself.

I try not having regrets about anything. My mum, when talking about her life, would say, she will never die with any, that every decision she made was right at the given time. I didn't want to give up on Carrie. I couldn't. For Sofie and Andrew, I couldn't. My family warned me not to fall for her tricks. They saw how I was too easily manipulated by her and wanted me to wake up. They all said not to take her back but I did. They wished I hadn't. This would soon end up being my wish too.

chapter eight

All Carrie's antics had now come to a head and this should have been her wakeup call. She desperately needed one, a loud one. One that would wake her out of her destruction. What she thought made her happy had actually made her ill. Her body was worn out, screaming for loving attention because it wasn't being listened too. Rows had ceased but I wasn't going to hold my breath. In hindsight, she probably didn't have the energy for them.

She had already quit her job at the hotel but kept her position at the banking office and used her unused holidays for time off. With her health improving and gaining back some weight, she was on the mend and even started to involve herself in the house and as part of the family. I don't think our relationship was fixed yet, far from it, but it sure did feel like the wife and wonderful mother was on her way to us.

Sofie and Andrew's relationship with her was good but with a slight distance. They didn't have the same bond with her, as they did with me, but with Carrie continuing to be who she was being right now, that bond would come. It just had to be nurtured. She still had a few nights out with friends here and there but they weren't causing any problems. Our evenings together were enjoyable. Even our intimacy as man and wife resurfaced. It had been a long time since love was felt. Many months passed with no issues indicating any holes in our family boat.

Carrie woke up late and joined me in the kitchen. Still not a morning person, unless she had work and she needed to have her coffee before anything else. I was with Marie, she had finished work so having a quick cup of tea before she left. Marie and Carrie's relationship had improved, ever so slightly. Marie knew it was my life and if I was happy, she was happy. She knew anything other than civil would only cause more problems so she set her feelings aside and gave Carrie the benefit of the doubt, on my behalf.

Carrie sat closed off and un-talkative, taking slow sips from her cup. She was quiet but not because she hadn't fully woken up yet but like something was weighing on her shoulders. Showing the odd smile, mid-conversation in the random stuff we were talking about, I could see something was amiss so I asked her if she was ok. She hesitated at first but between sips said she was wasn't going to drink alcohol anymore and that she didn't want to say anything yet. Bewildered,

"What do you mean"

"I didn't want to say anything. Not until I was certain"

She placed her cup down,

"I'm pregnant"

I was lost for words, literally. Nothing came out of my mouth, even though I thought I was responding to her. I then went into question mode,

"How long have you known? What about the birth pill? What is the point of using a birth pill if you're still able to get pregnant? Are you sure?

"I didn't want to tell you straight away, until I knew what I wanted to do. Whether I wanted to keep the baby or not. I'm still not sure"

I absolutely wasn't sure and still in shock. We booked an appointment at the doctors and it turned out she was over ten weeks. Regardless of what we thought was the right thing to do, we both agreed that the pregnancy was too far gone to contemplate a termination.

My mum blew a gasket when I told her the news. She said it was a bad decision and cursed Carrie, and myself also, for 'being so stupid'. She believed Carrie knew about being pregnant for a while and purposely kept it a secret until it was too late for an abortion. Carrie did know how I felt about abortions. I felt the same as her. We both had a cutoff point. The fetal stage at ten weeks was way over ours.

Sofie and Andrew acted oblivious when finding out. Not the normal response children should have when they're going to have a brother or sister but who could blame them. We were this crazily, messed up couple, who weren't even fully back on track, yet we were about to have another baby.

Regardless of how it happened, it was happening so it was a case of pull our sleeves up and deal with it. It wasn't going to be straight forward again either. Carrie gained weight rapidly and ballooned. With all the constant checks, it showed she was suffering with diabetes again and she was ill all throughout the pregnancy. Vomiting more times than she should be. Her feet would be swollen, toes would become blue and she regularly had to use insulin.

Chelsea became the new member of the family and Sofie and Andrew's response, when seeing their baby sister, was better than the announcement, thankfully. She was a teeny little thing that struggled putting weight on. Carrie tried breastfeeding but Chelsea wouldn't take to the breast and Carrie didn't have the patience for her. We changed to bottle formula and for a while there was no improvement in weight, in fact Chelsea would lose pounds rather than gain them.

After a few times bringing the milk back up, feeding settled and she slowly gained some weight and continued to do so. Carrie still had some health issues after the birth, regarding the diabetes and because of the excessive weight gain she was told by doctors to exercise more and look into her diet. As her health improved, her energy levels increased and, when Chelsea was six months old, Carrie said she was going back to work.

Life wasn't as terrible as it could have been. Yes, Carrie was still too much to handle sometimes and a lazy mother but she wasn't being a bitch, for want of a better word. I think the only way I can describe this time, was playing the cards I was dealt with. Letting life flow and trying to enjoy all the good bits, and if bad bits dropped in, well, just don't pay too much attention to them.

We even had another holiday. This time to Tunisia and it went smoothly. No hiccups or rowing and no 'accidents' with any of the kids. With Carrie and Marie burying the hatchet, she joined us out there too, with her new partner. I still ran around after Sofie, Andrew and now Chelsea, while Carrie sunbathed but, other than that, the atmosphere felt pure. All the kids had a fantastic time. Evening entertainment was great, with them all getting their faces painted and joining in with the stage entertainment. As a family, we looked perfect. Onlookers weren't able to see the invisible duct tape, that I kept using to piece us back together again. The trip was satisfying. If only there was a way of pausing the ambience. I wanted it to come home with us and have it continuously on loop.

As much as I didn't want to believe it, what happened on the holiday, stayed on the holiday. Back home, both of us back to work, back to family life, I could tell Carrie was getting bored again. Bored with us. I was a fool to think life could ever be how it should be! I started to think, maybe my mum was right. That Carrie did hold off on revealing Chelsea's conception on purpose.

How foolish was I?! She didn't come back after her gallivanting because she loved me, she came back because she had too. It didn't work out with the other guy, for whatever reason, and I believe Carrie knew she always had me here. Stupid me, manipulated at a click of a finger. Easily fooled, duped with hope. She needed looking after and she knew the only person that would do it was me. This wasn't love or even broken love that could be mended. Carrie didn't want me as a lover or a friend, and certainly not as a husband. I wonder if she ever did.

She wanted someone she could move around her game board. She wanted back in the family home and did whatever she could to do it. It doesn't sound dumbfounded to suggest that Chelsea was planned by her. That Chelsea was her cement. A way to stay.

Carrie knew I could never go anywhere, with a baby, and again, I would never tell her to leave.

With Carrie back to work and back to her ways, I laid in the bed I had re-made for myself. I always talked myself round to accept my idiotic decisions. I had got quite the expert at it. All I had ever done was grab hold of good moments, any chance I got, to stay afloat but I would end up capsizing eventually anyway. I was doing everything a textbook mum would do. This never ever changed. I was the primary in every aspect. With two children in school, and an infant, I juggled work and was grateful I worked from home. I found it a god send. I really don't know how I would have managed if work wasn't this way. I believe Carrie used this to her advantage too.

If I had to go out on any rounds and Carrie was out or in bed, Marie would have Chelsea in with her. It made work slower but we did what we had to do. The longer Carrie was back in her routine of independence, the more of her old self was resurfacing. Everyone was back to egg shell steps and Marie tending to Chelsea in my absence ended up being the only quality time she got with her. I remember returning one day and found Marie pressing hotel sheets while extending her leg out, keeping Chelsea to a rhythm while she drifted off to sleep in her bouncer.

Carrie still had follow ups at the doctors yet that didn't stop her trying to pick up where she, so often, left off. She just couldn't, and wouldn't, let go of that 'single young life', regardless of the negative effect it had on her, or even the children and myself, but her body wouldn't allow her to party like she used to so her shenanigans couldn't be as frequent. Not as much as she would have liked, anyway.

She was now dealing with polycystic ovaries and gall stones, on top of everything else and the doctors were trying to get to the bottom of it all. This didn't stop her alcohol intake when out though. No one can tell Carrie what to do. She began dictating to me again about anything and everything. Most of the things so pointless and ridiculous. It always starts like that. I'm sure she would have blamed me for the rainy weather if she could. Somehow, I would have done something to the clouds but at this point I had nothing left to give. Not only was I worn out by juggling every role that needed my input, but my brain hurt from trying to figure her out. The 'peacemaker' had packed his bags and ran. The 'defender of his corner' was fast asleep because he was worn out too. Blasé was all that was left. She could call me all the names under the sun, I didn't care. I didn't care anymore. Most of the time now, I would respond to any of her outbursts with "ok, Carrie" because I was so bored of her routine. I didn't want to try and be a good husband anymore, there was no point.

Sofie and Andrew's relationship with her became null and void. The root was never planted and watered by Carrie so one was never going to blossom. Things were different now. They had their own thoughts and feelings and had encountered their own run-ins with her that made them have the feelings they did. When back from school or on the weekends, they were helpful and caring. They would help me make dinner or tidy up or even see to Chelsea. They were growing up to be such kind-hearted kids. I loved that and oozed with pride, especially when their mother was such a cold character.

Sofie was fantastic with Chelsea. If Carrie allowed her to be, that is. One minute Carrie would hand out orders, the next she would curse Sofie for 'trying to be the mum'. With Carrie glued to the pc screen one evening, finding the social media site more entertaining and worthy of her attention than her children, beckoned Sofie. She was in the kitchen when her mum wanted her to move her handbag. On asking where it was, Sofie said no. Still with her eyes fixated on the screen, she shouted to Sofie,

"Can you just move my f****** bag please"

Sofie reminded her that it was right by her feet. That her bag was right by her feet yet she was ordering Sofie, who was about seven metres away, to move it! But It didn't matter. Carrie elevated her tone,

"SOFIE, SHE'S GOING TO GO IN MY F****** BAG"

It would have took Carrie seconds to just lean down and move it. It also wouldn't have hurt if she payed attention to Chelsea and did her social interaction later. Things like this were the reason Andrew would retreat to his bedroom, if Carrie was ever around. He just didn't want to be around her or get caught up in her webs. His bedroom was his safe-haven.

Carrie then put a wedge between her and Marie again, and other members of my family would visit but they were short lived. If Carrie was in, her mannerism would show she didn't like them being there, didn't want them there. The atmosphere of our house was laughter and love with this added scent of hatred, lingering around and seeping from every corner. Carrie couldn't prevent Marie coming, no matter how uncomfortable she tried making her. Marie had to be there in the week for work but that didn't stop Carrie from trying. She even started directing animosity towards Marie's kids.

Sofie, Andrew, Kaine and Andre have a strong family bond and are little mates. Kaine hated being around Carrie because she would "do and say mean things". Once, they were all in the garden playing because our work was busy and Marie needed to stay on later than normal. It started to rain but that didn't matter to the kids. They were having a laugh and messing about and the weather wasn't bothering them at all. If anything, it added to their fun. When the rain got heavy, Carrie called Sofie and Andrew inside but, when Kaine and Andre were about to follow, she told them they weren't allowed in the house because they were wet and that they had to stay outside until they went home. She shut the door on them. A loving aunt, a real aunt, would have given the children a towel to dry off and ushered them in the dry.

Now, what should have happened was I or even Marie, should have confronted Carrie and told her to stop being so spiteful but that isn't how things work with Carrie. We had all learnt over the years, it wouldn't have made a blind bit of difference. If anyone approached Carrie and told her what for, me and the kids would suffer the punishment.

Carrie, not being able to get a rise, or even fall out of me, began resorting back to her venom of 'taking the kids'. It had become tedious until she began throwing in an extra bomb. To tell Sofie that I wasn't her real dad.

When speaking about it in the very beginning, we always knew It was going to be something we would eventually have to deal with, out in the open. Selfishly, I wished we never had too but I knew that wasn't right. We had made Sofie legally known by my surname a long time ago but we knew one day we'd have to have the 'chat'. Regardless of how I felt, the right thing to do was one day tell Sofie the truth but in no way like this. Not in a heated row to gain points.

I thought, would she be that cruel? I know she could be, but would she? This was her new ammo, that she no doubt kept tucked away in her pocket for all these years, and when rows erupted, she did her hardest to prove to me she meant every single word in her threat. Her gritted teeth would reappear and I know she wanted me to be scared. I was but there was no way I was ever going to show her. This woman knew exactly how to hurt me and if hurting the kids hurt me, then well, they were just means to an end for her. So, absolutely I was scared. Her behavior, routinely erratic, I could never say for certain what she was capable of.

Our home transformed from bricks to shells on a regular basis. We would all tread carefully, like we were in the dark and not knowing what our surroundings were. Waiting. Hoping. Wondering what type of day we were going to have. Then, as if by magic, it would become pleasant and clear. Like a witch placed a barrier spell. Carrie would be good natured but we could never cherish these moments now because we didn't know what they were or what they meant. Most times they were due to Carrie wanting money.

I remember Chelsea's birthday party, with my family over, in the garden when the weather was nice and she joined us out there like the welcoming host. Portraying the perfect wife and perfect mother. Sometimes she was and it was so draining. I used to wonder if there was something medical going on with her, something psychological, something 'not right' but then her mood swings would always coincide with a 'sane', premeditated agenda.

Carrie was unable to put on a show. The most affectionate persona would surface but then it would crawl back into the darkness. I now personally believe she lived there and that her 'normal' moments never lasted long because she unable to keep up the act for a long period of time or she had got whatever she wanted out of being that way so the act was cut.

Life never unfolded naturally as I wanted it too. Which brings me to announce Adam. Carrie was due to have her gallbladder removed but had problems with her menstrual cycle so the doctors did a routine pregnancy test. Again, she was too far gone for a termination and the operation was held off. We were going to have another child and I felt like a deer caught in headlights. I couldn't blame Carrie because it takes two to tango but this really wasn't meant to be happening. It's horrible to say but I don't remember it as 'love making'. It as a night of fulfilling needs. I want to say a mistake but I would never say that about Adam. He would never be one.

Life was more like a movie with no script and scenes were just improvised. If it worked, it worked and if it didn't, well, the camera continued rolling regardless and you had to improvise some more to get back in the game. But with every movie, there is a director, watching over the characters, possibly taking notes. They know the ending before anyone else does. If my movie was ever to hit a big screen, Carrie would be there, out in front of the credits. I would take home the supporting actor award because I placed the camera, and the royalties, in her hands in the first place.

chapter nine

Carrie's diabetes was dangerous during Adams pregnancy, with the doctors now saying she probably had it all her life, that it had gone un-diagnosed. She would have to test her levels every few hours because it could rocket too high or be dangerously low, where there could be a chance of a diabetic coma. She collapsed once, one evening, at the bottom of the stairs resembling a drunk person and began hallucinating. I tried helping her up but she become incoherent, then told me to get away from her because 'I was trying to kill her'. I ran into the kitchen and got her injection needle and a sugary sweet for her to suck on but she wouldn't accept it, saying it was poison. Trying to make her stay focused, reassuring her, I enticed her into having it. After a while her sugar levels stabilized and I helped her to the kitchen. Coming around, she said, at the time, she didn't know where she was or who she was.

When asking her what her lifestyle was like, Carrie gave the doctors a watered-down version so I took one of them aside and told them the truth. They told her that it is imperative that she changes her diet and lifestyle. With the diabetes controlled and the pregnancy going smoothly, or as smooth as It could, Carrie got her strong mentality back and was back ruling the roost.

Her first target was Marie, who had now stopped working because of an operation on the tendons in her hand. Work was pretty tough for me, running solo, and my dad had relayed this back to Marie. She arrived one morning, now with her hand out of bandages and said she was here to see if she could work. She later said that she didn't want to hurt her hand but wanted to try because she didn't like hearing I was struggling.

Marie only had time to get to the back door before Carrie ripped into her. Marie had her hand on the door handle ready to open it but stayed in that position while Carrie picked at her. Like Marie was just there working out what to do. Carrie blasted how Marie doesn't care about me, that she just left me high and dry and hasn't cared how busy I've been. Marie faced Carrie and showed her hand. She was still unable to open it fully and was having physiotherapy to ease the tendons out. Reminding Carrie that leaving wasn't what she wanted but was needed.

Carrie continued shouting at her, cursing her. Marie told her that she didn't care that she was pregnant and if she was going to shout and scream at her, then she will do the same. Carrie continued,

"Are you here because your rent needs paying? Because you're not here for your brother, are you?!"

With that, Marie said to Carrie, probably what she's been wanting to say for a very long time,

"How dare you! All you've done, Carrie, most of your life, is sit on your fat arse, watching my brother run around like a blue-arsed fly. When I worked up to 10pm some nights, that benefited you all, WAY more than me so, HOW DARE YOU stand there insinuating that I don't care about my brother! But, ohhh, now you care about my brother?!"

Marie, in the end, left. She was done with Carrie and wiped her hands off her for good. The outburst was strange and ironic. Yes, I was extremely busy, running around trying to make the business and parenthood work simultaneously, on my own but Carrie could have made things easier for me. She could had parented too yet she directed all her anger at Marie like it was purely her fault why I was struggling. The row was left with Carrie making it very clear that once Adam was born, Marie was to have nothing to do with him or Chelsea.

The row had nothing to do with Carrie being a supportive wife, sticking up for her husband. It was to try and put a wedge in between me and my sister. I know that now. I know everything now. She was jealous of our relationship and also knew that Marie wouldn't always allow her to get away with treating me the way she did. I believe, Carrie not only thought I was easily controllable where the kids were concerned but also more controllable on my own.

As soon as Adam was born, Carrie seemed to turn her back on him. Uninterested, like Adam wasn't hers, but mine. At first I thought it could be postnatal depression. I read up on it but Carrie seemed different to how it was being described. She wouldn't just be unsettled by his crying, she would just completely ignore it, for a long length of time. Too long sometimes and would order me or Sofie to deal with him. Swearing and getting angry if we weren't quick enough. If she changed his nappy, it would be left on the floor until I put it in the bin.

The house was becoming disgusting because I had no time to keep on top of it. To me the state of the house was the least of my worries. I had a business and four children to contend with. Carrie wasn't bothered about the state of the place, she just continued to add to it. You knew where Carrie had been from the sight of overflowing ashtrays and moldy coffee cups. We started to row a lot over this, the last straw for me was having to put used sanitary products in the bin because she would just leave them laying around in inappropriate places. When told about the bin she would just swear at me, that, if I didn't like, I should do it.

Living with her now was a nightmare. Asking her to get up in the morning to help would awake a monster. She would just tell me no and if I continued to ask, she would tell me to drop dead. If Sofie and Andrew were in when she arose from her pit, Andrew would go to his bedroom and eat his breakfast, while Sofie would take hers outside and sit in the garden. I wasn't surprised, I didn't want to be around her either.

I felt like a slave and spent most nights looking at all four of my children thinking, what have I done and what am I doing and how the hell do I get us all out of this mess? The more Carrie shouted at me, the more annoyed I got because I didn't deserve it. If I showed any confidence, she threw her weapon of leaving with the kids. Once, while Sofie and Andrew were in the room, but they quickly stated to her that they would NEVER go with her and she couldn't make them either.

Carrie's threats about taking the children would always scare me and she knew I'd do anything to stop it from happening. She would have been right, a long time ago but I wasn't feeling like that person anymore. Sofie and Andrew were older now and in all honesty, I drew strength from them. It was like I wasn't alone, that I had back up. As they got older there became two sets of extra eyes in the house and I felt reassured. If Carrie was to ever do anything or say anything damaging to me, the kids were there to witness. I feel so awful writing my feelings in that description but it's true. We had each other's back.

The strong relationship between me, Sofie and Andrew was very visible and Carrie hated it. It didn't work in her favor so the more rows we were having, the more threats she'd pull out. How she was 'the muvva, 'the wife' and had 'entitlements' and again,

"You're not even Sofie's real dad, maybe she needs to know that!"

She started to go out with her friends again, demanding money. I would give her it, just to get her out of the house. Going out with friends should be a normal thing to do but it was what came after Carrie's socializing that made it anything but normal. She was more vicious, more controlling and unapproachable. She would moan about my dad being over some weekends and about his drinking. That is was "unacceptable behaviour" around kids. Pot calling kettle!

She loved his visits though, when she could get money out of him. She would purposely make me feel under pressure about not giving her any. I gave her forty pounds one night and she blasted me, for it not being enough,

"What can I do with that"

It was difficult to control any situation with her because you would want to stand up for yourself but also not want to rattle her cage. Most the time I didn't know what the best response was so I'd just do what I could to end or prevent conflict. Dad was the same, he'd give her money just so she would leave me and the kids in peace.

With Adam now three months old and life getting severely worse rather than better, I was finding myself no able to live like it anymore. I couldn't make my children live like this anymore. I was back in time. Back to Sofie and Andrew being young yet Carrie was different to back then. More powerful maybe. It was like Chelsea and Adam were the new versions of Sofie and Andrew but Carrie was a different mother all together. She wasn't just lazy and unpredictable with the odd temper. She was amped up.

On the next threat of revealing the truth to Sofie, I made the decision to tell her myself. I would never have wanted Sofie to be told in a bad way. It was a sensitive matter. Carrie would have dropped it out the blue. I can see it now, with Carrie about to walk out of the room and she would then look back and say "oh by the way Sofie, he isn't your real dad" and she'd continue to walk away, probably with a victorious smirk on her face while Sofie's left in dismay. I wasn't going to let that happen so I waited for the right time.

Carrie was not going to pour poison using this subject, I wasn't fair on Sofie. If anyone was going to tell her, it would be me. In a calm, caring manner. It was one of the hardest things I've had to do in my life. This little woman was my daughter. I felt no different towards her than any of my other children. I was her dad.

When Sofie would be out with me on my rounds, I'd casually drop a situation like ours in conversation. I suppose like testing the waters. Something came on the radio about a single mum and we got chatting about that type of scenario. We spoke about Kaine and Andre, who had a step father in their life rather than their biological one and we had an intellectual conversation about 'blood sometimes not being thicker than water'.

I knew Sofie was ready and could handle the truth. Honestly, I always knew she would be, I think it was more to do with me being ready and able to handle telling her. I then did. I told her everything. The how and why and that it didn't make any difference to me, that I loved her so very much,

"I may not have helped make you and I wasn't there the first six months but I've been there every day since. You are my daughter in my heart"

She had tears in her eyes, as did I. My little Sofie so grown up and strong. Stronger than me. Her response was just as adult as I thought and hoped it to be. Biological or not, it didn't change anything for her but she thanked me. Going by her memories of her mother growing up, and imaging not having me around, she said,

"If it wasn't for you, I would have probably ended up in care!"

Returning home, I then had the task of telling Carrie. I wasn't afraid. A part of me was pleased that I took that power away from her. Especially for the sake of Sofie. One of Carrie's threats was now invalid. She couldn't hurt me with it anymore and couldn't hurt Sofie to get to me either.

Carrie, of course, went mad. Her response was, I was totally out of order she cursed me for not sticking to what we had agreed. She meant that we were supposed to tell Sofie together. We did agree that but that was at a time where life showed a path of happiness, happy family, mum and dad, one day having to sit down with our daughter and tell her the truth. That wasn't our life now. This was Carrie, an expert at diverting blame onto anyone else.

If Carrie ever thought the truth would ruin my relationship with my kids, especially the older two, she was very much mistaken. If anything, her ways made our bond stronger. The more Carrie couldn't upset the apple cart, the worse her behaviour got and by this point our relationship was well and truly over. She segregated us like we were teams. Me, Sofie and Andrew vs her, Chelsea and Adam and this time it was in a battle sense.

On speaking about how we would split, Carrie would firmly and confidently say that I should go. Constantly repeating that she was the 'muvva' and who children stay with. Normally this was where I diffused her to gain back quiet time or control over the situation but quiet time was a myth, I don't know why I searched for it so long. My response changed. I told her to go! Reminding her that, it was my life before I even met her that got us, materialistically, where we were. It was my house. I said that loud in my head too. IT WAS MY HOUSE. If anyone should leave, it was her. She never wanted to be a wife or a mother so why stay? Then I knew why.

I've never seen someone so pleased with themselves when making a statement. Carrie gloatingly reminded me again how mothers have rights, mothers have automatic rights and also that she has rights being on the mortgage and deeds. I felt like I started to run towards freedom to only hit a brick wall. We were about to be in a head to head, I knew what I wanted, she knew what she wanted. I believe she knew what she wanted all along. She wasn't going anywhere and I wasn't either. She was staying put and ready to make my life an absolute misery, probably in the hope I'd walk out. I would NEVER leave my kids and especially not in the full care of somebody like her.

chapter ten

Two people living separate lives again and only brought together in conflict. Carrie has no interest in Sofie or Andrew. If anyone was lucky to get any of her time it was the little ones but it wouldn't last long. Boredom would strike and Carrie always ending up having better things to do, other than parenting. Her partying was in full swing, mostly coming home early hours or not at all. She quit work and was now attending college to become a social worker. A drum roll should have been announced before I revealed that. You're probably thinking exactly what I thought when I heard this. I'd never heard something so crazy and ridiculous. A social worker is there to help families and children yet Carrie was burning hers down to the ground!

With Marie back working, she stayed well away from Carrie. As far as Marie was concerned Carrie didn't exist and if the kids were around, she acted normal so the kids didn't feel uneasy. Unlike Carrie of course, you could cut the atmosphere she radiated with a knife. Marie was still not allowed any contact with the little ones and Carrie relished on it.

She still wouldn't care about parenting Adam in the mornings. Even at a young age, Adam was like us, had to do what Carrie wanted. If she wanted him up, he'd be up. If she didn't, he'd have to stay where he was. Adam, bored of waiting, started banging his head continuously on his cot but his mother's attention was never received. I found him one morning happy as Larry with his nappy was off. Amusing himself with his own faeces. The cot was covered where he had smeared it with his hands. Confronting Carrie lead to me being told to drop dead again and that the incident wouldn't have happened if I had changed him. I just kept altering my routine to make things like this never happen again while struggling to find a way out of this whole sordid charade.

The animosity towards Sofie and Andrew continued to get worse the less reaction Carrie got from myself. Andrew never gave her a chance to erupt anything with him. He would show her no emotion, giving Carrie nowhere to go with it but I could see how frustrated that made him inside. He would purposely stay out of her way. Something I wished I could do. So he didn't have to retreat to his room all the time being bored, I brought him an Xbox. Most nights now he was in his room being a 'normal boy', having a laugh and fun with Kaine online, away from any mess that was happening outside his door.

Sofie was more than capable standing her ground and Carrie didn't like it. She wasn't always able to overpower Sofie which made Carrie try harder. Annoyed that Sofie got to order out of our catalogue, Carrie had to order too because,

"Why should Sofie get something and not me?"

Like she wanted to prove to Sofie that she was more inferior. An open-backed dress inappropriate, in my eyes, for her age and was a few sizes too small. While out on the town one night, Carrie's friends used red lipstick and wrote on her revealing back 'free and single' and plastered the photos all over social media. You may not have been able to see it but these words were clearly on the back of her wedding dress too!

Life was carnage and the only person that seemed comfortable was Carrie. Still suffering with medical issues yet still doing exactly what she wanted and trying her very best to push my buttons. Her feet would still regularly be swollen and blue yet without fail, her five-inch-high heels would be put on and ready to party the night away. Carrie's life revolved around being in bed, at college, out with her friends or on the PC. Mine consisted of cooking, cleaning, working, washing, school runs - everything a parent does and my version of partying was strawberry picking with my kids. My life was great as far as I was concerned, apart from the annoyingly embedded splinter, being Carrie.

Sofie's birthday didn't even entice her to stay at home, she was up and out. I was hardly surprised, nor was Sofie. No special events brought out any niceness. Sofie did want to go to Thorpe Park but I couldn't afford to pay for us all. Carrie had heard this conversation between us the night before and, a few days after Sofie's birthday, tells me she's going to Thorpe Park herself, with her friends. She made sure Sofie was with me when she said it too, I know, just to rub it in Sofie's face because she came home gloating afterwards of the rides she had been on and what a fantastic time she had.

If money wasn't available, she still got her party nights which annoyed me because it showed she didn't have to ask me for any in the first place. I found a pawn shop receipt in the bedroom where she had sold her wedding ring and a gold chain I brought her many moons ago. I then made sure my own valuables were well out of her sight. Her party nights were obviously extremely important to her and there was no way she'd be out drinking, courtesy of one of my grandfather's air looms.

It was like having a teenage lodger. Rolling in early hours in the morning with no respect for the sleeping household. I never knew someone could make so much noise just by putting the kettle on. She would slam cupboards and clip-clop about in her heels, on the wooden flooring. No regards to the kids having school in a few hours. Waking me up, I'd go down to ask her to be quiet but she would just swear at me and made even more noise.

Her drinking made me nervous, the more it was occurring. She was a confident character without it, but once drink was inside her, she had more 'balls'. I started walking around at home with my mobile phone on voice record. I'd just go about my day to day routine with a little guardian angel in my back pocket. Watching over me, in case I had to prove my innocence. Things were feeling too familiar. Another thing added to my to-do list because I'd have to sneak, whenever I could, to get the files off before Carrie came home. My phone memory would become full and unable to record anymore and I knew my luck. It wouldn't be recording when it needed it the most.

I was amazed how Carrie juggled her day and night life. I'd be so tired in the mornings. Just buttering bread for packed lunches was a task, all on its own sometimes. How she managed to attend college classes in hangover mode, I don't know. Though, I suppose it's like what I said in the very beginning of my story. Working hard, putting effort in for results. It's just that Carrie's efforts were solely for her gain.

Regularly sat the PC, if home, 5pm-early hours. A mixture of college work and social media interaction. Carrie wanted us all quiet so she could 'concentrate'. Understandable to some degree but it never entered her head that this was achievable if she chose the timing correctly. Perched on the swivel chair, glued to the screen, it was dinner time. Adam was in high chair waiting for his noodles I was cooking while Chelsea played with the laundry basket, pretending it was her boat. Having fun and getting excited with it,

"Ooooow my boat is swinging, my boat is swinging" (swimming)

and she tilts the basket left and right. Carrie is not liking the noise,

"Shut up, you're p***ing me off"

I signal Chelsea to quieten down, but Carrie's too annoyed,

"SHUT THE F*** UP!"

Adam's now whining loud and getting angst in his high chair because his food isn't ready yet, which annoys Carrie even more.

"Sort her out because I'm gonna punch her in a minute", referring to Chelsea. I ask Chelsea to be quiet for mummy, as I dish up Adam's food and before I can do or say anything else,

"She's f****** rude, you need to sort her out. She gets it from the f******* rest of the kids".

Adam is now elevating his moaning and beginning to bellow, like he's mimicking Carrie a bit, so I'm trying to calm Adam down while trying to make Chelsea settle. Then, it's all my fault.

"You're taking the f****** piss".

"Carrie, I cannot look after the kids, cook and stop them screaming, and everything, at the same bloody time!"

I then state the obvious. Chelsea is four years old and Adam is under one. Surely their bed time would benefit her more. If anything, it would benefit us all. We could eat our dinner in peace!

Peace. Something I had long forgot the definition of. Carrie was on a one-way street and it was clear as day, she was the mayor of our town. I don't actually know if Carrie would of ever carried out her threat of punching but I didn't fancy the odds so I would take all four kids out on my rounds with me any chance I got, limiting the gamble. I had a busy evening and with all kids being with me and Carrie said she would go to the supermarket instead of me doing it. The moment my key entered the lock I could hear Carrie stomping towards the door. She verbally lays into me about ignoring her text. She had text me while we were out but I hadn't looked at it yet because I was driving.

She's angry at me because the text was to tell me to do the shopping instead.

"You're out in your f****** van, you can stop there, it's more than f****** easy for you to do that, you're out in the f****** van anyway, what's so f****** complicated about it, really!".

All because she couldn't be bothered to go and, again, it's my fault. I explain to her, what she already knows, that there's nowhere to park in my big van and she just gets even more irate.

"WHY ARE YOU GOING TO F****** TESCOS, ON THE F****** CORNER, IN A BIG THREE AND A HALF TON VAN ANYWAY? OF COURSE THERE'S NOT GONNA BE ANYWHERE TO PARK! WE'RE

TALKING ABOUT SAINSBURYS…….A SUPERMARKET……WITH LOTS OF F******* SPACES".

Talking to me like she's educating me on area. She wants me to do all my business calls at the other end of town, go to Sainsbury's with all four kids, contend with rush hour traffic, all in time to put dinner on. Commonsense straight out of the window because it doesn't work in her favour. Reminding her I was working is pointless,

"So f****** what! You've been working, so that stops you from going?"

She continues to argue her point, why she's in the right and I'm in the wrong. She texted me and the fact I didn't get it, wasn't her fault. It was mine for not reading it and that it makes total sense that I should go because I was already out. Trying to get through to her thick skull, if I'm working and she is only sat using the social media site, it was easier for her to go than me. She doesn't want to go and shouts it plenty of times. I tell her we need nappies and baby wipes but,

"It's raining and cold……..I don't want too!"

She then changes the argument all together and is now annoyed at me for not sorting out her MOT on her car! How, she must rely on public transport all because of my doing, my 'incompetence'.

This caper goes on for quite a while. It is one of, very many, recordings I saved. If she was the scared wife she made herself out to be, surely she wouldn't speak to an 'abusive husband' in the manner she does. I'm sure you can guess what the outcome was. I walked over and got the shopping and couldn't wait to go to bed! Sleep was the only escape from her.

Customers would ring quite early in the mornings and I'd often get caught with my hands tied. Asking her to take over changing Adams bottom, while I answer the calls was asking too much. Applying her mascara was far more relevant and that,

"Another five minutes more in a dirty nappy isn't going to hurt him".

She was too busy getting ready for college. She had a busy day ahead. She was now involved in a support charity who help families with young children deal with whatever life throws at them. They have volunteers, one now being Carrie, who support parents as they learn to cope, improve their confidence and build better lives for their children. The irony! I often said to Carrie that I would ring the charity myself, that perhaps they could help me!

Maybe Andrew's football presentation would have been a night to remember, on a more positive note, if someone was round our house 'helping'. Andrew is big on football and on his way to becoming quite professional at it. With his presentation evening coming up for his team's achievements, he stated straight away that he did not want his mother going. Carrie actually didn't even want to go but changed her tune the moment she heard we were popping into my aunt's beforehand for her birthday BBQ. She said she was coming and we all knew we couldn't stop her. Once there, our masks came out. My family wore them too. Keeping the peace, being civil for the children's sake. Carrie, wanting EVERYBODY to know she was 'in the building' was loud. Drinking excessively and used profanity in every sentence and embarrassed us all.

Not wanting her anywhere near the presentation I told her she needs to go home but she refused unless Adam went with her. I now needed to be in two places at once. Andrew's presentation was soon to begin but I also needed to be with Adam. Life was so god damned difficult and finding a solution was impossible at times.

Andrew, my dad, Sofie, Marie and her kids, walked to the hotel the event was being held at while I went home with Carrie and Adam. The distance between us was only three-hundred yards, thankfully. Once Carrie laid down she was asleep in now time. I settled Adam and waited until he was fast asleep then I texted Marie my plan. Carrie wouldn't have liked it but it was the only option I felt I had. I couldn't leave Adam or Andrew.

They were all there at the hotel making sure Andrew didn't miss any of the event. To show him support and to take any photos in case I missed anything before being able to get there. Once I felt ok to leave, I sprinted down to Andrew. As I got there, Sofie and Marie left to be in the house with Adam. As they were about to leave I got a text from Carrie which didn't make any sense. Jumbled up letters and words. Marie told me to concentrate on Andrew, that it was his evening, and went back to mine with Sofie.

Arriving at the house, Adam thankfully still asleep, they found Carrie hanging over the bed. She had vomited everywhere, leaving a trail. Trying to reach the bathroom, she had also hit her head. Marie let me know and said they'd deal with it but I felt guilty. It wasn't there responsibility to clean up vomit, especially not Sofie's, so once Andrew got his medal we headed home. On first sight, Carrie looked disgusting. Embarrassingly disgusting but the only thing I kept thinking about was the bruise on her forehead. A mark that she could very easily say I did. She had done it before. I played that evening cool, many evenings afterwards too. Kept my distance, spoke nicely to her, became her best friend, hoping I wouldn't give her any incentive to use it.

For a while I was on edge, waiting. I dreaded every knock at the door because I immediately would think it was the police back to put me in handcuffs. God knows what the postman thought of me, by the nervous wreck I would be in. Thankfully the police never made an appearance and I could calm my nerves. Never able to do that for long though because Carrie would sometimes take Chelsea and Adam out in the day to meet up with her friends. No doubt to keep up the pretense. Playing mum to the audience she wanted. My fingers would be crossed and I'd pray to god that everything would be ok and that Chelsea and Adam would be fine. I relaxed again when they came home safe and well.

Her actress skills were very good, I give her that. She would do the same when any of her family visited too. Mainly around her nan, grandad and aunty. All three I got on well with. More so her grandad. He said I was the son he always wanted. Memories I will cherish close to my heart because he is no longer with us. He told me the actual reason he had fallen out with Carrie all those years ago. She had stolen money from him, taken DVDs and before I was on the scene would always try to dump Sofie off on them. I wasn't amazed by this at all. He was a good man and became a good friend of mine and is very missed. Everyone had clearly suffered the wrath of Carrie one way or another.

Even Bushy couldn't escape her temperament. Especially if she was whining in her presence. Carrie was getting ready for another night on the town and angry because she couldn't get ready 'in peace' and disgusted at the little money I offered on her request.

She ordered Sofie to take Adam downstairs and wanted Bushy hushed,

"Shut that f****** dog up before I punch it in the face"

She was irritated and wanted more money from me but we just didn't have it. We didn't have the money she wanted for her nights, not without making a mess with the bills. The only amount spare was eighteen pounds and on hearing that, Carrie turned her nose at it,

"What the hell am I supposed to do with that?!"

Chelsea had heard and came to the bedroom,

"Mummy can have my money" talking about her two pence collection. But instead of saying something nice, Carrie replied with "no darling THAT'S NOT ENOUGH". As if she was patronized by Chelsea and annoyed that she offered very little too.

This was going to be our life and every time I thought 'I can do this', I couldn't. My business started to suffer because I couldn't be out of the house long enough for collections. I had got to the point where I didn't care what happened to work. My children were more important. Even so, I was finding that a task too. Carrie made me feel like I was an octopus, tentacles franticly moving in every direction, trying to keep hold of everything. The business hadn't been great for a while which made us seek help through tax credits. This only gave Carrie more of a reason to demand money and because her "name was on the claim".

I would lose sight on things too. Marie pulled me aside once letting me know Adam had been put to bed by Carrie in the clothes he had worn all day and not been washed, even though his hands and feet were dirty black from being out in the garden. So, there I was, running upstairs to amend her ways. Everyone close to me told me enough was enough and that I needed to put a stop to it. I knew that but I just didn't know how too. I had a difficult wife, that's what my manly pride told me and my manly pride wasn't helping me at all.

With Carrie still getting confrontational, more often than not, I made sure my mobile phone memory was never low. I started to stop off at Marie's to save everything on a hard drive. There was no way I was ending up in a police cell again, unable to prove my side. Carrie had learnt from the law and I didn't want to get caught in any more traps. We would row quite bad and it would always turn into a match. She wanted me gone,

"Get the f*** outta here if you don't like it! Why don't you just f******* leave?"

Constantly hearing this over and over again, grated on me and eventually I stopped scampering into a corner,

"NO! You F****** leave"

I just wanted her to leave! It was exhilarating but Carrie would then say she isn't going anywhere,

"What are you gonna f******* do about it? What you gonna do? Hit me? Go on then! Go on! You know you want too"

I'd ask her why she always talks like that and did she really want me to hit her? Of course, she wanted me too, oh how she wanted me too. She could then ring her friends and they'd escort me away again.

No man should hit a woman. In fact, no one should hit anyone but when I hear about a man hitting a woman now, after living with someone like Carrie, my first thought, however deemed wrong, is 'but what did the woman do'. We're men and yes, were supposedly stronger and more capable but when you're put under an extreme amount of pressure and stress, I understand how some men lose their cool. Please don't take that as me condoning physical violence. I absolute DO NOT!

'Grab your coats were going' is the same, to me, as my children dying. 'You'll never see them again' and that thought made me so angry and full of rage. Add that to the constant griping, goading and belittling, your life can become too much to deal with. So yes, I could have hit Carrie. I thought about it many times. Someone, purely through words alone, is able to destroy the very core of you and make you feel trapped in your own emotions.

Anyone has the ability to rage, I think it's built in. If someone entered your home threatening the life of your kids, the rage would kick in. Wouldn't it?! You probably wouldn't even recognize yourself. The protection element of our being would bring it forward. Some days I wished I could bring it forward. I wanted to stop her, so yes, I understand how men lash out in the end, who break when they can't cope anymore. Not that they're right but I will say this, I am not ashamed to say I deserve a medal for not physically hurting her. I only ever gave Carrie what she wanted in my head and inside I'd be screaming, doing everything in my power to end her. Her voice would fade out and all I'd hear is my own thoughts and they weren't very nice. Not nice at all. I'd play out ulterior endings, I'd grab her so tight round her throat and warn her to 'STOP'.

My thoughts would be graphic but I never felt guilty of them. I won battles against her many times but only my brain knew of the victories. I didn't break because of Sofie, Andrew, Chelsea and Adam. The thought of losing them was far greater than the need to hurt Carrie but my self-control was tested to the max. I prayed every night for strength. Asking for guidance.

This was my life and I found it not so difficult speaking to family about what was happening. Relaying things Carrie did or said to me, I approached like I was just 'having a moan'. I never addressed things in an emotional abuse manner. It was too embarrassing. I would always give off 'but anyway, I am coping so don't worry' persona but that was far from the truth. I was too embarrassed. The possibility of talking to a professional made me feel even more embarrassed, anxious too.

When I was arrested, I tried saying my part but ended up disheartened and felt dismissed. Life couldn't continue how it was and I knew I needed to do something. I needed to let go of any shame and emasculation. With the help of Marie, I arranged to speak to the police for advice. That's untrue. I didn't help, I was too afraid too. The police were the last people I wanted to be involved with. Marie set up the meeting telling me it's time to talk and end all 'this'. I was reluctant and on edge because I didn't want to open up and be made to feel a fool.

We met the officer around Marie's house as I didn't want Carrie finding out. I didn't have long and explained to the officer why. I was closed off at first. He spoke to me officially but then also like a human being. After stating what the law can and can't do, what textbook procedures needed to be followed, he spoke in a way that made me grateful. It was comforting to be able to talk to another male and not be judged or questioned. For a minute, he was my friend. Not giving out too much information, he told me of the situation he had been in. It didn't mirror mine but he had children and had split from his wife. Explaining how it took a toll on his life.

Then his exact words were -

"Write everything down, remember everything. Document it all and seek legal advice. If she won't change her babies bum and she's happy for him to stay soiled while she lays in bed, change it yourself then put that dirty nappy next to her pillow! I know how you feel, you feel lost and being in a bubble comforts you but it isn't doing you or your children any good. You need to come out of that bubble. You need to grow some balls!"

I am eternally grateful for this guy. He will never know how much our conversation meant to me. My friends and family said the same as him, in a roundabout way, yet what they said often went in one ear and out the other. Yet this stranger seemed to hit target and got through to me. He made me feel I could come out of the bubble, that I was allowed too. Most importantly, he believed me. Every word I said.

chapter eleven

Carrie would do her upmost to make me feel uncomfortable while I did my upmost to show her I wasn't uncomfortable at all. She would be really spiteful to Sofie, always showing her that she was the woman of the house and Sofie was nothing but "a silly little girl". She would go into Sofie's room and take her deodorant, perfume or lip gloss, I'm sure just to antagonize. Her and Carrie would always come to blows, with Sofie maintaining a sophisticated broad vocabulary, whereas Carrie was monosyllabic with a potty-mouth.

I was hearing about things Carrie had posted on her social media page. Everybody on Carrie's side totally oblivious to the truth, were praising her, showering her with sympathy. She posted once that she 'didn't appreciate being woken up like that'. Her bad, evil husband had woken her up by shouting abuse. Swearing at his poor defenseless wife and of course they believed the whole spectacle. Why wouldn't they? They were her friends. Why would they possibly think she was misleading them?

I tried not letting this bother me. I didn't need to care about their thoughts. I knew the truth and that was enough for me. I didn't need any social media approval or validation. I actually found

Carrie pathetic. It was obvious the types of things she would write anyway. In her eyes, she wasn't lying. That's what Carrie does, she takes snippets of the truth and molds it into her own clarity. She wasn't lying, she didn't appreciate being woken up by me and, yes, I cursed her but what she failed to mention was the soiled nappy art work incident with Adam. She wouldn't exactly write that, would she?! That wouldn't be the type of attention she was aiming for. A recent post, was Carrie and her friends having a subliminal conversation, clearly finding it amusing-

'Hope the husband enjoys his dinner tonight, I added something extra to the gravy'

Followed by 'hahaha' and ☺. Her friends joined in the giggle, with Carrie continuing to give them their laughs-

"Does that smell like chloroform to you ☺"

Coincidently, she had said to me one morning,

"Bad things are going to happen to you. I'm gonna make sure of it"

If I ever shouted at her, the same way she did me, she would have a patronizing tone,

"Be careful. You might have a heart attack"

She had made us dinner on a few occasions, which I thought was odd at the time. I have no idea if she did do anything to my food. If she did, it was pointless because I'm still here but on hearing about her posts, I kept an eye on my food.

I also kept tabs on her. It wasn't spying, well, I suppose I was, but it wasn't hacking or invasion of privacy. Carrie would post things publicly. Anyone could see it because she chose the whole public to be able too. What I did have to do though was have another social media account look at hers because she had blocked me and my whole family. I was determined to be one step ahead of her.

My diary became my sanctuary. My hideout. A place where I could talk freely, open and honest. It felt good to have a release but I often wished the pen and paper could talk back. I wanted to be open and honest here, in this book and thought about just copying out my whole diary but I didn't want to bore you with tales of hanging washing out on the line and the amount of ironing piling up on the chair. Most days I would just document Carrie's whereabouts, what I did with the children and jot my feelings down, instead of bottling them up but the diary always turned into a thriller. You could get the gist of the day I was having purely from my erratic handwriting. It wasn't even an actual diary. I wouldn't have been able to fit a regular one in my pocket. It was just A4 sheets of paper, per day, that I folded to make good of all the space.

Carrie liked writing too, expressing herself. Her college books would be laid out on the kitchen counter looking like they belonged to a secondary school student. Sofie luckily spotted them before Chelsea did. The books had graffiti on them and vulgar language, ironically on top of psychology, social work and educational textbooks. Placed in view for all to see, Carrie didn't see the issue with the child-like, art-work drawing of a penis ejaculating.

I tried again with the police. Again, round Marie's for privacy. This experience was totally different to the previous one. Two police officers came, one male, one female with the female seeming to take over the authority of the call out. I told them a bit of what was happening and it didn't seem to hit home so the recording of the laundry basket incident with Chelsea was shown to the female officer. I thought great, they're going to see this and say they will help me and the kids.

Quite the contrary. The officer wasn't impressed because the law doesn't 'approve of recording'. If they weren't police officers I would have read them the riot act. Was there more rules that helped bad people than good?! It was apparent to me that I had to prove whatever I say. Now that I'm proving, its wrong. A suspect can be brought in because they are seen on camera at the same time of a suspected burglary and they use that recording as 'reasonable doubt', yet my recording of a woman threatening to harm a child is meaningless. What if Carrie carried out her threat? Then what? Surely the law should prevent bad things from happening, as well as being there when they do? I wanted to say to the policewoman that she needs to put down her rulebook and work with a bit humanity. Perhaps it was too much paperwork for them. Maybe they didn't believe me, didn't take me seriously? Was it because I was man? Was it because the officer was a woman?

They say that a recording is frowned upon because it could have been instigated by the recorder. What an absolute cop out! I was arrested and put in handcuffs, maybe they should look at their previous reports for enlightenment. Carted away on hearsay, a woman's word and upon hearing me say I was going to kill her. This woman could walk into a police station while in midst of a phone call to me and they intercepted. There was no 'the outcome of the call could have been instigated' then!

She showed them bruises and they came to her rescue. I'm here saying she is abusive, unstable, an unfit mother and show a recording of her viciousness, which let's be realistic, contradicts every accusation she's ever made, and nothing! Like, let's have a cup of tea and forget this fiasco. This is exactly why woman, correction, some women, know they have the full use of the law behind them because they know how the system works. Not only do they know how it works in their favour, they know how to use it to their advantage. The law is messed up and most laws contradict the other, in my opinion, but never seem to give a man, especially a father, anything concrete to hold on to. The visit wasn't a totally waste. It made me determined to prove my side.

Carrie's now started, when taking Chelsea and Adam out, making it known to me that a male friend was going to be there. It was none of my business if she was dating again. I felt sorry for the guy if that was the case. He was more than welcome to take her off my hands. Take her away and do us all a favour! I made a point of her only ever wanting to take the kids out when people would be around. They would want a mum, not her friends and certainly not any new boyfriends of mummy's. All this did was make outings with this guy more frequent because,

"I'm going to make sure he is always there, just to p*** you off!"

Maybe she wanted me to be jealous. That was never ever going to happen.

I stayed focused. My appointment with a solicitor was coming up and I couldn't wait for it either. Biding my time, staying on the path that only had one direction, whereas Carrie's path was like the magic roundabout in Swindon. Traffic signs, all of a negative nature and she'd choose her route. Sofie was first in the fire line today. Despised by her mother over 'bags'. Carrie accused Sofie for their disappearance while Sofie didn't have a clue what she was even talking about. Sofie's way of talking bothered her. Carrie would see Sofie's tone as being spoken to like a child, when she was merely talking respectfully and precise.

They were head to head, with Carrie demanding her bags and Sofie demanding Carrie stays out of her room. Telling Sofie, repeatedly, that she's a silly little girl annoys her and she retaliated with how pathetic her mother was for stealing her daughters stuff, stating,

"Why can't you just be a normal mother?!"

I come into the room with my arms full of washing and try to remove Sofie from the conversation by changing the subject. I ask Sofie to get me her washing and to leave it now, walk away and ignore it. I'm then next,

"You need to sort the girl out"

I just ignore her too while she rambles on about her purple bag, how its disappeared, it was there and now it's not, then she comes back for Sofie, how she's a stupid little girl. When Sofie disagrees with that statement, Carrie threatens,

"Shut your mouth, shut your f****** mouth 'cos I swear to god, I'm gonna slap it out of you"

"That WILL be surprising" Sofie replies.

Carrie then threatens to take everything out of Sofie's room and that there isn't a thing she can do about. Sofie is determined to finish out the row, standing her ground, and Carrie seems like she's going to go on for hours, that she won't run out of steam any time soon, so I say "enough". Sofie listens. Carrie doesn't.

"You're a pansy, why don't you tell Sofie about herself?!"

Yes, I've heard it all before Carrie, I thought. I'm a pansy, I'm a 'scrawny pathetic man',

"Step in and be a man"

"So I don't smack the kids"

"It's all your fault"

"You're useless"

"You should be happy you're still married"

"You're lucky"

I'd hate to experience what unlucky felt like! Lucky was the last word that would cross my mind. Solicitor. That's the only word I kept repeating to myself. Andrew was now being threatened to be punched if he came out of his room mid-argument, especially if he stood up for me. The biological factor with Sofie was bringing out competition, with Carrie not liking the respect I was receiving, while she, the biological mother, received none. She didn't deserve any, she never could see that. The case of the disappearing bags was nothing more than Carrie forgetting where she had put them. Hanging on the bannister, yet an apology to Sofie was out of the question.

The bond between Sofie and my family (Sofie's family regardless) got to her too. Jealousy brings out such an ugly side. Carrie told her to be careful of us many times and was warned to stay away. Carrie, on another occasion, had grabbed Sofie by the chin,

"I swear to god Sofie, shut the F*** up"

And Sofie needed to be careful of us?! This woman was literally the most craziest, dislodged woman I had ever come across. Like when she ordered me to wash her leggings

"Do it, are you going to wash them or not? Yes? No? HELLOOOO?"

Then, when asked where her leggings were, Carrie looking around the bedroom trying to locate them, realizes she's wearing them!

Targeting Sofie always seemed a priority on her agenda. Sofie was probably on par with me. Carrie knew how to get to the both of us, I think. Sofie wanted to stay away from her mother but also didn't want to leave my side or the little ones. Andrew was very protective of the little ones too. Always keeping an eye on them, watching in the background. Andrew and Sofie had eyes like a hawk. Andrew would very rarely swoop in, whereas Sofie was the opposite. The more her mother's behaviour affected her, the more she couldn't tolerate it. She began doing her homework at the kitchen table, purely I think, to be around for us all.

An argument exploded between them and Carrie just mocked her,

"Do I abuse you Sofie, do I f****** hit you around? Do I neglect everything? Do I?

"Yes, yes you do!"

"No I don't Sofie, you don't know how good you've got it. You need to go and live in house where you are getting all them things done to you and come tell me, yeah! There's a lot more f******* kids out there a lot more worse off than you, so don't go sitting there pitying yourself"

Sofie just muffled under her breath and continued her homework.

"You need to take a long hard look at yourself Sofie and the way you speak to people"

Bemused, Sofie tells Carrie that it is not the way she speaks to people and it just leads Carrie into threatening mode.

"YOU KNOW WHAT, IM GONNA THROW THEM BOOKS AT YOUR HEAD IN A MINUTE, COS YOURE P****** ME OFF BAD.

When I enter the room,

"You're pathetic and useless! You need to tell your "f****** daughter to stop talking to me like that"

I'm amazed that this women could, soon in the future, end up being a qualified social worker.

She started to play loud music too. She'd sit at the kitchen counter with it blaring. I asked her to look what there was for dinner one evening and she just told me no. I then asked her to turn the music down and she just looked at me and increased the volume. A juvenile delinquent. Asking again she was just obnoxious,

"I wouldn't have to, if you didn't keep talking in my ear. I will play it over and over and again until you shut up"

"Why do you hate me so much, Carrie?"

"You're a p***k".

Her potty-mouth was directed at Adam too, eventually. She was feeding him one evening but he kept spitting the food out. Annoyed that it was taking so long, she kicked his high chair and called him a c***. Explaining her to my solicitor was comical yet worryingly alarming. On talking about the threats of walking out with the children he said yes, we can fight for custody. He advised that I try and speak to her amicably first and then go from there. I suppose like a last attempt, plus at this stage it was only hear-say to him. Sticking by the rulebook, I attempted. Obviously failed because Carrie saw nothing wrong in who she was. To her, I was the culprit and if I left, the household would be fine.

Carrie sought her own advice too, telling me she had been to the citizen's advice bureau. On returning she was different. I don't know how to explain it, just different. She had invited her mum down, which I dreaded. We had a party to go to the next day, not Carrie this time though. She was never on any guest list again and I knew with her mother about, things weren't going to go smoothly. They both strived on drama. Two women believing they own the rights to put the world to rights, however wrong they were. When she arrived, she didn't come alone. Carries sister, half-brother and his mate were in tow. Walking in like it was their house.

If I was a dog my hackles would have been up for sure. There may be a 'do and don't list' for us men where woman are concerned but it is totally different when its man vs man. We don't think of rulebooks in this type of situation. They walked about and stood arms crossed and if they thought I was intimidated in any way, they were seriously mistaken. You can't be a man and come in front of another man and expect to take power away from him in his castle.

Whatever he had been told by his sister, I had to give him the benefit of being allowed to believe whatever she had said but I couldn't help thinking, why a man would stand in front of another man and never say anything. When I found out a man laid his hands on Marie, I didn't do nothing. Granted, I didn't use physical force, even though I wanted too, but I made him know that he would NEVER be able to touch one hair on my sister's body if I was ever around.

Male testosterone filled the room but they were boys to me. Standing there, trying to come across 'hard', trying to make me feel uneasy. They just stood there, looking shifty, not giving off any signs as to why they were here in the first place. The protective element switched on and the rage was waiting. I would happily, however unlawful, show these 'men' what happens if you step into a lion's den. They had to be very careful in what they were thinking of doing or saying to a lion around his cubs.

Nothing happened. They left, except her mother who was staying the night. A pointless visit but not pointless to them, I just didn't know that yet. Later that evening I found out Carrie's sister had tried to make a conversation with Sofie upstairs, asking her, does she not think her dad is wrong for what he was doing. I wish I knew this while she was here, I would of asked her, so what EXACTLY am I doing?!

Party day arrived, just deep breaths, let go of all the poop and enjoy the segment of normality. Carrie was fine with Chelsea and Adam going. Odd and was quiet. Chelsea was overly excited about wearing her new party dress and couldn't wait to get ready, with the help of her big sister making her look like a pretty princess. Chelsea was already my little princess. My mum, down visiting and staying at Marie's, came to mine with Marie, Kaine, Andre and my dad. Carrie sat weird looking, with her eyes darting about. We were ready to ring the taxi when Carrie interrupted saying Chelsea and Adam were now not allowed to go. Chelsea on hearing this began getting upset. I just knew. I should have expected it. It just blurted out,

"For f*** sake Carrie, what are you doing now?!"

She didn't swear, raise her voice or anything. Just calm and collectively said they are not allowed to go, that she had changed her mind. Andrew spotted it before any of us. He points at her,

"Look she's recording!!"

Carrie's hand was placed on the kitchen counter but the phone was placed out of her range, more towards ours,

"Carrie, what are you playing at?"

"Nothing. You can't make me do anything"

Quiet on set please, actress Carrie is performing. Marie trying to contain herself, my mum looks like she's about to blow, Chelsea running off crying and I'm stood there with a puzzle, trying to put the pieces together. She calmly and cleverly, without instigating herself begins antagonizing Marie. Marie knowing full well what was unfolding, warned Carrie to not underestimate her. Patronizingly with a smirk, Carrie replies,

"Perhaps, Marie, you shouldn't underestimate me!"

My mum blew. She walked towards the kitchen counter, Carrie being on the other side and the phone is in the middle of them. My mum swore at her, directing her voice to the phone, telling Carrie to record her and that how cruel she was for waiting for her little ones to be dressed, ready and excited, before saying in front of them, that they weren't allowed to go. This brought Carrie out of the evening's character and she put her phone away and was now the real Carrie,

"They're not f****** going, because I said"

I looked at Marie, she asked me if she should. I said yes. While I'm talking to Carrie trying to reason with her, she is outside on the phone to the police. Really, just to document the event and to double check that if I take the kids and Carrie phones them, will they turn up at the party and arrest me. The law said I could take them, so I did. We had a lovely time, the kids had so much fun, dancing about and when the night was over I went to bed knowing first chance I get, I'm ringing social services.

The following day Carrie's mother played the dotting grandmother, she most certainly is not. Carrie being on her best performance behavior says she's going to do the food shopping. Playing out her scene, I give her forty pounds and she takes Chelsea and Adam with her. When gone, Sofie and Andrew said they were asked to go to the park with them but obviously declined and couldn't understand why on earth they would think they would go with them. We got on with the day and waited for Carrie and the little ones to get back.

It was getting late and Carrie had been gone for hours, too long in fact, and even Sofie and Andrew were getting miffed by it. Sofie went upstairs and it wasn't long before she come rushing down saying all the little one's clothes had gone. I knew she wouldn't be lying but I had to see for myself. I ran upstairs, missing steps, and went into their room and she was right. Their draws were open and empty. All the times of threatening, she had actually followed through with it. They were gone and at that moment I could have been a woman. I felt exactly what it would feel like if your child was ripped from your womb. Two of them and I was frantic.

I ran back down stairs and phoned Carrie but my calls would just ring out, leading to her answer machine. I kept trying. Until I couldn't because my calls were then going straight to her answer machine. She had switched it off. I then dialed 999. There was nothing they could do because 'she was the mother' and that I should seek legal advice. I rang social services and they said the same. Standing there helpless, I just kept thinking, too much time had passed already and these stupid phone calls were taking up valuable time, that could be spent on getting them back. I couldn't ring the solicitor because it was a Sunday. I just didn't know what to do.

Sofie and Andrew were angry at her. Andrew just wanted to be close to me, holding me, with me holding him. Sofie's anger was red. She went up to the bedroom and saw Carrie had left some of her clothes behind. She began ripping them, tearing them apart, destroying them,

"If she's not coming back she doesn't need them!!"

As much as I know it was wrong for Sofie to do this, I understood her rage. She couldn't rage at her mother so the clothes were a substitute.

chapter twelve

How long had Carrie been planning it? It all made sense now, when Carrie changed her mind letting the little ones go to the party. I believe she was going to go that night. After hatching a plan with her family. Actually, I believe they were going to go when her brother and everyone arrived the night before but none of them had the balls to carry it out.

Like Carrie would go and do food shopping! Why was I so stupid! Her recording stunt was to get something tangible on record that she could use for her get away. A little scene she could use to provide enough evidence to back up a story of this mother desperate to escape her evil husband. She had to ask Sofie and Andrew to go to the park, making her story look 'real' to her mother and sister. She knew the older two would say no. Carrie's family gullible, believing her concoction.

They took two children but left two behind. Why did they leave two children with a 'man like me' if that's what they really believed? Were only two children worthy of saving? Why weren't

Sofie and Andrew forced to go? Because Sofie and Andrew couldn't be used in Carrie's game play!! It not rocket science. Chelsea and Adam were young enough, innocent enough, easily manipulated than the older two. They were just Carrie's little props.

Why did no one want to listen? Why was she allowed to take them when they knew of my worry? Was my worry not worthy either? An insignificant parent vs a mother. This day could mark the very day I never see my little ones again. That's fair? That's right? I couldn't focus or get my bearings. I wanted to just shut down and break. To fall apart and let my emotions free because I was hurting so badly and struggling to hold myself together.

That corner I spoke of at the start, I'm there. I'm worried, lost and feeling alone. That magical ball isn't coming any time soon. I was suffocating and falling, and would take my kids down with me. I was dying inside but that wasn't the father Sofie and Andrew needed. They were hurting too. They were scared too. Daddy wasn't worried so you don't have to worry, that's how I had to be. Somehow.

Come night time, placing my parent badge down on the side, now just me, alone, I crumbled. So much, that I thought my eyes would burst from crying too much. They were blood red. I held my face in the pillow as hard as I could and let out any sound my emotions needed to make, praying Sofie and Andrew wouldn't hear me. Images of Chelsea and Adam flickered through my mind like a slide show. I missed them so much, it was like they were gone a lifetime already and I worried for them. Nervously worried, telling myself Carrie wouldn't hurt them. I found no comfort in it because I knew there was a chance something could happen accidently or neglectfully. I couldn't sleep, no matter how hard I tried and no matter how utterly exhausted I was. Were they ok? Were they eating properly? Where they being bathed?

Walking round the house early hours in the morning, like a zombie, pacing up and down. I then went in and checked on Sofie and Andrew. Both asleep which I was relieved by. I didn't want them seeing me a mess. Andrew was not in his own room though. I found him in Chelsea's bed, holding one of her t-shirts as he slept, which ripped my heart out even more because I had said goodnight to him while he was in his own bed. How could Carrie do this and not think of how it would affect the older two?

She wasn't just taking my children away from me, she was taking their brother and sister away from them and what about Chelsea and Adam? How were they feeling? I just couldn't function. I paced and I cried then I sat on my bed. Cried again and paced some more, watching the morning appear through the window.

I wanted to get into bed, close my eyes tight and hope this was all just a bad dream, that I'd wake up soon. It was the first time I hadn't heard the little ones in the morning and it was strange. Eerie. I was supposed to be up doing their breakfast, getting them dressed while Peppa Pig played on the television, on repeat. It was their favourite. It was my favourite. I wanted my favourite back. The house was wrong and the thought of this 'wrong' being forever was frightening. It was like I was mourning, like my babies had died.

I waited impatiently for 9am, all morning with my phone in my hand. I couldn't work, my brain couldn't deal with it. I'm thankful for customers, that had over the years became good friends because they understood my reasons for cancelling on them.

Through this whole process though, I lost a lot of other business and my earnings were lower than they had ever been.

There was no formal "hello this is...." when I phoned the solicitor. I simply said three words –

"I need you"

He was my last hope.

"Ok, you were right. You saw that coming" he said, as he tried to calm me down over the phone and tried to make me listen carefully with a sound mind to what was going to happen next.

He said that we needed to make this incident serious. Make it serious? I thought, it was already serious. I had no idea where my children where or how they were! The normal family court route would of taken months and there was no time to file for legal aid because that would of taken too long as well. Carrie wasn't capable overseeing herself for months, let alone children.

Our first port of call was an emergency court hearing in London. The only option for a quick intervention. The cost was six thousand pounds. I borrowed half off my mum and sold my motorbike to raise the rest. I would have sold my soul if I had too but why did I have to pay to show the severity? To make the right people listen, I had to pay. Money talks while a concerned father is muted. To say I was a mess is an understatement. My heart felt like it had been put in a vice and darkness was turning the handle, making it struggle to carry on beating.

We had a hearing in a few days but for me it was a few days too long but there was nothing I could do, except wait. We tried getting on with the days the best we could, but all three of us,

Me, Sofie and Andrew, just walked about like headless chickens. Carrie eventually answered her phone. Me and Sofie had been trying a lot. The first call, Carrie handed the phone straight to Chelsea. Chelsea answered and I closed my eyes. For a split second she was right next to me. Her voice melted my heart but I know my princess, she wasn't happy.

How could Carrie never feel any remorse? As long as she punished me, it didn't matter who she used to do it. Chelsea didn't seem herself at all,

"I don't want to speak to any of you"

Her tone of voice came across confused and it seemed like she was being told what to say. I aimed to come across 'normal', asking how her and Adam were but with every question I asked, Chelsea paused before answering then gave long confused answers. It wasn't her words, it was Carrie's and I could tell my little girl was uncomfortable. I just stayed placid,

"Daddy will see you really soon"

The call ended. Trying to call back got me nowhere. Carrie wouldn't answer the phone.

The next day we were up early and gave the house a good clean. I think just to feel like we were accomplishing something. I didn't sleep very well, I only had a few hours. My body just collapsed. If I hadn't of slept, my eyeballs might have popped out of their sockets. I couldn't face work again either, I was on reserved energy as it was. My brain couldn't organize itself to sort out call outs and routes. Being on the road, with the state of mind I had, would have been dangerous. My concentration was at an all-time low.

With the washing machine ready, I put a load on while Sofie phones Carrie to, hopefully, speak to the little ones and it was answered straight away but with a cocky tone. Informing her that Chelsea didn't want to speak. Sofie got upset and asked why,

"Maybe it's because you've been whispering things about her mummy in her ear"

Shocked, Sofie stuck up for herself,

"I have not been doing anything of the sort!"

She then questioned Carrie, why she would have the little ones around her, 'her' being Carrie's mother, who she heard in the background, that 'nan' never has anything to do with them, that they hardly ever see her.

One-upping Sofie, Carrie responds saying, the same can be said for great nan (Carrie's nan) and Carrie's aunt, who Sofie, all of us, get on well with, except Carrie of course. Family that we are in regular contact with. She just ridicules Sofie's statement and deems the letters her great nan sends as 'nothing' and 'only' letters. The call ends.

I come in from doing the washing (my children aren't that messy, in case you're wondering why I'm forever washing. I have customers washing too) and find Sofie's distraught and she tells me what happened. I ring Carrie myself but she just cuts off my call. Letting it just ring isn't enough. Knowing that I know she's purposely cutting me off is way more entertaining for her, so I just leave a message on her answer machine, asking her to explain to me what had just happened. Later that evening she made contact but had her phone on loud speaker.

It was a circus. Nothing being resolved, just childish antics. There were a few people in the back ground, clear as day, laughing, egging Carrie's performance on, with her laughing along with them. I could hear Chelsea and Adam in the background, then Carrie's brother shouts out k**b. Comical because this lad said nothing when he was in my presence. Telling Carrie that this behaviour, from her and her family, was not only childish but damn right despicable, lead her to be even more bolshie and the call ending. The emergency court hearing was the next day and I was raring to go. I wanted my children back where they belonged.

Up at 5.30am and, boy, was I ready! I tried my hardest looking respectable but I just looked appalling. Gaunt, red eyed, pale and I stood out like a sore thumb amongst the regal fixtures of the High Court of Justice. A magnificent building. I had never been to this part of London before. I was in a beautiful building feeling ugly, about to address something ugly. It's quite an intimidating place too, super high ceilings showing how small you are in comparison. My solicitor assigned me a barrister, who was waiting on my arrival. Nerves were kicking in and I felt dizzy from the scenery and having not eaten much since my babies left. He briefed me on what was going to happen and we brushed up on what we were going to address.

The judge seemed understanding at first but then gave off the impression that it wasn't as much of a big deal, as it was to me. My barrister explained Carrie's behaviour, that she doesn't parent the children and spoke about Carrie's college, her whereabouts more important than her children. The judge quickly stated,

"Well, mothers ARE allowed a life and they are entitled to an education"

Like it was more of a personal view. The judge was a woman. I didn't expect this to make a difference but I felt like it did. My barrister, seeing my reaction, went into more detail. On hearing my concerns, she said she couldn't comment without hearing Carrie's side but she did agree that the children needed to be back home and that Chelsea needed to go to school. It was like I walked out with second place. 'Yes, the kids need to be back but I don't believe what you say yet', that's how it translated to me, that what I felt I had won. I was rewarded a parent card, but it wasn't worth anything until I presented it again, this time in front of the almighty mother. Again, this feeling of dis-acknowledgement, the feeling of people not listening to me because I was a father, just made me know I had to shout louder. While the judge put in place an order for Carrie's court attendance, I headed home.

We were able to speak to Chelsea and Adam when we were back, with Carrie answering and passing the phone over. Chelsea sounded so pleased to speak to us this time. She asked if she could play on her trampoline and I told her very soon and that I loved her very much and to be a good girl for mummy. I wanted the call to be as normal as possible so we spoke about Adam's Birthday coming up. Chelsea knows that she always has a little surprise on any of the others birthdays and all vice versa, so I reassured her she will still get one. I babbled a bit with Adam and told him I love him very much too and to be a good boy. Though I missed them dearly, the phone call put me a little at ease and fed my aching heart.

The following morning, my solicitor called to say Carrie's location had been found. I knew she was most likely at her mother's but I never knew of the address. She was to be served papers, not only to attend court but to bring Chelsea and Adam with her. Even though the circumstances were no doubt going to be disorientating for them, I couldn't wait to see their little faces. I couldn't wait to hold them. I phoned Carrie but there was no answer so I waited a while before trying again.

I also received a letter in the post regarding a mediation meeting that had been cancelled and rearranged. It was the first I had heard of it. Carrie must have set this up at some point. Maybe this was what her citizen's advice bureau meeting was for. I called her again, just gone 12pm but again, no answer so I just text asking if I can please speak to the little ones. She replied straight away-

'No, because you have upset them'

I tried calling again, still no answer. I tried all through the day but nothing. Even Sofie tried and was ignored. I didn't see the point in trying anymore that day. We were soon to be in court, I just had to bide my time. Hoping Chelsea and Adam were ok, me and the older ones went to Tesco's and Argos to finish off Adams birthday gifts.

9:30am, the next morning, I try again. Still no answer. It's so frustrating. At times I wanted to throw my phone but always stopped myself, because even though I could hardly speak to them, there were times I could. I imagined Carrie, looking at the phone as it rings, seeing my name and smirking to herself, which only frustrated me more. My last attempt was 11.40am with no hope. I tried not to stress, telling myself I will see them soon enough and hopefully they'll be home and these games could end.

Carrie phoned back shortly after. I will talk to them when she says so, that was the clear deal she had made on my behalf.

Condescendingly, she asks me why I keep phoning. I wanted to scream down the phone at her. What sort of question was that? She knew damn well why I was phoning. I wanted to call her a bitch and tell her to stop these stupid games but I knew It wouldn't have got me anywhere. Plus, knowing Carrie, she'd run to the police saying I scared her and that she was now too afraid to go to court, which meant there would be a possibility I wouldn't see the littles one as soon as I hoped. I remain calm, biting my tongue. I'm surprised it never bled,

"Carrie, I want to speak to the little ones"

"No, you can wait until Thursday"

Biting even harder,

"Can I not ring on Adam's birthday?!!

"I'll think about it"

The call ended.

I felt like a donkey. Carrie waving the little ones in my face like they're the carrot. I couldn't stop thinking, what if things were the opposite? What if I took off with the kids and behaved the way she did? I'm no law expert but I'd bet my life that I'd be arrested within hours and brought back. If a father had equal rights this big top spectacle wouldn't be taking place. I would have been helped by social services and the police, and the little ones would be brought back home before they even got a chance to hit the motorway.

Dangling her carrot, she rings me in the evening asking if I want to talk to Chelsea. Tongue still not bleeding, I speak to her. My little princess, her voice settled my heart and broke it at the same time.

I missed her so much. I missed them both so, so much. I was on speakerphone so knew we had an audience. Their whispering was hardly discreet.

Chelsea sounded distant again and took long to answer simple, everyday questions. It was killing me. I knew what Carrie was doing. Using her little prop. That prop is my little girl, no doubt scared and confused and I hated it and I hated Carrie for putting her through this. The vision of Chelsea in my head, her little sweet face, was destroying me. I couldn't help her and I just really wanted too. Struggling not to cry, I asked her if she was ok. There was whispering in the background and Chelsea began stuttering, sounding confused again.

Remaining calm, when all I wanted to do was jump down the phone somehow. I wanted to be where she was and remove anybody around her pressurizing her into not being herself and she burst into tears, crying uncontrollably. I'd never heard her like that before, not to that extent. My heart pulsated with pain and was crying for her. Crying with her.

"Please don't cry Chelsea"

I hear her not able to catch her breath,

"I miss you daddy. I want to come home. I want my Peppa Pig bedroom"

I wanted to cry with her, I wanted to let her know I really wanted that too.

Holding back, hoping my tone would reassure her, while fighting the urge to blurt out that I'm coming for her and Adam and that people are going to help daddy,

"Stop crying now Chelsea, You need to be happy. Nice will come. Remember, you're my little princess"

I sing to her. What we always sing together, the first song she ever learnt. The Barney song,

"I love you, you love me, we're a happy family"

It worked, her breathing steadied and her crying wasn't as severe and I then promised her, I will see them both soon, that they're just on a little holiday. Still sobbing slightly, she replies,

"Daddy, I don't like this holiday"

I then hear Adam in the background singing our song, which he obviously heard through the speaker. Before I get a chance to talk to Adam, Carrie takes over the call. I have spent every single minute with my children and to take them away in the manner she did was wrong on so many levels and she didn't care. True Carrie style, she tells me,

"It's your fault I left with them. I felt threatened by your family. That's why my family came down"

"Absolute rubbish, Carrie!"

There was no need to take the little ones, if there was any truth in what she was saying. Spinning deception so easily from her calculating mouth. One, my family were not round that day and two, this had been planned,

"I know you had this planned for some time, Carrie. I know for a fact!"

This woman is cold and hard as nails with her feelings, she's not the type to feel threatened. She's the one that does the threatening!

The phone goes dead.

Waking up in the morning knowing it's your little one's birthday and they're not there with you is hard. All the presents and love that you want to provide but no one to give them too. Ringing Carrie in the morning is unavailing. I don't believe she isn't answering because she's being a spiteful bitch. She's no doubt still in bed, fast asleep, as per. That in itself makes me worry too. Who's looking after the children if she is asleep? Are they left in a room on their own until someone comes to fetch them? How long have they been awake for? Are they hungry? The little ones wake at 6am most mornings! I couldn't turn off parent mode if I tried!

We eventually get through at 10.30am. It was by Sofie's call and she was allowed to speak to Chelsea. Sofie could hear Carrie telling Chelsea what to say. A little into the conversation, Chelsea started to talk on her own accord but Sofie could now hear the background. She could hear Carrie's mother playing with Adam. Highlighting her voice, beckoning him,

'LETS.PLAY.WITH.YOUR.CAR"

Sofie could tell it was staged. She said every word was pronounced precisely and automated. That 'nan' wanted to be heard. Sofie was definitely on speakerphone because Adam heard her voice and called out her name. Grabbing moments, however messed up, Sofie continued to talk as normal as she could. She then asked if Chelsea wanted to speak to daddy. Chelsea paused then said no. The background was noisy and Sofie didn't hear correctly so she repeated herself. Again, Chelsea paused but this time elevated 'noooo'. Sofie reluctant, asked if she was sure and Chelsea's tone softened and said no again.

Sofie knew what was happening. Even someone as young as Sofie knew this type of behaviour was fallacious so she asked Chelsea again, one last time, if she was sure. She wanted Chelsea to know that it was perfectly ok to talk if she wanted too. Chelsea then became excited and animated saying 'yes' continuously, so she passed me the phone,

"Daddy, is 'arnty' Maree there?"

I let Chelsea lead the conversation,

"Yes princess, she is. Kaine and Andre are here too and they all send lots and lots of love to you and Adam"

I knew I didn't have long, Carrie wasn't going to let this lovely, real conversation happen and I had heard her tell Chelsea daddy will speak to her later so I spoke swiftly and wished Adam happy birthday, before passing the phone back to Sofie.

Carrie was on the other end now, telling Sofie she needed to hang up because another phone call was coming through. Sofie didn't want the phone call to end,

"Don't go yet! Five minutes isn't long enough. I haven't even spoken to Adam yet and Andrew hasn't spoken either. We haven't seen our brother and sister for so long. Please let us talk longer?"

Begging Carrie, hoping to tug on any heart strings, was senseless. Carrie did not possess a heart,

She ended the call.

I tried to call later but there was no answer so I just kept myself busy. I washed all of the bedding while waiting for dinner to be ready then I tried again but this time Carrie had turned her phone off. I text her, later on, saying I had been trying to call and she text back straight away-

'Yes. Battery dead. You already spoke today so why call again? Love to Sofie and Andrew. Tell them I miss them'

I wanted to reply 'what a crock of s***', every part of that text. I wanted too but didn't,

'I only called because you told Chelsea I would talk later'

'No I didn't, a misunderstanding, I meant tomorrow ok'.

Misunderstanding my bottom cheek. This whole fiasco was ending soon. Hopefully. Court day was around the corner. Three days and counting. I felt like a child awaiting Christmas. I really couldn't wait to see my little ones.

chapter thirteen

Sofie tries calling Carrie all through the morning but she wouldn't pick up. I worry what effect this is having on her. I suggest she leaves the calling for a while, it's a nice day, sit out in the garden. Anything, other than spending all her time trying. I wanted Carrie to understand that me and her need not talk, unless it's an emergency so I text her, explaining just that. I ask if I call at 12pm, could she please just pass the phone to the little ones. I had no reply and when I phoned at twelve, there was no answer.

Me and the older two try and do our normal family stuff, though it's hard when some of your family is missing. We would sit and have a conversation about random things but the conversation always lead back to Chelsea and Adam. I tried Carrie a few times more but with no prevail. Sofie and Andrew are just as worried and sad as I am. We had no contact at all today with little ones. My parent brain is on a hamster wheel. Where are they? What are they doing? Is there drugs around them? Has Carrie gone out partying and left them with her mother? Are they being fed? I don't even bother getting settled for bed, I know there will be no sleep tonight.

On edge all night, carrying it through to morning. Sofie wants to get out of the house which I think is a good idea. I drop her into town and ask if she wants us to join her but she says she wants to just be on her own. Andrew has Kaine and Andre round playing Xbox, being clowns. It's nice to see his mind distracted. Andrew is a lot like my dad, out of sight out of mind. He can easily switch off. I don't know if this is a good thing or not, given the circumstances. I think this is why Andrew never wants to speak to the little ones as much. I think he can't handle it, holding his emotions in, so he just chooses to keep a distance.

I pick Sofie up later in the day hoping that her fresh air and alone time would help her feel a tad better but she didn't enjoy her shopping. Well, she did until she saw one of Carrie's friends. She made Sofie feel uneasy, glaring at her in a horrible way across the street. Like Sofie had done something wrong to this woman and the woman had a problem with her. Who does that?! Who does that to a child?! I tell her to shrug it off, to ignore people that don't matter and that if an adult behaves like that to a child, there is something wrong with that adult, not Sofie. They are the one who has a problem! Sofie calls Carrie and is short and sharp with her, still annoyed from her town experience. She is allowed to speak to Chelsea but is told they will call later so Adam can talk. There was no other call. If it wasn't for court day being tomorrow, I would have tried ringing. Instead we had a cozy night together on the sofa, watching television and I prayed for a decent night's kip. I wanted to be on form for tomorrow.

Carrie being with her family is a strong indication that they will arrive with her at court so my dad and Marie demand they are coming with me. I was thankful because the taxi drive to London is better when you have company. My mind races a hundred miles a minute, having them with me slowed me down slightly. I had conflicting feelings. I was tired but full of energy. I hoped the little ones would be coming home today so eagerly took their car seats to court. My fingers and toes were crossed as we sat in the main hall waiting for my solicitor. Then I heard a sound. A sound so familiar and annoying. Like finger nails on a chalkboard. Clip-clop, clip-clop. High heel shoes, loud and echoing through the tall ceilings. I didn't want to look in the direction because I knew who I would see but I could see my babies. I couldn't not look! It was Carrie but she was alone. As if by slow motion, she walked passed us, heels louder the closer she got and she looked terrible. Old faded leggings with big heel pole dancer shoes, looking like she had just come from a corner which dawned a red light. This was the first time I felt total shame. Ashamed at all the things I had allowed her to say and do. They all flashed before my eyes. I was ashamed that this woman was the woman I married.

My solicitor, along with my barrister, arrived and we waited to be called in. I'm on one side of the waiting area, Carrie is on the other, sat with her solicitor. Then I see them. My beautiful little babies. They are walked in to where Carrie is, by one of Carrie's female friends and a guy. The guy later revealed as the same guy Carrie wanted to 'p*** me off' with when she would take them out. I first noticed the Happy Meal boxes from McDonalds they were holding and munching on the contents. I found it quite embarrassing. This is the high court of London, a little bit of decorum wouldn't have gone a miss. I was soon drawn back to their faces. Chelsea and Adam looked tired and scruffy. They smiled but awkwardly, looking around at Carrie then back to me. Probably to see if they were allowed to smile at their daddy.

My solicitor went over to Carrie's, to introduce herself and debrief and I asked if I could go over and see them. I just wanted to hug them, even just for a second. A quick squeeze and I would have moved back to where I was but it wasn't advised. I could only look. My dad and Marie did a little wave to them. Carrie was busy talking to her solicitor. While my solicitor was waiting for their conversation to end, I just stood there staring at them, thinking to myself, 'this' is going to end today.

The solicitors didn't talk for long, mine was soon back over to me,

"You're safe and need not worry"

She had overheard Carrie talking to her solicitor. He asked her to comment on the domestic violence and Carrie replied saying there hadn't been any violence for quite a few years. This was one of the subjects that nerved me the most and Carrie had just landed herself in it. Make up your mind Carrie. Am I being violent now or a few years ago? It can't be both! Her family are under the impression I'm violent now. How many stories does she want on the go?! That's the thing about lies, you have to keep up with them. Keep them rolling and if you tell too many you risk losing track of every little story you've told. It was also overheard that Carrie was in contact with a woman's refuge charity who were helping her move and she was arranging schools for the little ones. She was never coming back.

My first thought was, how easy it clearly was for her to receive help. Did the charity not question anything she said? There are women who desperately need to seek sanctuary and there's the likes of Carrie among them. Like being among sheep, kitted out in their clothing, while concealing her wolf-teeth. I find it disrespectful to these women who go through such awful ordeals while Carrie had the ability to sit in par with them. Like she knows what they are going through, like she was the same as them.

In the court room, Carrie sat with her head down, looking out of place and not so cocky this time. This is the moment I hoped she knew that I would never stop fighting for my children. I felt sorry for her solicitor too. He seemed out of his depth and couldn't understand some of the legal terms that were spoken. I don't know if it had anything to do with him being a free solicitor from citizen's advice, that maybe he hadn't been in this type of court room before or he was new on the job. Maybe he was getting in a pickle with words because everything contradicted what his client had told him. He was probably under the impression that it was an open and shut case. There are always two sides to the story, always! The judge at one point got frustrated, having to repeat things, so my barrister explained in layman terms. I think she felt sorry for him too.

The judge states that this needs to be addressed in a family court with the relevant authority's involved. The judge asked what Carrie's life was like at home before she left. The reply she received, on behalf on Carrie, was,

"The marriage was over, there was nothing between him and her, no violence and she mostly slept on the sofa"

I wanted to applaud. Absolutely there was no violence from me and, without a shadow of a doubt, our marriage was over. Finished. Kaput!

I knew I wasn't walking away with custody today, I still had to prove myself but everything was in motion now, people will hear me and people will listen. I was hoping that Carrie would be advised to move from the house while this is all dealt with but that's as farfetched as the magical ball. I asked if the little ones could return home with me and Carrie refused but said she would come straight home. The judge noted down that the 'respondent' stated she will return home immediately upon leaving court. Carrie then got her solicitor to ask for clauses to be added. She wanted none of my family to be allowed in the house. On my behalf, my barrister objected as it wasn't warranted and also Marie works with me. Taking on board that our house is jointly owned, me and Carrie are placed on a non-molestation order until the family court hearing. She's coming back to the house.

No threatening behaviour. No violence. No harassing. No pestering. No derogatory comments, even to other family members, to name but a few of the conditions. Any conditions not adhered can lead to an immediate arrest and possibly up to six months imprisonment. I plead with my solicitor and barrister when we are given the outcome. Carrie is illogical, unreasonable and self-centered. This is not going to work. I cannot live with her anymore. This woman doesn't care about rules and regulations. My solicitor assures me that today's result is a good thing.

Firstly, Sofie wasn't biologically mine and, in the eyes of the law, I had no parental rights. Even though Sofie was at an age where she had her own voice, Carrie was her mother. She could never be forced to go anywhere with her mother but Sofie always worried about this. My solicitor requested parental responsibility on my behalf and I was granted it. The little ones were also coming home and my solicitor highlighted that, now I can address matters properly. I'm trying my hardest to feel thankful but I am totally uneasy with the result.

Leaving court, I get the taxi driver to rush us back home. I needed to get home before Carrie and have time to explain to Sofie and Andrew what had happened. I knew they would feel exactly like I did. Happy to see the little ones but dreading Carrie coming back. I arrived home at 5pm and sat down with them. They were angry and really didn't want their mother back in the house but like me, put them feelings aside because they had their brother and sister back with them. When pulling up at home, both were peering out of the window, eager faces waiting to see their siblings. Now talking to them about the order and what will happen next, I felt proud at how much of an adult approach they both had. My mum who sat with Sofie and Andrew while we were gone, left with my dad and Marie. Me and the older two sat impatiently and excitedly, waiting for Chelsea and Adam to walk through the door.

Coming up to 6pm, Carrie texts-

'I've missed the train'

I text back asking where she is and she says the tickets got messed up. I text again asking where is she,

'Victoria is 6.06pm'

She didn't get the train back straight away like she was told too, like she said she would. Again this is Carrie, no one tells her what to do. Another text from her comes through saying she took the little ones for something to eat. Maybe she thought I'd forget about seeing them eat McDonalds in court.

With Sofie and Andrew still perched at the window, it's now 8.15pm. Carrie and the little ones are nowhere to be seen. The older two were looking forward to spending some quality time with them before bed and so was I, but again, Carrie knows how to manipulate any situation. This stunt is Carrie continuing to show she will do what she wants. That she can. Like always. Missing a train is feasible. A good mother will feed her children when they're hungry. That's how her brain works. The order isn't worth the paper it's typed on because in Carrie's world, she didn't type it. I know what life will be like when she walks through that door and I'm dreading it. I will draw blood on my tongue this time, for sure.

I said and did nothing other than hold my little ones when they were eventually home, with Chelsea crying saying how much she missed us.

(once the court order was received in writing, it stated that she had to be home by a set time. Contradicting the "immediately" statement. The order gave Carrie, and her reluctant journey home, just cause but, she didn't know of this part yet. She took so long purely on purpose)

My routine is back. I get up as usual to Adam, its 6:30am and we go downstairs ready for breakfast. I've missed little people sounds in the house. If they made a lot of unnecessary noise now, it wouldn't bother me. Make as much noise as you like, my ears would just listen and be soothed by it because I missed it so. Carrie asleep, hears us and awakes, suddenly jumping off the sofa, rushing towards me and Adam in the kitchen. She states that she's making his breakfast and goes into mummy mode fixing it up. She's not herself. She's a different person, different personality. I back away and let her get on with it, thinking to myself, now you want to make your son his breakfast?! I've never seen her move so fast!

Have court proceedings made Carrie see the error in her ways? Highly unlikely! She's behaving like there's CCTV in the house and she's painting a new picture of herself. Late in the afternoon, she takes over changing Adam's bottom too. It was like watching the Stepford wives. A different personality in a hollow shell. Remote controlled. She struggles with Adam, who won't stay still so she gives him something to occupy him. Within minutes Andrew is shouting,

"DAD!!"

I turn and see Adam, arched back and choking, while Carrie seems oblivious. I dash to him, lifting him up and over and bang his back. Thankfully he was ok. Andrew turns to Carrie,

"Why on earth would you give a baby a coin to play with?!"

To settle Adam, Carrie had handed him a 10p coin which then dropped down his throat. I tell her she was stupid to allow him to have it, and even worse when he's laying down, while thinking, 'this is what happens when you pretend parent'. Her take on the incident was Adam had it in his hand and she took her eyes off him for two seconds,

"And, It's not a big deal, kids do things like that"

Carrie tries keeping up her 'mother of the year' demonstrations. Every morning she would jump off the sofa as soon as she knew me and the little ones were up. Her persona now was grating on the older two's nerves. Seeing straight through her act, she agitated them. I just laughed it off, I knew what she was doing. I had clocked her mobile phone near her every time a 'show' commenced. No more traps, I was going to be guarded and focused. She's had no doubt gone through the non-molestation order with a fine-toothed comb, looking for any loop holes she can work with. Still wanting to prove to me that what she says goes, I had to bring the little ones back from taking them to the beach. I had a set time so she could then go somewhere with them. Yet on return, still slumped on the sofa, Carrie changes her mind and doesn't go anywhere at all.

As requested by the court, social services visit the house and interview us all. Their report advises that it is in the best interest of the household that Carrie finds alternative accommodation. These people are just 'people' to Carrie. They possess no faculty. She sees it as they 'advised' not 'ordered' so she didn't have to go anywhere and anyway, It was me she wanted gone.

Clearly not used to the little one's early mornings, Carrie's starting to slow down. She's not jumping up as fast. But when up, she barges in on any roles and I give her space to do them. She even resorted to housework. Full blown housework, being a domestic goddess but only seems to be on occasions when she's going out, alone.

I'm confused too, how she comes home with items she's purchased because I am completely skint! This then makes total sense, when I receive a letter from the mortgage company saying we are behind on payments. I realize just how neglectful I've been with the finances. Things are tight with work not bringing in an substantial amount of money but I knew, or hoped, we could keep our heads above water. Even if it meant using credit cards and help from tax credits until life improved. I was under the impression this was the case until I was made aware that Carrie had made other plans.

Going through my bank statements showed no tax credits had been credited for some time. No wonder the mortgage was in the red. I phoned them and was told my claim had been cancelled. Carrie had ended our joint claim when she left and set up one for herself, claiming for her, Chelsea and Adam. Child benefit was now under investigation because two people were trying to claim for the same children. I couldn't believe it! I argued with the tax credits representative but got nowhere. Carrie was allowed to stop my claim yet I wasn't allowed to stop hers.

Now with money, Carrie's evenings out became more frequent. She seemed to be struggling going back and forth, between her real persona and her fake one. When home. she was very strange. Sometimes looking like the lights were on but no one was home. There were times where you could tell she was holding back her true nature. She was being secretive too, eerily. She'd sit out in her car for hours in the driveway. Sometimes on the phone, sometimes crying and when the call was finished she would come inside acting like she was on a script.

The more times she 'played' mum, the little ones were starting to fight against it. They weren't used to this 'mum' and I think it was confusing them. I had to intervene on any bath nights that Carrie took charge over because I would end up hearing Chelsea crying for daddy. I'd go up and find Chelsea distraught because Carrie was pouring too much water over her face and getting annoyed that she wouldn't stay still. Water over the face was something Chelsea hated. It scares her. Carrie would have known this if bath time with them was a regular occurrence. If she knew her child! I'd calmly suggest to Carrie that I'll help so she can get on with bathing Adam. Just to stop her terrorizing Chelsea and desperate to keep the real Carrie in her cage.

Chelsea was struggling with Carrie's change of nature out of all of us. Me and the older ones kept a significant distance, as many times as we could, but there is only so far you can go when you're in the same house. Our routine when dinner was finished, would be to go upstairs and stay there together. Keeping well out of Carrie's way. Majority of times, Chelsea and Adam would join us in the too.

Me and Carrie began bickering about money. She was free to spend hers yet eating the food I was providing. We only had something to eat because my mum was doing our food shopping and there was Carrie, spending on herself. I would ask her to not leave the television on all night. One, to save on electric and two, because if the television broke, I wouldn't be able to replace it. Sometimes I would come down for a glass of water and she would be fast asleep so I'd switch it off but no longer than five minutes later, I would hear it back on again. Repeating myself every morning,

"Please don't leave it on"

Carrie prepared dinner occasionally. One time I asked if she was also sorting out pudding. She is fully aware that I record now and vice versa,

"Can you please stop standing so close to me!"

I am nowhere near her.

"So…..are you gonna change your sons bum, seeing as you've left him in a poohie nappy all day, or what?"

Crazily inaccurate, I just hum a random tune, trying to ignore her efforts of goading,

"Are you?.....yes?...no?...yes?...no?....or would you like me to do it, on top of everything else I've had to do today?"

Trying so hard to pick a row with me, knowing full well her mirrored comments could make me bite,

"Carrie, stop saying stupid things"

"Well, you started it"

"Carrie, I only asked if you was doing pudding!"

Changing the subject, she now moans that I don't allow her to do her washing. Our washing machine is out in the shed, which I lock up at night. I tell her she has all day to do any washing. She cuts me off talking,

"Are you still talking....you're boring"

I'm there looking at her, thinking, how sick and tired I am of her and how she speaks and I bite a little. Telling her how she hasn't been verbally abusive since she's been back and how very odd it was. I question her mental state but apparently, I'm the one with a mental illness. We carry on bickering and I stand firm, telling her I can't wait to go to court and that she's only making up stuff because she's scared of the truth.

"Bollocks, You don't scare me....one little bit"

And there it was! The first swear word that had left her lips since returning. It must have been so hard for her to curb her vocabulary,

"Ahhhhh, the real Carrie now! You will break eventually. The real Carrie will come out!"

Somehow we get onto the subject of a time when Marie and Carrie went out in the evening. A long time ago. Marie's friend was down and had never met Carrie before. Carrie got drunk and was aggressive, getting in a mood because Marie went to the bathroom with her friend and not her. Riled by it, she barged past Marie's friend, nearly knocking her down some concrete stairs. I must have been talking about her aggressive nature to bring this up and how she comes from a violent background.

"Is that what you're gonna try and use? You're family are just t***s, your family come from mentally unstable people! Oh, oh, oh...murderers...oh, oh, oh, paedo's, molesters...who knows what you're doing with my daughter"

My mouth drops,

"Oh my god! Now, you are sick in the head Carrie"

My face shows her just how disgusted I am and at the fact that she felt it acceptable to shout out in front of the kids,

"You make me physically sick Carrie, I don't know how you live with yourself"

Sofie walks over, telling Carrie she heard every word and she's appalled. Carrie says she will be bringing it up, no doubt meaning in court, and tells Sofie to be careful of my family again. It would take me two minutes to shut her mouth for her, I really want to. A vile and shameless mouth, nastiness spewing from it. I tell her how dare she and she pushes me as she walks past.

She's then suddenly placid,

"Can we both together discuss things with the children?"

Andrew jumps in,

"You just pushed Dad!"

"Carrie, you're ridiculous and behaving the way you are because you're guilty"

"I don't want to talk now" and she pulls her phone out. On seeing Sofie and Andrew watching,

"A private text, that's NOTHING to do with you"

Adam is near Carrie and he cry's suddenly, rubbing his back.

"WHAT DID YOU DO CARRIE?"

"Nothing"

"You know what, Carrie, you say I'm lying, I say you're lying. Let the court decide. You are as mad as they come!"

True to form, showing the extent of her vicious nature, I soon after this day, receive a phone call from child protection services. A worker from there department tells me they will be interviewing the children as an allegation has been made against me by Carrie, questioning my relationship with Sofie,

"Are you kidding me?!!!! You're kidding me right? Is this a joke?? Sofie is with me right now, her mother couldn't have been that worried leaving her with me!"

He wasn't allowed to go into detail or tell me when the interviews would take place but did go on to say they would need to speak to Chelsea's school because of her age. I was mortified. Disgusted and sickened. Embarrassed too, thinking what on earth will the school think.

The child protection team carried out their investigation, at some point, then called me to say they wouldn't be taking matters any further, that their investigation was over. They queried if Carrie had ever been diagnosed with bipolar.

chapter fourteen

The order also states, we cannot upset the normal running of the household and not intervene with it either. The order was hard to live by, especially confined in these walls with Carrie, more often than liked. Her behaviour was becoming even more erratic and weird. You would get goose bumps whenever she walked by you. I was feeling the bizarre atmosphere and I could tell all the kids, and any visitors we had, were experiencing it too.

Something occurred between Carrie and Chelsea which resulted in Chelsea being put up against the wall, like it was a naughty corner. With Chelsea crying, she looks scared and confused. When seeing me, she reached out her hand and tried coming towards me but Carrie forced her back to the wall. I ask Carrie what this is in aid off,

"I've been doing this type of discipline for quite a while"

A complete lie, I have never, ever, seen it and it was apparent that it was new to Chelsea too. Chelsea still tries to run to me but Carrie won't allow her,

"Daddy isn't going to help you Chelsea! You need to say sorry or you will be on the wall longer"

She continues to cry, looking around, not knowing what's happening,

"I love you daddy!"

Carrie, keeping her against the wall, so she's unable to move, repeats herself,

"Daddy is NOT going to help you!"

Chelsea becomes even more distraught,

"Daddy! Hug!"

I walk closer to Chelsea and try to get Carrie to stop but, she quotes the order,

"You must not intervene!"

My little princess needed saving, I wanted to swoop her up in my arms and tell Carrie 'enough of this now'. I also wanted to throw Carrie across the room. It was like there was a force field and if I stepped over it, I'd be penalised. I wasn't allowed to enter unless Carrie allowed me to do so. If I did anything, she would get me arrested for breaking the order. I tried everything verbally possible to make Carrie see sense, but it only made her stamp her law more,

"Chelsea, just say sorry to mummy"

But she wouldn't listen to me. The closer I got, the calmer Chelsea was becoming but Carrie didn't want me near her,

"Let me deal with this please, go back over there"

Chelsea still defying Carrie's method, I ask again for her to say sorry. Chelsea still crying and trying to get away from the wall, to only be pushed back. Struggling to keep Chelsea in place, she then asks me to help,

"Ok Carrie, let me talk to her then"

"NO! I want you to support me!"

Seeing an opportunity, I calmly tell her that's what I'm trying to do. If she would just let me. The barrier comes down and I'm allowed to talk to Chelsea and be near her, though Carrie still has her pressed up against the wall. I soothe the situation, softly asking Chelsea to stop crying,

"Calm down now, just say sorry to mummy and you can move"

Carrie just pulls faces at me,

"You're not helping, Carrie"

"I didn't want you talking to Chelsea while she was doing her time".

Sofie and Adam are now in the room from hearing the commotion. Chelsea shyly says sorry and then tries to move but, again, Carrie forces her back, with Sofie now yelling at her,

"MUM! Let her go now, she said sorry"

Carrie disagrees, she didn't hear Chelsea and she must say it again. This makes Chelsea cry again. Still near, I tell Chelsea,

"Just say it again" goading her with my eyes, and she does. This time, Carrie moves away,

"That is good" she says, responding to Chelsea's apology.

Carrie walks away and I grab Chelsea as quick as she grabs me. This moment, I had seen the true darkness in Carrie's eyes. The controlling evil. Cold and ruthless. I strongly believe she was hurting Chelsea in the hope I'd kick off. Or there is something seriously wrong with her!

When things are settled, I try to reason with Carrie, explaining my feelings about what happened with the 'naughty corner' and about our recent situation, what had unfolded,

"How did you sleep at night after taking them? When Chelsea came home, she sobbed saying how much she missed us. How could you have done that?"

"You're lying, that's not what Chelsea's been saying to me"

I then go into more detail, asking her to explain the upsetting phone calls while they were away but she deflects the request,

"Chelsea was only calling for you when she was on the naughty corner because she was being disciplined by her mother. It had nothing to do with Chelsea loving you more, because that's just ridiculous"

She's confusing, making remarks like she's having her own separate conversation. Totally different to ours. It's either she's absolutely nuts or her mobile phone is recording in her pocket.

I see Chelsea fall over so I leave the conversation and tend to her but Carrie isn't finished yet. It jumps to her aunt staying over soon and the topic of the clauses in our order are brought up. I remind Carrie that at first, she didn't want any family members around.

"I said to my solicitor that family were allowed but not on a daily basis"

"You did not say that Carrie, your solicitor, next to you, in front of the judge and my barrister, requested no family"

She continues to disagree with me. I'm done talking now, she's hurting my head. My last words on the subject,

"The children's happiness is all that is important to me"

But Carrie far from finished,

"OH, PLEASE, stop going on like you're some master, it's all fake with you ok, everything is fake with you. Your whole family is fake".

Green eyed monsters are never pretty. I tell her this is where it all stems from. Jealousy. Jealous of my relationship with my family, with some of hers, with the children but that jealousy does not condone her behaviour. She chooses to be who she is. I respond with,

"Yes Carrie, no Carrie"

Showing I really don't want to talk anymore and that my life has only ever been about that. Three bags full Carrie.

"You should have divorced me years ago then" she smirks

"Oh, I wish I did, believe me Carrie. I would have in a heartbeat if you didn't keep threatening to take the kids away from me"

Apparently now untrue. Carrie now says she has never threatened using the children,

"It's all lies!"

I look at her hand, close to her pocket,

"Are you recording by any chance, Carrie?"

"Its only to protect myself. You only want the children so you can pay for the mortgage".

Anytime she's in the house, things are unpleasant and before long, she's having her evening antics again and her balls are hanging large. The bitch is back. The bitch never left as far as I'm concerned, she was merely hibernating. I walk in on a row with her and Sofie, with Sofie telling her mum she's aware she's been recording the moment she returned and that she's been pretending the whole time,

"Oh well, just wait Sofie, its fine"

"Wait for what, mum?!"

"You need to speak to someone Sofie, you have a lot of issues towards me"

She then brings me into the conversation saying she wants something drawn up by the solicitor that states money will be split in half. I wanted to curse her, how dare she think she's entitled and I wanted to call her out, saying money has only ever been what she wanted. She was only ever after what she could gain. Not love or family, just money,

"Ok Carrie, I want something drawn up saying you should pay your way here"

"You also have to, as your wife, you have to support me as well, were not divorced yet"

Someone sounds like they're quoting! Divorce. I never even thought about that. My brain has been so wrapped up in getting this custody sorted and the date for it seemed to be taking forever to come through. But yes, without a doubt, a divorce was inevitable. Seems like Carrie's more focused on that now. Money or children? A no brainer really, which Carrie will choose to fight for. Talking of our separation, how we can't possibly separate under the same roof, I remind her what social services advice was but it goes over her head,

"I'm here to look after the children"

In the midst of this, she hands everyone dinner but the older two refused to eat anything from her. She's fine with that, showing them it bothers them more than her,

"I will just cook for Adam and Chelsea then"

Andrew retreats to his bedroom.

"Can you not see why they are behaving the way they are?"

I don't know why I keep bothering. Wasting words. She doesn't want to see. All this friction between me and Carrie, the lies, the abuse, how she's been over the years, is getting to the older ones now. She proceeds,

"And what about all the times you forced me to have sex with you".

"OH MY GOD" says Sofie

"Carrie, how can you talk like that in front of your thirteen-year-old daughter! That was inappropriate and disgusting! I am sick of your story telling! I just want to get back to a NORMAL life"

Something I'm not going to get any time soon and being under this order is making me feel like I've got my hands tied behind my back. Carrie's now rummaging through my grandfather's cupboard demanding 'documents'. She is hell bent on antagonising me today.

"You can't just take my keys and open it. I want to see what you're taking. Its locked for a reason, all you had to do was ask, not go into my wallet and take the key. You can't do that!"

"Yes I can"

Carrie wants all documents on life insurance and the mortgage and the little one's red medical books,

"What's owed on the mortgage? I also want the house valuation details and my passport too"

She is heavy-handily riffling through everything, making a mess,

"Can you please have a little respect! There's old photos in there!"

Actually, my grandfather's unit is filled to the brim of photos, Carrie knows this. Old stamps that were handed down to me too. She's just rough with it all and demands that she really needs the red books, that she wants everything.

"Do you want all the information about money owed on the mortgage too Carrie? What about our debts? Do you want all documentation for them also?!"

She's moving things out the way, photos are falling out of the unit, she's crumpling up things as she moves her hands about.

"If it wasn't for me Carrie, there would be no photographs at all, no memories of the children"

Handling them like there meaningless pieces of paper!

Juvenilely she says "oh sorry, they fell" to any photos now scrunched up on the floor. I tell her, all she has done is continuously, purposely, hurt me throughout the marriage.

"Ok, let's see what you have in your shed!"

As she makes her way to my shed, I run ahead of her. I have a safe in there with evidence I've collected. I believe this is the real reason why she's snooping. If Carrie ever found the recordings or my diary she would destroy them, I know it. I get there quick and stand by the door holding it shut,

"You have no right going in there Carrie, no need either"

"You can't stop me"

"Yes I can"

I continue to hold the door shut, with her now up against me trying to force it open. I stand firm as she tries to enter, moving forward, using all her weight. My diary is my lifeline, there is no way she can snoop around in here. I will not let her and I now know I must find another hiding place. Eventually she gives up and walks away.

We have a little party coming up, a belated party for Adam. Carrie's aunt is due and a few of my family members. What could possibly go wrong? Being civil, wanting the day to go without any bangs, I asked Carrie if she wants to help. Party food, decorations etc. While doing so, she's bickering, comparing this party to all the others we've had. She then asks who's coming so I tell her the usual. Her aunt has already arrived at this point and taking the task of cleaning. This is her normal self. Very helpful, very 'mummy-fied'. She's bleaching everywhere. The house sure does need it but Carrie isn't impressed and seems to get the hump with her aunt, mumbling under her breath,

"Cool! Saves me doing it"

Marie arrives with Kaine and Andre, my mum also. You could cut the atmosphere with a knife again. Carrie is not happy they are here, even though no one is showing her any rudeness and she knew who was coming prior. They all mainly stay outside in the garden. Carrie then starts to follow me around the house. Not speaking, just lagging a few steps behind me and it's making me feel weird. I go out in the garden to the play house, where Chelsea and Adam are. Carrie's aunt is with them. We play about and I tell her aunt that Carrie's making me feel really uneasy. Her aunt says the same.

Carrie, poking her head through the play house door, like the shining movie,

"What you doing?"

I can't do it, being near her is making my skin crawl and I get up to walk out but her aunt says not too. Her aunt tells her how she's making me feel, how she's making everyone feel and how she's behaving but Carrie disagrees and doesn't see what the 'big deal is',

"I've only come over to talk to the children"

I try and stay out of her way but I have to then intervene when she says something to Sofie that alters her mood,

"Anyway Sofie, no matter what you think of me, I still love you."

The statement disowned by Sofie, she just tells her mother she doesn't want to hear it. Back to me she asks if my dad is staying the night,

"Because if he is, I don't want him too"

"Yes Carrie, no Carrie, three bags full Carrie"

I'm sick of her!! So, so sick of her and her weird, manipulative, crazy games. I honestly believe she wants something to kick off. Digging and picking to get a rise out of me or anyone. I thought it was fine dad staying because she had already said she was going out in the evening. So, yes, my dad was staying and there shouldn't have been a problem with it,

"We will soon see about that, won't we!"

She has a personality that's high on ego. Her ways to overpower gives her a boost I think. She happily sits next to anyone she knows she can make feel uncomfortable. She does it to Marie, my mum and her aunt, who stop talking the moment Carrie sits by them. Close to them. She might as well sit on their laps. It's hard to deal with, especially when you can't have a normal reaction. To tell this person to move the hell away from you! In the end, Marie and Carrie's aunt seek solace going to the supermarket. It gives them the opportunity to talk too, about what's been written over social media and keep the aunt up to date on the current situation. Something obviously best not spoken of around Carrie. While they are gone, Carrie tells me again that she doesn't want my dad staying the night,

"It wasn't part of the agreement"

"Carrie, you're not asking me, you're telling me"

"Well, if you don't agree I'll have to bring it up next time"

I literally have no idea what she means and luckily Adam comes inside so I can divert from her

"Let's just enjoy Adams birthday shall we" and I coo over him as he's walking about, grabbing all the party food he can fit in his teeny hands.

"It's not his birthday though, IS IT"

"It is to me Carrie, you kidnapped him, remember!"

"Anyway, I don't want to talk to you, I never wanted to talk to you"

She's the one following me about, scurrying behind me, questioning who, what and where, yet she doesn't want to talk?! She walks out of the house.

A short while after, Carrie returns and asks me where my sister is. I know exactly where she is and I know exactly what has just happened because Marie has already phoned me.

"Where's your sister, she was here and now she's not. There's nothing wrong in asking that, is there?"

Carrie is on one. I haven't a clue what the 'one' is, where it will lead to or what Carrie is wanting to get out of it. I know she has searched for my sister and her aunt at the shopping centre. She sat watching them in her car before approaching them.

Carrie says they are both 'gathering evidence', that they've been listening to recordings and the aunt has been handing over photos. I tell Carrie, whatever they are doing is none of anyone's business and there was no need to follow them. Carrie denies doing this, saying she went over for cigarettes and she would have given her aunt cash to get them but she only had her card,

"Why did you feel the need to sit next to them on the bench then Carrie?"

"I just noticed that they were there and needed to go to the cashpoint for money"

An implausible response. I stop her wriggling out of her madness, telling her she's intimidating and it's none of her business what other people are doing,

"Am I not allowed to do that then? And it is my business if my aunt is handing over photos of my children to Marie"

"Did you see photographs, Carrie? Has anyone said they were photos of the children, or even photos at all?!"

"Ermmm, it will ALL become clear so it doesn't matter"

The reason Carrie doesn't know where Marie is, is because she's in our shed. When hearing how Carrie behaved over the shop, I asked them to get back quick, before her and ring the police for advice. Marie is on the phone to them while I'm having the conversation with Carrie. I needed to know where we all stand regarding the order because Carrie and her barmy, unbalanced self is just too much.

chapter fifthteen

The house is quiet for a few days, with Carrie feeding her mundane appetite with college work and evenings out with her mates. While home, she continues to sole-parent the little ones, or tries too, without my input, but always fails because of her ineptitude. I'm glad that she's going out a lot. It's more time spent away from us and we all prefer it that way. We're able to relax.

It's a rainy day, we're stay home and I'm eagerly awaiting her departure. Her mood is shining bright, or should I say dark. She's annoyed that I cancelled her mobile phone contract. I never cancelled the actual contract, I only stopped the direct debit coming out of my bank. She knows this too but denies we had a conversation about it a few days ago. Sadly, showing my life, I have it on recording. I record anything and everything to disapprove any lies that leave her lips. I stopped her car insurance too. The bank of 'me' has started to close its doors.

I remind her, constantly, that she stopped my family tax credits and it's now financially impossible for me to pay for everything. Why should I, anyway! I only get the little money that's coming in from work and £33.70 which is child benefit for Sofie and Andrew. If it wasn't for my mum, we would starve. She's not even entitled to a reason for my actions, why should I pay for her bills? She's eating the food my mum's supplying, while she spends her incomings of whatever she likes. She believes I'm wrong for cancelling things so I test her, asking if she will do some food shopping any time soon, seeing as she gets money for herself and the little ones but no, Carrie's unable to do so because she has a two-hundred-pound phone bill.

I'm guessing she was under the impression I'd continue to pay her bills for her and it wouldn't surprise me if she ran up the bill on purpose. Oh dear! If so, its backfired on her. As much as she deserves it, I never cancelled for malicious reasons but that said, I deserve to inwardly cheer myself on. Proving her stature, she's resorted to only cook for herself and the little ones while I tend to myself and the older two. With herself in charge of her own outgoings, and I believe to just one-up, she starts buying food and then orders the older two not to touch. She puts yogurts in their faces and says they must not eat them because they are Chelsea's and they are her favourite. Rose watered with bits in. Not your average kiddie yoghurts, they are higher end. Something we all know Chelsea would never eat. In fact, the yogurts never get eaten.

Me and the older two just hold our breath until she leaves and then it's all hands-on deck. Cramming in as much normality, cosy living as we can. Her nights out are a blessing because we get to have movies nights, stuffing our faces with popcorn, instead of sewing them shut. They haven't spent a lot of time with my dad and they're missing him not being round as much, so on weekends when I know Carrie's going to be out, he comes over. Marie's relationship with Chelsea and Adam is on the verge of being non-existent too. On Carrie's orders, they are still not allowed to interact with her. Carrie feels this is warranted after Marie's 'behaviour' the day they had words. The time Marie had an operation on her hand. Marie shouting back at Carrie should not strip Marie of her aunty role. Sofie noticing Marie not engaging with the little ones, prompted her to question her mother. Marie is not allowed any relationship, what so ever, with them because,

"Marie was going to kill Adam"

Her thought process, her irrational logic, Carrie believes everything that comes out of her mouth.

My birthday's approaching but there's no excitement. As you get older the fun factor fizzles out, I think and anyway, even if I wanted a fun celebration, with Carrie about it would be out of the question. My aunt's putting on a little spread for me and I made sure Carrie knew in advance. Doing so is the same use as a chocolate teapot,

"Oh, by the way, I am taking Chelsea and Adam to a birthday party Sunday"

Yes, it's easy to guess, it just happens to be the same day as my birthday. How convenient! I tell her my aunt has gone to a lot of trouble to make the day special, more so for the children. Doesn't matter to Carrie, she says the children are going to party to do with the guy's name that she keeps bringing up. One that Chelsea often mentions when they've been out with her. Perhaps 'this' guy will take her off my hands!

As requested by the court, we attend a mediation meeting which just ends up like a comedy sketch. Carrie makes herself look brainless. All she mainly speaks of is money, that when we separate she wants half of everything. The mediation lady probably had as much of a headache in the end, as I did. In one sentence Carrie would say she wants me to leave and all children should live with her but then says if she did leave without them, she wants the house put on to the market, so she gets her share.

Carrie's true natured character was just oozing from her mannerism. She showed no real concern for the children. When it was my time to talk, there were no 'buts'. No money or possessions would ever alter my plea. I would never contemplate leaving and, like I've said a million times over already, I will never leave my kids.

She spoke about how controlling I am and how I use to be violent. You could tell by her face that she knew she was losing the mediation lady's side, so this was her attempt at bringing her closer. It didn't work, Carrie just can't help herself. She knows what she wants. She soon tiptoed back to the subject of the house and wanting it to be sold. The lady asked her, where would the children live if that was the case, and Carrie just stared blankly. She was thick, stupidly thick and I shook my head at her. She was making a complete fool of herself. With the first session over and another one to follow in time, we left and no sooner as the door opened, she had something to say,

"You do know none of this is legally binding"

I could tell she wanted to shout, even swear. I know when she's getting angry. She froths at the mouth. Saliva builds up in the corners of it. This was always the sure sign she was ready to let rip. Clearly not happy with what happened, or what didn't happen in the meeting, she's seeing red looking at me. Going by her remark, I tell her I will not attend anymore sessions and I get in my car and drive off.

The following day I'm guessing Carrie's been to see Citizens Advice. She returned home behaving amicable. She asks to discuss court, how she wants to stop the proceedings and wants joint residency for Chelsea and Adam. In the mediation meeting she wanted four children, now she only wants two? It's not hard to work out why she wants, needs, the little ones. Money and housing! Without them, things wouldn't happen so easily, so effortless. I also wonder if this has anything to do with her solicitor not representing her anymore. Getting ready for matters to go further, both solicitors exchanged evidence, matters they would be addressing in court. Its coincidental that the solicitor is now not working on her case, the moment all this is shared.

I refuse her request and make it known that I will NOT agree to her terms and that I WILL stay on this path and fight for full residency for all FOUR children. She tries to butter me up, admitting she was wrong for walking out and leaving with the little ones. I don't care. Acceptance of what she did means nothing to me. Realising she isn't getting anywhere with me, she retreats to her car and makes a phone call. She spends most of the day there. I wished she slept out there too.

The children are full of beans this morning. Chelsea wants a piggy-back ride downstairs and asks if she can see aunty 'Maree', who is already here working. I peek in the front room and see Carrie fast asleep, catching flies, so we sneak in to Marie. Love over flows from them both. Family is so important! The children need this type of love in their life. They laugh and giggle and hug, then we quickly go back in the house before we get caught.

With Carrie now up, she's showing no signs of wanting to talk or interact with anybody, which makes my day. The little ones come out in the van with me while the older two are still asleep. They always enjoy the ride. We have the radio on and they attempt to sing every word of the songs playing. They like seeing my customers too, who they've come to recognise. There isn't a day where they don't come home with a sweet or little gift from a few of them. These are the customers who turned into great friends and helped me through this whole process. They were there for me and very much appreciated. Their friendly ear and warming shoulders.

On returning home at 10am, Carrie is up and ready, standing in the drive. No sooner as I pull in, she's at the van door and taking Chelsea and Adam out of it. I ask her what the rush is and while placing them in her car, says she's taking them out. Eager and in a rush and she drives away. I go inside and have a tea with Marie and I curse the hell out of her name. Offloading on Marie, letting off steam and getting things off my chest but I soon change the subject because Andrew and Sofie come downstairs.

Within half an hour, there's a knock at the door. Low and behold, it's the police again. They arrest me and take me in for questioning for breaking the non-molestation order. Boy, that section that reads "up to six months imprisonment" probably rang in Carrie's head like a lottery ticket. The longer I was kept in, the later it got and Marie didn't know what to do with Sofie and Andrew. Both of them refused to go back to the house without me. The order states the children reside at our address but Marie wasn't sure about them staying over the night with her, if need be. Sofie and Andrew didn't want their mother to prevent them from staying out so she phoned the police asking for advice on it. She got nowhere because the constable wasn't entirely sure what the non-molestation order entailed and were waiting for it to be faxed over to them.

The first allegation was, I assaulted Carrie by nudging her. Spinning her tale of the red book incident, when she wanted all documents, trying to get into the shed. She then must have sat in the police station and thought 'let's push the boat out a bit' and adds in snippets of her delusions, saying I am stalking her, following her around in my van. Carrie contradicted her first statement admitting trying to get inside the shed, showing that if I was standing still and she was coming at me, who, in fact, nudged who?! Her claims of stalking were also squashed because the times and dates she stated I was 'stalking', I was nowhere in the area. I had proof that I was picking the children up from school and would not have had time to get to where Carrie was, within a two-minute time slot.

Twelve hours later and more money spent using my solicitor, I'm released with the police reminding me how serious the order is. I met Sofie and Andrew round Marie's and I am fuming that Carrie could put me in this situation again. She, as always, can do and say as she pleases. The police were finished with me but I certainly wasn't finished with them. I rang them,

"Now can you arrest her?"

Take her away and let her spend hours in a gloomy police cell for lying. Criminal Law act states-

'It is an offence to cause wasteful employment of the police by knowingly making a false report, either orally or in writing'

She had already done this once before. It was easy for her to get me arrested so it should be easy for me too? All I get told is the case has been resolved, so they can't bring her in. Coming across like they are trying to make me feel better, they say she was warned how serious things are, how serious the order is. A warning, I thought. A warning? I get carted off in front of my children again, spend hours locked up and mighty mouth Carrie walks away with a warning?! How many times do I have to feel cheated?!

Taking Sofie and Andrew home, Carrie is there. Bold as brass with a slight guilt on her face because I'm walking through the door. I am boiling up inside, clenching my jaw. My mouth's dry and I'm tensed. If we were at the top of the stairs, I'd want to push her down them. I feel a colossal amount of hatred brewing and Carrie needs to stay the hell out of my way. Twice now she's done this and twice she was allowed too, with no repercussions. I'm seething! Angry at the justice system and I'm angry at her. Before I head upstairs she looks at me. I look her straight in her demented eyes,

"As god as my witness Carrie, you WILL pay for this".

chapter sixteen

Agitated by my presence, and no doubt annihilated by her own cock-up, Carrie isn't a happy bunny. Her joyful image of me wearing prison attire, gone up in smoke. She then comes home after being out mostly all day and sits eating a Chinese takeaway while me and kids have beans on toast because the food shopping delivery my mum's ordered isn't due until tomorrow. Before she left she said she was buying Chelsea's school jumper but this doesn't happen,

"I couldn't get it in the end. I had to pay for my car insurance"

Looking at her scoffing her Chinese, I want to tell her she's actually eating the school jumper. My mum's already helped me get most of what Chelsea needs anyway and Marie has helped me out with Andrew's.

The day then arrives. Happy birthday toooo me! The children make me feel so loved in the morning. As they do every morning. The first thing on my birthday agenda is to ring the tax credits office, for the millionth time, trying to sort out a claim but I hit a brick wall every time because Carrie's overrides mine. Giving up, I get on with washing. It's always diabolical but I suppose with four children it would be. I'm sure the little ones change their clothes at least four times a day. The clothes Sofie ripped of Carrie's have made their way downstairs. Carrie says she wants to keep them as 'proof'.

It doesn't take long before one of her event arises either. I hear her scorning Sofie for tending to Adam,

"You're not the mum, stop acting like it".

One minute she orders Sofie to do 'mum' things, the next she's blasted. Do it, don't do it, all of us are pulled in multiple directions. Carrie had left a hot drink unattended on the edge of the unit and Adam attempted to pick it up to drink it. It spilt all over his face and he started to cry from the contact of hot fluid. Sofie noticed first and went straight to his aid, which is when Carrie bites at her. I rush over to strip his clothes off and place a cool cloth on his, now red, face and after a while it soothes and there's no harm done, thankfully, with Carrie saying,

"It's just one of those things that happen when you have children"

I get Adam dressed again and me and all the kids head out for a fun filled day at a marina, meeting up with Marie, my mum and dad.

When we return, me and Andrew go straight upstairs and the little ones follow. In tow is Carrie,

"Are you gonna give me a cuddle Chelsea?"

She then looks at me, showing her gritted teeth,

"You've had her all day!!"

"Yes, I know, and if you remember, you had me taken away yesterday and I didn't see them all day either!"

I then just tell her to go away. I've had such a lovely day and can't be bothered with her nonsense but she just stands at the bedroom door. Andrew, playing Xbox trying out his new microphone, gets told by her to turn it off. Targeting Sofie again,

"You're not the mother of this house Sofie, you're just a silly 13yr old girl"

Now her rant at me is about not being able to do her washing and, I again, tell her the shed is open all day! I'm not even using the tumble dryer anymore to cut back on costs and I bring up the TV still being left on and how tight things are. She just smirks at me. I don't understand what she finds so funny. If it wasn't for my mum, I would have been so behind on the mortgage, they could have repossessed the house. What would Carrie do then? Is she fine with cutting her nose off to spite her face? She's even letting the dog sleep on the sofa, which we have never allowed since a pup. Sarcastically, the wonderful world of Carrie and her defiant digs.

Sofie comes up with a birthday cake she baked herself and Chelsea is all excited like it's her birthday, wearing a smile from ear to ear and wide eyed. The candles are lit and all the kids are about to sing,

"Haaaaaaaaaapppp....."

They don't get the chance too. Carrie leans in and blows out the candles as Sofie walks past her.

"Why did you do that Carrie, that was just damn right nasty! And you wonder why your children don't have any time for you?!"

Sofie's upset but Carrie just sniggers at her,

"I guess that's what happens when you make up lies Sofie"

Remarks like this obviously stem from Carrie knowing some of what has been said to Social services,

"Have you been telling people that I always smack you?"

Sofie's looking nervous, Andrew's angry and Chelsea is now crying. Adam, luckily, hopefully, doesn't understand what's going on.

Sofie put a lot of effort into the cake and extremely proud of herself. Carrie just can't help it, always resorting to spitefulness. Sofie chooses to ignore her and goes back down stairs to relight the candles. Carrie doesn't realise, doesn't care, that hurting me hurts the children. Not even caring that Chelsea is crying,

"Daddy, why did mummy blow them out? Me and you were doing it"

Carrie crawls back to where she came and they eventually get to sing, with Sofie presenting her yummy masterpiece and Chelsea helping me blow the candles out. We both make a wish. Chelsea's is probably for a new doll she's seen advertised on the television. I wish for Carrie to disappear. That she walks out, gets in her car and I never see the devil again.

Quoting from the Bible, Timothy 6:10:

'For the love of money is the root of all kinds of evil. Some people, eager for money, have wandered from the faith and pierced themselves with many griefs'

It would never enter my head, or my heart, to trade any amount of money for my family but Carrie is a different kettle of fish. Adam and Chelsea wake at 6.30am and we head downstairs. Something happens between Carrie and Chelsea and she kicks her mum. She's told off but Carrie isn't interested in Chelsea. Regardless of being kicked, she's brushed to the side. It's my attention she wants and asks to speak to me amicably. Here we go again!

"It is impossible to talk to you like that, you don't know the meaning of the word. There really isn't any point"

But there is for her,

"I want £25,000 and then I might consider giving you full residency for all for children. Providing I can leave and walk away from all the debts"

UNBELIEVABLE!!! This is her version of amicable. Any normal person of a sound mind would think this was a joke. That surely a mother wouldn't sell her children down the river for a measly £25,000. Carrie would and Carrie wants too and if I gave her the money, she'd be gone like a shot.

Getting what she said straight, I debate with her,

"That's a lot of money and to do that, I will be left with a house with no equity, £20,000 worth of debts, I owe my mum £15,000 where she's fitting the solicitor bill AND NOW you want £25,000, how is that amicable? How is that fair?"

"I think it's reasonable"

A part of me wanted to be able to throw money at her then throw her out the door. It would all be over then. She basically wants to take the money and run so she doesn't have to be accountable for her actions, in court. She knows I'm going to win, truth always does! Truth always should! I may have to jump through many hoops but I will. I will jump, I will climb, I'll do whatever I must. It's not about money, it's about well-being. The children well-being.

We're at a kiddie market, with her trying to haggle with me and not only does it make me feel vulnerable, but odd. She's dangling the kids in my face and it's like she wants me to tell her how much my peace worth to me, how much my kids worth to me. She then starts sobbing, saying her college course is going 'all wrong'. It is on record, obviously, that she took the little ones, and it's causing conflict with her studies. Hardly surprising. After all, she is training to be a social worker!

In all honesty, I'm torn. She's in front of me telling me she will leave, something I greatly want and saying it will be known that the children reside with me. Something also I'm aiming for and all I keep thinking is, if I give her the money, our life will be ok. It can get back to normal. We can be free. Carrie then saying she will give me the house makes me seriously contemplate her terms. It's one of the things that I worry about. I had plans to build an extension, do the house up and its possible in the future the equity would increase a lot, especially if the market value increases. The thought of years down the line having to give her 'her share' annoys me.

Putting Carrie on the deeds was a big BIG mistake. We could end up having a peaceful life and she could go off living whatever life she wanted but there would always be that chance of her coming out of the woodwork demanding her share, demanding a sale. If anything was to happen to me, the children, not only would have nowhere to live but wouldn't benefit from a sale. She would give them nothing. I want to be in the position of helping them with their first down payment on a house or first car. Sole equity would work in my, but mostly the children's, favour. With future benefits in mind, I ask her,

"What if I raise £10,000?"

"What am I supposed to do with that amount? The kids, car, your business and living in the house is worth at least £20,000 but, actually, I won't agree to come off the deeds of the house"

I've participated in tarnishing my children's past, I know that but I won't ruin their future. I end the conversation saying we will go to court. I go upstairs to the children, she goes out.

Feeling free, I go back downstairs and get comfy watching a movie. It's not long before she's back and starts making loads of unnecessary racket. She wakes Chelsea, who has now come down stairs and sitting with us. Carrie starts being O.T.T with her, over dramatic playing and Chelsea gets excitable. She starts licking Carrie's arm, who at first finds it amusing until she starts kicking her. She's out of playing mode then and drags Chelsea to the hallway, leaving her there,

"You can stay here. In the dark now"

I disapprove and she then tells me, Sofie and Andrew that she's tired so can we go to bed now. The movie only has twenty minutes left but she's "very tired" and won't let us finish it so we all just go upstairs, including Chelsea. Carrie is that 'tired' she spends most of the night watching TV and interacting on her social media page.

Up early as usual with the little ones and no pouncing off the sofa by Carrie. She's supposedly taking Chelsea and Adam out to the party she mentioned and while she gets Chelsea ready, I sit with the sewing box. Sofie's given me five pairs of leggings with little holes in, so I sew them while placing Andrew's school badge onto his blazer. My mum taught me to sew when I was young. I'm glad she did, it's come in handy, being a domesticated father.

Carrie changed her mind now, she's not taking Adam and she goes into the fridge, taking food out then crisps and fruit from the cupboard. Not to eat, to take with her!

"It's for the party"

I ask her not too, purely because she's taking excessive amounts. We've hardly got anything as it is! Not to mention, the fact that she didn't pay for any of it, plus what she's taking is meant for school packed lunches. It's not my job to supply party food. Why would she decide not to take Adam? My guess is she's going on a picnic and whoever she's meeting, will see her with her little prop. I want to say she's not allowed to take Chelsea but I know I can't. She'll still take her and there will be no stopping her. I've also got a strong feeling she's meeting up with a man friend. If so, should Chelsea really be involved, given the situation?! I can't say no because Chelsea will get upset. I just have to let things play out.

I get all the ironing done then sit a make a memory box for Chelsea. The school has requested these as something the children can look through, if they feel uneasy at school, as it's there first time. I decorate Chelsea's with Peppa pig, pictures I've cut out of old magazines and when she's home she can decide what she wants to put it inside it. It's getting late, I hoped Carrie would have brought Chelsea home by now, seeing as she's got school in the morning. I make the school packed lunches and look forward to an early night. At 7pm Carrie and Chelsea are home.

Piggy-back rides downstairs with Chelsea seem to be our new morning routine. A tad tired for it this morning though, from Adam waking me at 5am getting into my bed. I sort breakfast and make sure Andrew's set for his first day in secondary school. He looks very handsome in his blazer, very posh and excited to go. Carrie's awake but doesn't move from the sofa, a sofa that's now starting to look very grubby. Sofie doesn't start school till the afternoon so after quickly putting a load of washing on, I take Andrew to school and the little ones come with me.

I have to pop into Chelsea's school for a quick chat with her teacher before her starts. I explain the situation at home and she's very supportive. I'm getting good at this talking malarkey. I feel more confident speaking out loud. I don't feel like I'm drowning as much. The teacher is so kind and understanding and asks if I've got all the uniform ready and I tell her I just need to get a cardigan. Before I leave, she hands me a bag of uniform and I'm very grateful for her charity. We are going to have regular talks, keeping each other up to speed.

When we get back, me and the little ones hang the washing out then I make them up some bubble solution to keep them amused before lunch. Carrie, still glued to the sofa, not dressed and I'm guessing not washed either. I first ask her to PLEASE stop leaving dirty sanitary products in view. It's so awful!! I then talk about her leaving but she doesn't show any interest in engaging with me other than telling me to talk to my mum regarding money. She's still determined to get this £25,000. The sofa really is starting to look disgusting, I call it 'her sofa'. If she does leave, it's going with her or down the tip! I imagine the roof opening and down comes a big crane claw and it lifts her out of the house while she sleeps and she wakes up in a random place. Preferably deserted island.

She literally spends the whole day sofa sitting, mainly on her phone. I'm amazed how she's able to be constantly on it, how she keeps it running. When I'm using my mobile, I make super quick calls to prevent a huge bill coming through. I even try and make my calls to my solicitor as quick, for the same reason and obviously because his time is a tariff all on its own.

When I pick up Sofie and Andrew from school, I also speak with their teachers. Again, explaining home life. They have student services where they can talk but Andrew says he doesn't need it. He just wants to focus on school but me and the teachers make sure he knows that if he ever needs to talk, people are there to listen and he agrees to do so if he feels the need too. On to Sofie's school and her school says the same after being updated. Sofie is very verbal in the conversation and her issues of resentment and anger are very transparent. She finds it easier and better when she talks so she's allocated a counsellor. The end of school runs are complete, dinners prepared and eaten, washing is ironed and put away and the little ones have been bathed. It's now Adam's bedtime, before getting into character, whichever book Chelsea chooses tonight. My day to-do list has many ticks on it, whereas Carrie has moved her legs, upright position to stretched out, with toilet breaks in-between. It's a hard life being a mother!

The next day actually goes ok, even though Carrie's in the house. It's like there are two lanes. She stays on hers, we stay on ours. I'm able to work a little, with the littles one out in the van with me, tidy up and do normal things, with no evil interruptions.

Andrew and Sofie come home to a peaceful house, with Andrew going upstairs to play with his mates online and Sofie making chocolate cornflakes cakes with help from the little ones. The nicely clean kitchen is not so nicely clean anymore, as you can imagine nor are the little ones but there was no interference from Carrie, so the mess is trivial. Quite different to the last time Sofie was in the kitchen. Carrie finds it amusing standing up against the cupboards while Sofie tries to get a bowl out. She pushes her leg against it and Sofie has to prise the door open.

Carrie's clearly up to something or miraculously had a personality transplant, she's even going food shopping today but what she ends up buying will only last about two days. She spent twenty pounds, if that, but she did what she said. The money side of things is still annoying the hell out of me. Tax credits have giving me a rotten headache, trying to organise a claim and my headache worsens knowing Carrie has her own entitlement and the household isn't gaining from it. I feel she should not have been able to make a claim. Child tax credits, let me highlight the word: CHILD, yet what child is benefitting from it?!

With the little ones asleep, I sit and sort the name tags for Chelsea's uniform, with the older two sitting downstairs with me. Carrie is on her way out. It's not hard to fathom why she spent so little on food shopping now. I'm glad she's going out. I didn't want commotion the night before Chelsea starts school. I want tomorrow to go well for Chelsea but, on the flip side, I'm hoping Carrie isn't going 'out out'. She's doing Chelsea's school run with me in the morning. I don't want to walk in there with her anyway but walking in with her, a mess from her night out, will be worse.

chapter seventeen

What is it with the first school uniform your child puts on? It manages to turn our babies into tiny little grown-ups within a click of a finger!

"Oh Chelsea, stop being silly, get changed, you're not ready yet"

In hindsight, it's me that isn't ready. She looks so cute ready for her big day and the morning's gone good so far, until I'm sat doing her hair. Carrie's awake, getting ready upstairs for the school run. It is wrong that I hoped she wouldn't have come home last night? I'm not looking forward to walking in with her, at all. She comes downstairs, followed shortly by Sofie who has a disgusted look on her face. She says there's vomit in the sink. I ask Carrie about it and she just says she'll clean it. Could it not have been taken care of before coming downstairs? Or did Carrie leave it, purposely, for Sofie to find? Perhaps she thought Sofie hadn't washed yet. I thought her lack of using a bin for her sanitary products was bad enough, but vomit?!

I do not want Chelsea's mood lowered so I divert and coo over her. She's loving her uniform and feeling like a big girl. I take her to the hallway and she poses for 'my first day' photos. Carrie notices and when I'm beckoning Chelsea to say cheese, she gets her phone out and does the same. All the time with me thinking, if this day marked parental pride for her, she wouldn't have gone out drinking last night. The copious amounts of make up on her face, is not hiding the rough night she had.

Entering the playground, Chelsea is attached to me, holding on to my arm and leg. Carrie is uninvolved and disconnected, sat with Adam while I play with Chelsea in the sand pit. A few other children were there so I spoke to them and got Chelsea to interact. Once it was time to go in, I spoke to the teacher who allowed me to stay until we both thought Chelsea was settled enough to be left. The teacher got an idea of the relationship difference and I'm guessing every onlooker in the playground noticed too.

When home, Carrie goes upstairs with Adam but later comes back down on her phone, leaving Adam up there. Showing no signs of going back to him, I go and he has a really smelly bottom. When downstairs, I make a point of it to Carrie but she's fixated on her phone. Someone's either got better things to do or didn't want to change their son. If I had a pound for every time I shook my head at her, I'd be a millionaire by now!

The morning goes quite quickly, with Chelsea only attending mornings to start with. Me and Carrie both go to collect her. Her little face is a picture, all the children's faces are. They all have obviously enjoyed their first day. Stood with all the parents waiting, Carrie spots Chelsea and is over dramatic and picks Chelsea up. The whole playground is drawn to her noise. I don't know what's worse. Carrie being false or uninterested. Chelsea had a great morning, I'm so pleased and when we arrive back home, she runs into the office to Marie, telling her all about the day she had at her big girl school. Carrie pulls a face but doesn't react.

Not long after, she tells me she's done the washing up and leaves in a hurry because she's forgotten her doctor's appointment. I haven't heard anything health related since she's been back. Again though, I'm glad she's out again, I can get on with the day. Her idea of washing up though, was placing the dishes in the dish washer. Which she knows I rarely use now to save electric!

She arrives home with a pair of pyjamas for Adam and a pair of school trousers for Chelsea. I make a point of them not needing them, that food would have been a better choice. As I'm saying this, she pulls out a brand-new pair of boots for herself. I just want to grab them off her and throw them! I'm so frustrated with being shown that her money is her own. I will always provide food for my children one way or another, but I'm annoyed that I'm feeding the little ones on barely any money, when she has money for them and doesn't!

She wipes down the kitchen sides and then gives the little ones a bath which I have to intervene with again. I go up and, again, Carrie is pouring water all over Chelsea's face while attempting to wash her hair. She knows Chelsea doesn't like it!! What is wrong with her?! I ask her what is wrong with her! She's angry and rushes them out of the bath and goes to sit in her car on the phone while I get them ready for bed. Her sitting out in the car makes me feel on edge. I'm just sensing something. I don't know if Carrie's doing all these little things, like how she baths Chelsea, the vomit, spending money etc., in a bid to make me want to get rid of her. In a bid to get the money she wants out of me. An hour later her car's gone. The quick wipe in the kitchen and the rush bath was because she was going out. Her guilt controls events. She does things so she doesn't feel or look bad when she's going out or she does things to cause a debate with me so she can leave, having me as the excuse.

Her car conversations are happening all the time now. Numerous times throughout the day, if she's home, and they make me nervous. I hope that she's just doing it to have private conversations but I can't shake off the anxiety it brings me. I watch her sometimes, through the window and I see her change moods a few times. She'll be crying one minute then be in fits of laughter. Mostly coming back in doors stressed or with a deviant look on her face. The anxiety I get from it, makes we wonder if the police are going to arrive soon. Especially when she sits out there for a few hours then drives away. Still being on the non-molestation order, I've made sure I've done nothing that could incriminate myself or be twisted into something tangible.

Before we have to collect Chelsea from school, Carrie goes to Sainsbury's and takes Adam with her. Three hours later and no shopping in sight, they're back. Adam's face and t-shirt are messy and Carrie grabs the baby wipes. We've got five minutes before we have to leave but the baby wipe she has in her hand is to wipe her shoes! I get Adam cleaned up and go to grab his coat. I have to then re-wipe him because she thinks now's the time to give him chocolate and it's all over his lips and hands. These types of things she finds funny, I know what she's doing. It's all fun and games to her. As I wipe Adam over, we both sing 'twinkle little star'. Carrie then decides she wants to wipe him now too. I really wish she would just leave me alone!

Making dinner for the little ones, Carrie tells me to make sure I put 'that' in. Speaking about my diary, that she's obviously aware of now. Thankfully I get a telephone call from my uncle so I'm able to ignore her, walking out into my office to answer the call. When I'm finished, I walk in on Sofie questioning her. Carrie had her ear up against the air vent in the toilet listening in on my conversation and Sofie caught her. Carrie's wanting to start something again,

"Where do you take the little ones when you go out? You're taking them to parent classes aren't you? Or a play centre"

"No, I haven't. Why on earth would I go to parent classes?

"You're lying. Someone saw you"

I am certainly not the one that needs to attend parent classes! I don't know if this is just a way of her sparking a row or she's unintentionally telling me someone is keeping an eye on my whereabouts.

She spends most of the evening upstairs getting ready then tells Adam it's bedtime, half hour before his normal time,

"It's a bit early Carrie"

'It's not early for me, I'm going out"

Drained by her pathetic childish attempts to annoy me, which I'll say she's achieving, I tell her I can put him to bed but she just tells me no,

"Carrie, if I can get up at 4am to get some milk to settle him, I can put him to bed at his normal hour"

"NO"

She puts Adam to bed and walks out with a bottle of wine. Exhaling her presence, I get on with dinner for me and the older two. They're both sat at the table doing homework and Chelsea is sat with them pretending to do some too.

When all the kids are in bed, I lay in the bath for ages. Thinking and going over everything. I can't stand Carrie and I just want her to go. She's tiring on my emotions, that bounce from anger to anxiety. I hear her come in. I dread the sound. When I go down to make a cup of tea, she has the TV on full blast, the PC running and every single light on available. All because she knows it's things like this that get to me. I'm trying to save money, she's trying to spend as much as she can. I go to bed but for a second I stop at the downstairs toilet where the fuse box is. Playing out a scene in my head of me taking the fuses out and leaving them under my pillow until morning. She'd probably get me arrested for theft.

Morning arrives, after having an unsettled night, with Adam waking up at 3am. I'm still trying to be that rising whistler. It seems like I do it now though, in the same sense people sing 'rain, rain go away'. I hope the rain cloud downstairs walks out the door as soon as possible. It's not even 8am yet and I'm having to deal with her. She's left a hot drink unattended on the unit again and Adam's about to make a move for it,

"Carrie, how many times are you going to do this before he gets hurt"

She just shrugs me off. Adam and Chelsea then run around the house with Carrie's handbag,

"Kids, go and get daddy's wallet and run around with it"

Carrie doesn't come with me taking Chelsea to school and I'm so flipping relieved. Once there, Chelsea doesn't want me to leave. The teacher, sensing Chelsea's anxiety, allows me to stay a while, reading her a story. Me and the teacher then sit with her, doing some drawing and I go when she's ok for me. When me and the splinter collect her from school, the teacher advices that Chelsea should do another week of attending 9-12 because she isn't ready for full days yet but does say that Chelsea has made a lot of friends and becoming very chatty. Carrie leaves saying she's going to see her solicitor. I don't know if this is too make me feel uneasy or a lie or she indeed is. The last I heard, she was refused representation.

Come Adam's bedtime, we have to wait. Carrie's up in the room getting ready to go out, music blaring. I ask how long she's going to be because Adam's crying but she's either ignoring me or can't hear me over the music. First, she wanted him in bed early because she was going out, now this evening, he can go to bed late! She leaves the wet dirty towel on the floor and soap scum around the bath and heads out.

After having a peaceful evening, Me and Adam get woken up at 5.30am by noise, showing us Carrie has returned home. I go to get him his milk to settle him back down,

"Oh sorrrry, did I wake you?"

Not wanting to give her the satisfaction, I tell her I was up already with Adam. She looks an awful mess and behaving like she still has alcohol in her system. As I'm warming Adam's milk,

"Don't worry. I haven't been round a man's house"

I sense her cocky-ness and really do not care where she has been,

"It's none of my business Carrie"

"Well, just in case you think I'm a dirty stop out"

She still tells me all about her night, like I'm interested! Walking back from somewhere far, getting into fights with people. A normal night for her then.

After getting a little more shut eye, Me and Adam go down for breakfast at 7am but she's unhappy with us doing so. She wants to sleep in peace. Her feet are poking out of the duvet and are sore looking and black. She gets up at around 10am and I notice she has a little mark on the left side of her face and her lip is swollen slightly. Alarm bells ring and I quickly jot it down in my diary, not wanting to take any chances.

She's going out tonight so I use the opportunity to have my dad, mum and Marie over. We're going to have a movie night. No cooking, just buffet food on the table, helping ourselves. Carrie's fine with this but makes sure she leaves her mark on the house before she leaves. She cooks herself a fry up. All pots and pans are left on the side, half opened tin of beans, oil splatter all over the cooker and a dirty ring around the bath after her use. She says she isn't going out until 8pm so, after tidying up, I wait to put out the food, not wanting her to do something childish and try to ruin my evening. Half hour before she leaves, I start organising the food,

"What is this all about?"

God help me! Grant me the power to ignore this vermin!! She knows, damn well, what my plans are! It's frustrating, having to talk nonsense for her amusement!

"You know what I'm doing Carrie"

"You're lying. You're celebrating something"

I want to tell her I'm celebrating her going out! I never know her motive or if there is one. Sometimes it seems like she just wants to put me in a low mood. A little bit of chiselling so she gets to walk out of the house knowing that she's annoyed me. Maybe it makes her evenings out that much more enjoyable.

With Carrie, mostly on her mobile phone, the following morning, I go about my day. Washing, ironing and cleaning. Such a rock and roll lifestyle. The weather looks nice and being the weekend, me and the kids go out in the garden for a little tidy up and water the plants. Carrie stands at the kitchen door having a cigarette just staring at us. She's taking the little ones somewhere today, saying they are just going 'out'. While I load up the recycling, she gets them in the car. I wait a while at the front door waving at them and I see Carrie turn and say something to Chelsea. Whatever it was made Chelsea stop waving and her face turned sad, showing her bottom lip. I go to the car to see if she's ok and while I'm talking to Chelsea, Carrie winds the window up, starts the car and drives off.

What did she say to Chelsea to alter her mood so quick? Again, hurting Chelsea hurts me. She enjoyed winding the window up. How can a mother see that they're the cause of their child's upset and not feel an ounce of guilt? I've caught her whispering to Chelsea a few times and it worries me what she's saying. I can't focus that well, when she has the little ones, more so today, now she pulled off another one of her cold-hearted stunts. I must have washed this kitchen floor about ten times, where I'm trying to keep busy. You could eat off it! I wish social services ordered her out the house. I wish I could chuck her out the house. I want to change the locks and barricade the door.

Coming up to 6pm, the little ones are back and I'm smiling. Apparently though, that's not correct behaviour, with Carrie annoyed by it,

"Why do you keep smiling?!!!"

This bloody woman!!! Am I not allowed to smile now?

"Don't look at me if you don't like it Carrie and stop talking to me"

As she walks off, me and the older two notice she's left books on the kitchen side. Revision material about abuse. It makes Sofie uneasy,

"She's put them there on purpose. For you to see Dad, to get at you"

"Don't worry about it, ignore it"

Revision on abuse. Carrie should have just asked me for my diary. Looking at the books I want to pick them up, go over to her and show her exactly what abuse is. She so badly wants me to do something and she makes me want too. I want to give her what she wants. I want to do what she's forever lying about. Then I'll be able to say,

"There! Now you're telling the truth!"

7am with Peppa pig on the telly before school, Carrie's not happy with it being on, or the light for that matter. She's now in a foul mood. Andrew couldn't finish his banana, having a little left so asks Adam if he wants it. He goes to give it to him but Adam turns his head and says no. Carrie takes the opportunity,

"Maybe it's because he can sense the horrible-ness Andrew"

Sensing her tone, I believe, Adam then asks for me,

"Where's daddy?"

"Let's hope daddy has gone to button moon"

"Carrie, Stop!"

Pick, pick, pick, dig, dig, dig. Twanging at my nervous system like it's a guitar and I want to use her head like a drum. She is such a nasty vindictive being. Not deserving of the word 'human'. My mood drops at the tone of her vicious voice. She then wants to annoy Sofie before she heads off to school,

"Love youuuuu Sofieeeeeee"

Sofie just tells her she's weird. I really don't want to walk to school with her and I thank my lucky stars that my wish is granted. With five minutes before we leave, Carrie still has a towel round her head so I get to do the school run in peace. I know a lot of the mums at the school so we have a natter in the playground. I'm relieved that she isn't here, making me feel uncomfortable and probably making the crowd I'm talking too feel the same.

When I return, Carrie is washing up. This time properly washing up. So many patterns in her behaviour. I believe, in Carrie's mind, washing up makes up for not being ready to take Chelsea to school. I need to pop out and Adam wants to come,

"Is it ok if I take him?"

"Why do you need too?"

"I don't need too, Carrie. He likes coming out with me in the van".

Adam cries saying he wants to go with daddy,

"Yes, he cries when I go out too"

With her competition comment, I want to tell her it's complete bull****,

"Why is the conversation turning like that? All I asked is, is it ok? A simple yes or no was needed"

If I ask she starts, if I just take him, she starts. Always turning one thing into another. Opportunist! She now wants to know if I turned the TV off last night. I tell her obviously not because the TV wouldn't have been on this morning. She says she woke up in the middle of the night and it was off so she turned it back on,

"So, you were asleep, you woke up and turned the TV back on, then went back to sleep?"

"Yes"

"Knowing I keep asking you to not leave it on? Just leave me alone Carrie"

She knows I never came down in the night, she just wants me to know what she's doing, gloating that she leaves it on, on purpose.

chapter eightteen

I can't bear to do Chelsea's school run with her anymore. She makes me feel so jittery and I really don't want us to be the gossip of the school playground. Suffering her in the house is bad enough, without having to walk the street with her too. She's showing no enthusiasm coming along in the mornings anymore, thank god, so I say she can collect Chelsea on a few days, on her own. This doesn't last longer than 2 weeks, with the school phoning me saying Chelsea is sat in the office waiting because no one had collected her. Carrie didn't even have the decency to phone ahead to say she would be late, she just didn't show up! Twice! The first time she was apologetic but the second time there was just silence. Luckily we don't live far from the school so, on both times, I ran down there. Chelsea little face sat in the office, looking so timid and fragile. She thought no one was coming for her. Not just her mum but her dad too,

"I thought nobody was coming", she sobs,

"Daddy would never ever leave you, ever! I will always be here, always"

I tell Carrie she isn't allowed to collect her anymore and if she doesn't like it, then tough! She has to accept it. How can she not? What's she going to do, ring the police and tell them I'm 'intervening' or 'intimidating', I'm breaking the order? They can ring the school and the teacher will explain what she did.

It's made Chelsea nervous now, she's crying not wanting to go to school. Leaving her in the mornings is extremely difficult,

"Daddy please don't leave me"

I spend most mornings sat on the teeny chairs waiting for her to feel comfortable enough. When parent evening arrives, I'm dreading it because Carrie's coming. I'm there first, along with Adam, so I openly fill the teacher in on what's happened since we last spoke. The teacher suggests that Chelsea could really benefit from play therapy and possibly counselling because they've noticed a change in her behaviour. She's doing well but has become very shy and showing low confidence. A nervy child. I love that people are wanting to help but it hurts me so much that they have too. I know this is down to Carrie leaving her at school. At home with me, Chelsea is fine. She's probably spending all her school day worrying that she will be forgotten about. Carrie turns up half way through the parents evening, with a bottle of pop and eating a packet of crisps. No apology to the teacher, just brazen.

Still continuing, and getting a rise out of, being a bitch, Carrie says to Sofie one evening

"It's ok Sofie, I've found your things"

Sofie has, or should I say 'had' a secret hiding place in her bedroom. Carrie must have snooped really hard to find it because it was concealed or she possibly squeezed it out of Chelsea. It leads me to row with her and I start off with this, then go on to when she was disciplining Chelsea on the wall and she doesn't like what I'm saying and she tells me,

"I will get the kids as far away from you as possible"

She then walks out of the house, gets into her car and sits looking at paperwork. Two hours later she comes back in.

I think she's trying her hardest to scare me into giving her the £25,000. To push me to the limit, where the kids are concerned, so I hand it over. I'm upstairs with Sofie and Andrew, with Sofie crying saying Carrie's invading her privacy and that she can't have anything to herself, talking of her perfumes and lip gloss that she hides. I comfort her and want to make her feel better, which I know I can for this moment but not always. Not yet. Sofie says she doesn't understand why Carrie is so nasty and wishes she would just leave. I don't want to feel pressured into handed money over to the spiteful cow downstairs but at the same time, I'm feeling like I want to do anything, just to put a stop to it all quickly.

Adam wakes at 5am and gets into bed with me for a cuddle. Chelsea's already in bed with me, from waking up in the middle of the night. Andrew done the same because he's at the bottom the bed too. When they're all awake, including Sofie, we go downstairs for breakfast. Carrie eventually is up and uses her bottom to keep the cupboard door closed when Sofie goes to get a bowl for her breakfast. Sofie manages to squeeze a bowl out through the gap,

"Why do you keep doing this?"

Carrie ignores her. Me, Sofie, Andrew and Chelsea go upstairs to brush our teeth and Carrie goes into the bedroom. Chelsea and Adam go in there after and Sofie follows,

"Do you mind Sofie, I'm getting dressed'

Feeling awkward, Sofie replies "oh, I was just seeing Chelsea"

"She is with her muvva!!"

It takes a while to settle Chelsea, who's crying not wanting to go to school again this morning and Carrie's saying she's coming this time too. The drop off goes ok, with me walking home and Carrie going to Sainsbury, supposedly for nappies and baby wipes. She returns two hours later asking me if I want some money for Sofie and Andrew. It annoys me! Why now? and I bring up my feelings on her cancelling my money. She obviously turns it into a loud debate and I leave it, getting worried by her comment,

"I can't wait for you to get kicked out of the house!"

Come evening, I'm sat with Andrew talking about school and also with Sofie about G.C.S.E's. Carrie is in a good mood, being all fun with the little ones. Andrew goes upstairs to play online and I follow him to have a chat as he seems quieter than normal,

"Everything ok mate?"

"Yeah dad, just a bit fed up. I hate being around her. I prefer it up here"

I knew this. He is so much like me, blocking things out and I know this isn't good. I teach the children it's good to talk about things. I should lead by my own example. He says he plays his Xbox to take his mind off everything and I feel such a hypocrite. It's all my fault, why we're in this mess. Putting up with the situation for so long. I really didn't know what to do and I blocked out how bad things were, and still are, and just concentrated on being the best dad I could/can be but I'm failing. I'm allowing Carrie to cause them upset. I only have two options. Wait for court proceedings to commence or give her the money.

The splinter continues to cause discomfort over the next few days. She asks Chelsea if she wants mummy to read her a book. This wouldn't be so annoying to me if it was real. The story doesn't get finished because Adam bugs her. Her mannerism shows she doesn't want to read to him, doesn't want him involved, only Chelsea. Adam then tries to get Carrie's attention with a magazine but she isn't acknowledging him so I tell him he's a good boy for reading.

Andrew's online subscription has run out which means he can't play with his friends or Kaine and Andre. My mum finds out, as she's down staying with Marie again. She talks to Andrew through Kaine's microphone so she buys him it. She also says it's Andrew's only escape. I feel horrid that I can't afford to buy things at the moment. I miss my life before, being in control and financially stable. How can I know I'm a good father but feel like I'm failing as one?

Come evening, Carrie puts Adam to bed early and while me and Chelsea are having a cuddle, she comes over, kisses Chelsea and says she's going out. Here it is again. Reading to Chelsea, putting Adam to bed early. Every time she ends up going out in the evening, she does little gestures beforehand to make herself feel better. Like she's done enough. Same old, same old.

After carrying Chelsea to bed, asleep, me and the older two watch TV. Coming up to 10pm, Carrie returns and sits on the other side of the sofa, her side, the dirty side, doing whatever on her mobile phone. Ignoring her presence, as she is us. Not long after, she turns the TV volume down so we can't hear it. Before I have a chance to react, Sofie does,

"Who do you think you are, coming in and turning it down while we are watching it? Why are you so rude?"

I asked Sofie to leave it. Why? Why do I keep doing this? Then I remind myself of the non-molestation order. It's that which tight lips me, which makes me want to keep the kids tight lipped too. I can't retaliate how I want too, how a normal person would and I can't let my kids retaliate because something may happen and I'd have to retaliate on their behalf. Which I can't! We listen to Carrie's reason, why she's allowed,

"Cos I'm the muvva".

I'm sick of how she says that. So common and authoritative. I really can't stand that word! Muvva! It's her slogan.

She has 'somewhere' to go so can't come on Chelsea's school run in the morning. I like these days. When she leaves, Marie comes with us because she pinkie-promised Chelsea she would, at some point, come and see her new school. She talks to Chelsea about the times she's been too upset for her daddy to leave,

"No more crying Chelsea, ok. You have to be a brave little girl. School is fun. I wish I could go here instead of work"

With that, Chelsea proudly, and confidently, shows her around her playground, pointing out who her friends are and where she plays,

"Wow, it's so lovely here! I like your school. Chelsea, you know what you have to do? When school starts, you need to tell daddy - Will you go now daddy! Go, I've got school to do"

They giggle with each other,

"If you can be a brave little girl and pinkie-promise you won't cry today, I will buy you a brave girl gift"

Chelsea smiles asking for a magazine and Marie pinkie-promises back that she will get it,

"because I know how brave you can be"

We left Chelsea entering school, smiley and happy, and no tears and she did, she told me to 'go now daddy'. Carrie doesn't come on the pick-up and isn't around so Marie's able to be waiting outside Chelsea's classroom with a Peppa Pig magazine instead of me giving it to her,

"See, you did it Chelsea! I bet you had a really fun day today too"

She did. Limited family contact is having a knock-on effect on the children. Grabbing snippets of love when it's convenient and safe to do so, is wrong and unhealthy. Family should be part of life's routine, not something you have to sneak about doing. For the sake of herself, Carrie would prefer Chelsea and Adam missing out rather than watch them happy.

Carrie has an opinion on everything, mostly brought on by that crazy mind of hers. A big sister can't even do her little sister's hair on request, without it turning into a competition,

"Why don't you stop playing mum?! And, why don't you stop letting her play mum and replacing me!"

If things like this really do bother her, why doesn't she just change? Be a better mum. In fact, just be a mum! A normal one! I'm bored of the constant nagging when it isn't us that need to alter our ways. Social services are due out again so I just tell her to make sure she's here when they arrive,

"OH, DON'T WORRY I WILL"

Like she's ready to put the record straight or something. That she's looking forward to their arrival. I get nervous about visits like this, even though my actions as a parent don't warrant it, whereas Carrie's able to sit in front of them and act like everything's rosy, that she's doing no wrong. They see through her though, again saying it's in the best interest of everybody that she leaves. Why can't they just remove her? And why 'everybody'? It's not everybody! It's in the 'best interest' of me and the children. We're not the ones hurting anyone. I wonder if Carrie takes note of what they've repeated. Sooner or later she has to realise that she isn't going to get what she wants. I will NEVER leave the children!

It's seems history is repeating itself. Carrie looks worse for wear regularly and is losing weight. Her body is showing her, like it did before, that she's being too excessive. Andrew spots her sitting outside a pub, drinking with a guy, on his way home from a half day at school. Her behaviour when she's home is tipsy but when asking if she's been drinking today, she says no. The guy she was with is the same guy that came to court, the same guy the little ones mention from time to time. Going by Carrie's track record, I know she's dating him. I wonder if this means she'll be leaving soon? Like she did before. Let's hope so!

"So, where are you taking the kids?"

"Andrew's football tournament"

"Well, just remember I'm taking them out!"

Like I'd forget. I hate the little ones going anywhere with her, it's not something that leaves my mind. Yet, when I return for the hand-over, she's changed her mind because she's ill. She really does look it too and is very chesty. Déjà vu. Maybe she's going to end up in hospital again.

It would be nice if illness muted her, we'd have a couple of weeks break, perhaps, but no such luck. Even if Carrie was ever on her death bed, she would still be a cow. All the way until the end. Then she'd haunt you and mess up your life until it's you time to pass. Then she'll annoy you in the afterlife for eternity! There would never be any escaping and being in the same house as her, there is nowhere to hide. She chooses to sit at the dinner table with us all. Something she has never done and you just know that it isn't because she wants to eat her dinner comfortably or sit and feel like a family. She starts moaning at me, putting me down and blaming me for the older two not wanting to eat her food. I want to just scream in her face, WILL YOU JUST F*** OFF.

I'm fed up of it all. You can't even feel pleased about sticking up for yourself because she just goes on and on and on. She is Groundhog Day. Chelsea starts crying and tells Carrie she doesn't love her. I promise myself that I'm not going react to her sly comments anymore, that I will just ignore her but I find it impossible after a while. She's ill yet got all this energy to blast me. She kicks off again in the evening when I'm sat nice and quiet with the little ones,

"Everything you've done will come back to haunt you and it's because of your lies"

Jesus Christ! I want to hold a mirror up to her and tell her to talk into it. She can project her shadow upon me as often as she chooses, there will NEVER be any resemblance between us.

Watching her in and out of her car, having her 'chats', running to collect any mail before anyone else does, her goading and maliciousness, I'm on the verge of breaking point. I constantly feel like I'm going to pass out from my brain not being able to compute. I know she's struggling finding someone to represent her. Hardly surprising, given the contradicting rubbish that comes out of her mouth but the more stress I think she's getting from it, the worse she is towards us. She is trying her hardest to win and she brings up the deal she wants to make again.

I will not agree to £25,000 but I know she knows she will lose in court and the thought of dragging this process out even longer makes me want to resolve it quick. I tell her I will pay rent on a property for a year so she has somewhere to go. I look at adequate accommodation and, going by the market, I offer her £5000.

"Will you be my guarantor?"

"Absolutely not! The last thing I want is a landlord ringing me up telling me I need to pay for damages you've made"

She says she won't walk away from the entitlement on the house but at this point, 'now' is more important than 'later'. Financial matters can be dealt with in the divorce.

"How about two years rent?"

"No! My finances are in a critical condition, the same goes for my business"

"What about at a later date?"

"Carrie, do you even realise the mess I'm in? Mainly because of you! I have no way of knowing what my finances will be like in a year down the line. I can't agree to that right now. If I can, and going by how things have been then, I may think about it"

Basically, implying she has a year to sort herself out and reminding her that our situation cannot go on any longer. It isn't fair on the children. She agrees for my solicitor to draw up a court order plan. If she's happy with it, she will sign it. The children reside with me and she wants the little ones every other weekend, to share the school holidays and one overnight visit a week. I'm contacting my solicitor first thing in the morning.

Even though I felt like sunshine was about to burst through the dark cloud, I was wary of the terms. The order is scary but my solicitor says it really is the best way forward, stating I have spent so much money already and further court proceedings will only add to the amount. He says it shows I'm trying my best to resolve things and I need to play things safe. We both knew the order would never work with Carrie being who she is but the order didn't feel like I was 'playing it safe' for the kids. It was more like a huge gamble but, at the same time, the order would give me power. Power to say no. If she was drunk or aggressive or showing any signs that the little one's well-being was at stake, I could say 'no' at any point, without any back lash.

I knew what would unfold, purely by Carrie telling me,

"Just make sure your solicitor puts the £5000 in the order"

That was her ultimate focus. Everything else was just to make herself look good or feel better. It wasn't about the children, it never has been. She signed the order, it was passed through court and approved and the money, borrowed off my mum, was transferred into Carrie's bank account. The non-molestation order was no more. She didn't leave straight away though and continued to upset the house. Her last stamp on us maybe. Especially the older two.

She chose a different property, a more expensive one and the money she was given ended up only covering half a year's rent. She took her awful sofa with her and she left. I let out a prolonged sigh and it felt like I was breathing fresh air for the very first time.

chapter nineteen

Freedom is a feeling and I felt it, in the morning, the moment I opened my eyes. The splinter, that was once embedded for so long, has now been wrenched out and the invasive abrasion can heal in a clean environment. The splinter is now just in sight and I will try my hardest to let things play out as respectfully as possible. The best outcome would be for Carrie to grow up, see sense and instead on focusing on herself, focus on her children and make things better. I won't hold my breath though, only time will tell and I will always be looking at the clock. The children have been through enough as it is. There is no podium for her now, no high horse she can mount and trample over me with. I can't say for certain that there will be no bad days, Carrie changing overnight would be a miracle, but what I do know is good ones will override any because they will be more plentiful.

All the children have taken her departure well. Sofie and Andrew are over the moon that she is gone, happy they don't have to deal with her anymore. Carrie wanted to be the one who spoke to the little ones, explain what was happening. I wasn't allowed to be involved in the conversation but I was told by Chelsea that mummy has gone to stay with her friends for a bit. I'm not sure if Chelsea said this from trying to make sense of it herself, or she was told this by Carrie. If so, I don't know why Carrie didn't relay the situation better, more truthful. That she was going to have her own place, where her and Adam can visit. I suppose it doesn't really matter what was said, as long as the little ones were ok and they were. They were fine with it because they are so used to their mum going out and hardly being around. Carrie leaving wasn't a big deal. They were used to having daddy all the time and 'mummy' sometimes.

The first thing I needed to do was sort out a claim for tax credits and the call to them was a lengthy ordeal. I still couldn't just make a claim, like Carrie did. I had to send them a copy of the order to prove all children resided with me. My claim was eventually granted but it left me bitter. The procedure I had to go through was clearly because I was a father. It had to be. Did Carrie have to prove to them she had the little ones? I'm guessing not.

Week one went without any major blips, other than Carrie not keeping to the times set, even times she set herself. She would always be half hour to an hour late than stated.

"Carrie, in future, can we try and keep to the times. Not only so we both knew what we were doing but also to establish a routine for the little ones?"

"You need to be grateful that you have my "f****** kids"

The new order was put in place to, hopefully, make life better. The little ones didn't need to see mummy and daddy at loggerheads anymore and her type of language outbursts weren't going to make this transition any easier.

The first day of week two, Carrie told Chelsea she would call her but it didn't happen, with Chelsea then asking me why. So early into the order and Carrie's already not sticking to things. If she's not going to do what she says, I wish she would just not say anything at all. Carrie doesn't even acknowledge her forgotten phone call and just texts me to say she wants to change the pickup from school to another day and how she will collect Adam in the morning beforehand.

With Adam ready, Carrie doesn't show up until the afternoon school run. She tells me they will be back at the "usual" 6pm, obviously not knowing the definition of the word. This is just a routine of speech for her.

After the school run, she brings them home at 4.50pm and tells me she's collecting Chelsea from school again tomorrow. I refuse, saying she can't keep picking and choosing as it's not fair on the littles ones, never knowing what they're doing. Also for me too, I have things to get on with and I plan around the children, more so now because of her contact. I want to be organised. I can't get through to her that all I would like is a routine that makes all our lives stable. She just gets defensive again,

"You're just trying to f****** keep the kids away from me"

'Carrie, will you please stop shouting and swearing in front of them!"

She just walks off saying she will take them out on Saturday. Surely in the little time it takes to drop the children off, she can curb her vulgar language?!

There's no contact for a few days until a text comes through Saturday morning asking how the little ones are and if any mail has come for her. She then says she won't be seeing them today like she said. Me and the kids get on with our day and once we've had lunch we're going to the park.

There's a knock at the door 2.30pm, it's Carrie to take the kids!

"You can't just turn up! Why don't you understand the importance of a routine? For all of us!"

"I'll be round tomorrow at 9.30am then!"

So much defiance in her facial expression! We've got fireworks already organised but I try to be amicable in the hope Carrie would also be. Like getting blood out of a stone, asking her if they can be back by 4pm so our plans can continue.

A morning text arrives at 9am-

'I won't be collecting the kids till 12pm. I'm busy'

I then have to amuse them because they were ready to go out. I don't know what to do. Do I stop telling Chelsea and Adam when they're going with their mum, in case she doesn't turn up or should I spring it on them last minute saying they're going with her? If Carrie can get to college on time, sticking to that regime, it shouldn't be that hard to stick to parenting?

Andrew has a football match so Carrie has to collect the little ones from there, with me walking them to the car park as Andrew doesn't want to see her. She tells me they will be back at 3.30pm, we both agree and they go off. Yet she returns at 4.10pm

"Carrie, we both agreed 3.30pm!"

"I'm their f****** muvva, if I wanna see my kids I f****** will"

This isn't Carrie wanting to spend more time with the little ones or she's behind on time. This is her, still letting me to know that she can do what she wants. Order or not. Purposely unorganised, just to prove that point.

Week three consists of two days contact that go peacefully, other than her annoying reluctance to turn up on time, which follows into week four with her telling me she is collecting Adam in half an hour. With him ready to go, she hasn't arrived yet. Adams been fidgety the whole time and starts getting upset because he wants to leave so I telephone Carrie to find out her whereabouts. She's at her friend's house,

"I'll leave soon"

I want to tear my hair out! Is she sat round her friend's, having a good giggle at my expense or does she generally not care what she's doing?! The latter must be true because effecting me is effecting the children. I'm not the one crying for her to turn up, Adam is! Just before 1pm she arrives and sees Adam's mood which her late arrival caused,

"Carrie, will you please just think of the kids?"

"I don't get what the big deal is".

Saturday morning, the little ones are ready. Carrie's coming for them at 11.30am but text comes through at 11.40pm-

'I'll be there at 1pm'

If I grit my teeth any longer, they will wear away! The little ones have been sat with their coats on, waiting to go and I now have to tell them they're not going yet. I make up an excuse that mummy's running behind so they don't get unravelled. I hate lying but I know the truth is worse. When Carrie turns up, she looks a mess. Her hair is raggedy. She tells me she had a few drinks last night, I wanted to tell her I could tell and that's obviously the reason why she changed the pickup time. With the kids waiting half the day for her, the last thing they need is her shouting the odds at me, so I keep schtum.

Leading into week five, she asks if they can stay overnight and the thought of it makes me nervous. I know I have to allow it but I really don't want too. I think it's too soon. I feel like I've shot myself in the foot with this order but I need to remember why I did it. I need to do things the right way, I know that. I need to do whatever I can, be the 'amicable parent', show willing, so I agree to try. I have to give Carrie the benefit of the doubt and if the order doesn't work, Carrie only has herself to blame.

Chelsea wants to go to mummy's but is scared to sleep there and starts crying. I settle her down and I can see hatred in Carrie's eyes. It's either because she's jealous I'm able to settle Chelsea or she thinks it's my fault why she's crying, not wanting to sleep over. Carrie gets agitated trying to get them in the car and I can tell by Chelsea's face that she's not happy so I walk over. I don't get far because Carrie winds the window up again and drives away.

I shouldn't have let them go. It's hard knowing what the right thing to do is. I want to ring the little ones but I know Carrie will say it's her time. Annoying her while the kids are in her care is definitely not a good idea so I just sit and hope all goes well. It doesn't.

I get a call from Carrie at 9.30pm and I can hear Chelsea crying and screaming in the background that she wants to come home.

Adam is awake also and making a lot of noise and it sounds like he's running around. Carrie passes the phone to Chelsea and I settle her. While I'm attempting this, Carrie is screaming at Adam telling him to get away from the cooker because its hot.

Chelsea calms at the sound of my voice so I ask her to pass me back to mummy,

"If you try and force the sleepover, it could push the little ones away from ever settling at yours"

"Oh, ok, you have all the f****** answers don't you, what do you suggest?"

"Your aggressive tone and language won't help for a start. I suggest I come and get them and we try again another time. Carrie, it's nearly 10pm. They have school in the morning. They can sense your mood which will only make them feel more uncomfortable. Of course, they would prefer to come home!"

If Carrie settled, just stepped back a bit, the little ones may have felt at ease. She could have cuddled them, read them a story and they may have slept.

"What do you f****** want, a f****** medal?"

Yes Carrie, that's really the best move to make, shout and swear. Medal?

"Just my kids happy would be enough Carrie"

When they're home, Adam's nappy is heavily soiled,

"He was crying for his bedtime milk, daddy, but mummy didn't have any"

I'm guessing that's why he wasn't changed either, she didn't have any nappies or she just didn't want too. I sit with them both until they're asleep and It doesn't take long. Who knows how long they've been crying for, they are no doubt exhausted.

Chelsea was fine in the morning and wanted to go to school, something I would have expected Carrie asking about. Perhaps a call in the morning?! But that's what you would expect from a caring parent. I wouldn't know what type of parent to class Carrie under without writing something untoward. If she cared, she would have phoned. I told Chelsea's teacher what happened and she said she would keep an eye on her. Carrie, however, did make contact in the afternoon-

'I'll pick up the kids Saturday at 12pm. Could you give me some money, I haven't got any left'

I know she gets college funds and I really can't see how she has nothing left, or is she just testing me?!

She actually does arrive on time and is friendly, agreeing that Chelsea will need more visits before she's settled with sleepovers. Carrie leaves happy and the kids do too. This is how it's supposed to be, this is how I would like it for the kids' sake. If it could stay like this, everything would be ok but it's too much to ask. Plus, the niceness is for a reason. Carrie texts me at 4pm-

'Chelsea is upset and wants to come home'

She makes it very clear that she isn't happy with Chelsea feeling this way,

'I'm not going to keep doing this but on this occasion I will bring them back early'

When they arrived, Chelsea ignores her and comes straight in the house. Because of how the sleep over went, I tell Carrie that if Chelsea, or Adam, say they want to come home, to let them,

"Ignoring their request will only make things worse and make them want to come home even more. They need to feel safe. Chelsea, especially, needs to get comfortable in her own time otherwise she will take longer in feeling content"

Carrie just stays arrogant "Chelsea will just have to get used to it"

"Yes" I tell her, "but in her own time, stop being so selfish, if four hours is long enough for her, you should show her that's ok"

She leaves and I'm sure I'm right in thinking that Carrie's good mood earlier was because she's desperate for money. Buttering me up because two days later she texts, only mentioning money! She does contact the following day asking to have the little ones but we've already made plans and are not home.

Week six starts off with her coming round for……. money. I agree to give her ten pounds but make it known I am not going to keep doing it. We have a pickup day with no hiccups but then Carrie says she is unwell. She's not sure when she will have them next but wants some more money! When Carrie is nice, you know she's after something!

'Can I come to the house to see the little ones and oh, can I bring some washing with me?'

Is she wanting to do her washing so she can see the kids or wanting to see the kids so she can do her washing?! She is fully aware of Andrew's and Sofie's feelings towards her and that her presence will not be wanted. Not wanting to have the conversation over text, I phone and discuss their feelings with her but again, she gets defensive and says she will collect the little ones tomorrow and then puts the phone down on me.

We are now at the start of the seventh week into the order. Carrie doesn't come for the little ones like she said yesterday but I had a feeling she wouldn't. I could tell she said it because she was annoyed, so I didn't mention anything to Chelsea and Adam. Instead, she texts early evening moaning at me because I didn't tell her about Chelsea's Christmas play. I, in fact, told her two weeks ago and I remind her that when I did, she told me she had spoken to Chelsea's teacher about it. She either forgot or she's wanting to use it to start a row, so I tread carefully, wording my text politely but precise. I tell her it is not my responsibility to keep reminding her but I was planning on doing so if she hadn't put the phone down on me yesterday. She finishes up with saying she will be at the school play in the morning.

I hated being next to her. So many parents were there cooing over their children. Proud mums and dads. I know we don't know what happens behind closed doors, but, at face value, all the parents seemed to have their stuff together, while I'm sat next to the mother of my children, who I can't stand to be around. I just focus on Chelsea looking cute on stage, playing out her part and I smile at her showing her she's doing a great job.

I have to pass on bad news to Carrie afterwards. Her Aunt has let us know her grandad has passed away. She isn't talking to Carrie. With the older two at school, I let her come to the house so I could speak to her about it. She wasn't even bothered. She was blank, uncaring while I had tears in my eyes telling her. He was such a lovely man, but Carrie's response showed she felt nothing.

"I won't be collecting Chelsea from school. I've got no money"

She leaves but texts late evening, 10.20pm-

'What have you got planned for this Saturday?'

Not waiting for a replying, she then phones. I'm on the phone to mum. She sends another text through-

'You seriously need to call me!'

I finish my phone call and go to sleep. I don't 'seriously' need to do anything. Its late at night, I'm about to go to bed. If it really is serious, she'll call or text again.

Finishing up the week, she wants me to help her sell her car so, as you can guess, when asking for help she is friendly. A person's true nature can never stay hidden for too long though.'

"The kids aren't allowed to go to granddad's funeral"

She's angry. I know this is out of spite, as her family have told her she is not welcome there. Not after the way she has treated everyone. They don't want anything to do with her. She says again, they are "NOT" going and before putting the phone down says she's coming for Adam tomorrow at 12pm.

chapter twenty

I wonder what the eighth week will have in store. Taking out the dysfunctionality brought on by Carrie's appearances, life isn't bad. We are all so comfortable in our surroundings now, enjoying the atmosphere. We have music on, we dance about and be silly, we bake and enjoy each other's company, with no one scorning us for it. It's a happy household, where we walk bare foot, safe in the knowledge that nothing will cut our feet. There's a huge positive difference in Andrew, who's still an avid gamer but he plays nowhere near as much as he did when Carrie was here. He's not limited to his bedroom anymore and I can tell he's liking the whole run of the house. He's doing well in school and making steady progress.

Sofie's the same, more relaxed and pleased she no longer has to hide her things or sand bag herself against her mother's outbursts. Academically, she's doing exceedingly well. Very intelligent and her school reports show how at ease she is with all her subjects. She still has regular talks with the school counsellor, which I don't pry on. It's Sofie's private time but she knows if she wants to talk to me, I'm always here to listen.

Chelsea is a bit half and half. When home she's a typical kid. Playful and content but when there's a Carrie incident, her mood changes. It's like she takes one step forward but as soon as Carrie creates something, she's many steps back. Her schooling is ok, still very shy and any advice I'm given from her teacher, I take on board and act upon. Adam is probably the easiest to parent. Not that the others are hard, he's just so young and life, our life, doesn't seem to be hitting his surface or affecting him. Or that's what I'm hoping. We're easing into toilet training slowly but surely, and so far, so good. All of them are great kids. I know I'm bias but they really are. All so helpful and kind loving. I'm a proud dad. Just not proud of the mother I gave them.

When Carrie's due to collect Adam, she rings me an hour before,

"Can you bring him to me? I don't want to walk"

"I can't, I need to be at a customer's house soon"

I just want to be able to get on with my call outs. I should have guessed this would happen after she asked about selling her car. I'm naive to think she will sort another way of collecting the kids, it will just be another job put on me.

"Ok, I'll walk to collect Chelsea and then we'll have to all walk back to mine then"

It's freezing outside! She knows I wouldn't allow the little ones to walk that far a journey. Trying to gain back control, I tell her I will drop them to her's but on Saturday, two days from now. She agrees. Obviously not that bothered about seeing them, otherwise she would had fought me on it.

Saturday goes without any bother but Carrie is asking for money again. She has no idea how precise her behavioural patterns are. She tells me she is really desperate for money and could I please find someone to buy her car. I agree to buy it off her which I will then sell on to get my money back. Quite funny really, I'm buying my car back, seeing as I paid for it in the first place. I don't look at it like I'm helping her. If she wasn't the mother to my kids, I wouldn't care if she never had money again. It wouldn't be my problem but she is their mother and they are in her care sometimes. If she doesn't supply what they need when she has them, again, she only has herself to blame. What she's gaining from her car will put food on the table. If she chooses to use it for that.

When I take the little ones to her, Chelsea gets upset and says she doesn't want to stay with mummy. Without batting an eye lid, Carrie's fine with it and agrees for me to keep her with me and to collect Adam at 4pm. Me and Chelsea have a lovely walkabout around town, stopping off at a café getting lunch. We also buy Carrie Christmas gifts so they can wrap them for her. Adam was happy on collection and we head home.

Exhale and inhale. Carrie phones a few days after and her argumentative and cocky nature is raring to go,

"What's this I hear about you taking the kids to the funeral?"

I tell her she made it very clear not wanting us to go. She also wouldn't have phoned if she had not heard rumours. She tells me she will have the kids 10am tomorrow but to pick them up at 4pm as she's going to her friends. EXHALE!

Chestnuts roasting on an open fire, correction, we have an open fire but were not fond of chestnuts. Its Christmas!! And even though week nine feels like week fifty, we're in the festive mood. I love this time of year! Up bright and early, seeing if the little ones have made it on Santa's good list. They always make it on his list.

Carrie calls in the morning wishing them Merry Christmas. She says she isn't going to talk for long so they can "enjoy their gifts" but will call back later and then see them Boxing Day. Luckily Chelsea and Adam forget, in awe of their presents and the day they're having and Carrie not calling like she said she would, doesn't interfere with their day.

12pm Boxing Day she texts-

"I'm just waiting for my friend to drop me home then you can bring the little ones to me"

She phones an hour later saying she's ready for them,

"Can you give me an hour to get them sorted? Family are round to give them presents and I don't want them to just take the presents and leave"

Carrie certainly isn't full of festive cheer,

"You're taking the p***"

"Carrie, I have so much going on as it is, without it being the Christmas period and the added fact of, now, being your bloody taxi service"

"You have had the kids all Christmas. You should bring them here straight away!"

"An hour is not a lot to ask for Carrie! And stop dictating all the time! You decided to go to your friends. You could have had them this morning"

Always having herself to blame but wanting to push the blame onto someone else. Christmas, of all days, I would just like a little peace,

"You expect me to jump Carrie"

She puts the phone down on me. Never being able to handle the truth. She probably thinks it bothers me, that she puts the phone down. It doesn't now. I'm glad her voice stops ringing in my ear.

I stay calm and collective on the drop off. I want to be in and out, that's it. She says she will text when I need to collect them and I walk away. Two and half hours later, she sends me the text. All that fuss over not seeing them at Christmas and the little ones' time with her is over already,

"I will text when I'm not busy and can see them again"

A few days later, obviously 'not busy', she texts asking to have them. I've got a busy day ahead, sorting the kids' bedrooms and they want to help me so I ask if tomorrow is ok-

'Why is that? Is it cos you're at the funeral? You better not be'

'You're ridiculous and paranoid. If I say I'm at home then that's where I am. I have no need to lie'

When I drop the little ones off the next day, she takes a while to come to the door. She eventually answers half asleep. Their time with her goes soundly, with Carrie calling at 2.30pm for me to collect them. When I get there, she looks tired and unwell, complaining of a bad back.

We then have two weeks of very limited contact between Carrie and the little ones. On the days she doesn't have them, it's due to her, supposedly, not being well or having too much university work to get on with. On two more occasions, she tells Chelsea she will phone but doesn't. She also tells her she has two days off so able to collect her from school. This doesn't happen either. There's very little contact leading into week twelve, until Carrie texts asking for them to be dropped off at 2pm. I have to give her different times because we've got football with Andrew. Carrie chooses 1-2pm, saying it's better for her. I'm sure it is!!

I collect them at 5.20pm and the kids aren't fully ready yet. I would prefer if they were. I want to limit contact between me and her. While the little ones are getting their stuff,

"So, how's Sofie and Andrew doing?"

"Really well, I spoke to their teachers the other day, they're both........."

Carrie butts in, now angry because she remembers Sofie saying she doesn't want her mum involved with her schooling in any way,

"It's your f****** fault"

"I can hardly see how"

At this point, Chelsea has come downstairs, now upset by the shouting,

"Stop mummy"

Adam follows and I try getting their shoes on quickly so I can get out of there. This is exactly why I want them ready to go when I arrive. I don't want this nonsense! Coming to the door, never knowing if things will be nice or not. She just continues to swear at me,

"You what Carrie, if you're not happy, go and seek legal advice. I'm doing my best. Not only am I sticking to my side of the order, I'm doing your part too!"

"Get the f*** out of my house!!"

Chelsea wants to take a toy that Carrie brought her,

"No, you're not taking it"

Chelsea starts crying,

"Oh, just take it then! I don't care anymore"

A routine of limited contact is set, with Carrie "too busy" most times to see the them. She requests them to be dropped to her after school today, but I tell her it's too out of the blue.

I'm sure she thinks I just sit around waiting for her,

"I'm quite busy, I've got a lot on. Adam isn't very well either. He's been poorly during the night with a sickness bug"

Concerned about Adam, she asks how he is. I'm joking, she didn't. As if she would ever be concerned! Even though I know she would never be, it annoys me every time that she's not, '

'Oh, I just won't see them then. I'm going away for the weekend'

Is she trying to make me feel guilty? It will be my fault she doesn't see them?! The quicker she learns of her own guilt, the better.

She texts at 2pm asking to come to the house to see them instead. Explaining all over again about Sofie and Andrews feelings-

'I only wanna come for an hour. What's the big deal?'

'Sofie and Andrew feel it's a big deal. We must think of and respect their feelings. They will do things in their own time. I feel that letting them work on it, in their own time, will help them make more progress. I work with you when you want to see the kids'

"I don't want to argue but I need to see my kids and if Sofie and Andrew don't want to see me, then they should just go upstairs'

I'm not surprised by her disrespectful and cold response. Has she forgotten that Sofie and Andrew are her children too? There's no trying to build back a relationship with them-

'I have never stopped you from seeing the little ones',

with her stating her 'need' to see them, like I've prevented it-

'You see things so differently to me, Carrie. You shouldn't have to come into the house anyway. You told Chelsea on Sunday that you would see her after school Wednesday, but you didn't arrive. You pick and choose when you want them and it's unfair. I work hard on a routine for them and I help you when I can Carrie. I'm not bitter and angry, so there is no need for us to argue. I'm not being unfair. Me jumping when you say jump isn't fair'

A lie, I am bitter and angry, you can't help not feeling that way, when having someone like Carrie to contend with-

'Can you at least phone me so I can talk to them, my phone credit has run out'

She seemed calm on the phone. Mostly sounding put on or there was possibly people around her,

"I will text over the weekend and when I do, can you call me? I still won't have any credit"

In my head, I said 'No I bloody well will not, don't buy any wine, buy some credit' but out loud it was,

"Yes of course"

Low and behold, the weekend passes and there isn't a peep from her, until a text five days later, asking for me to ring so she can speak to them and if she can have them for a few hours Saturday and Sunday. Saturday morning brings a short text of-

'Hi ya, is it ok to bring kids round bout two as over slept damn it thxs'

Fifteen weeks since her leaving, her erratic time schedule with the little ones seems to be how life will be from now on. Disorganised. They are just fitted in whenever it's convenient for her or whenever she's bored. Her lifestyle has no time for children and it takes first place, with the little ones on standby.

I'm guessing she doesn't like the little ones talking about me when in her care, I use the word 'care' loosely,

"Daddy, mummy says you're stupid. I don't like her saying that"

"It isn't nice to call people stupid but don't worry about it"

On Andrew's birthday, we get a text late morning-

'Hi ya, I'm ill and gotta wait for doctor to come round, so there is no way I can get to yours to give Andrew his card, can you let him know that I got him one and that I'm thinking of him and wish him a happy birthday, please can you also give love to others thxs'

I don't reply to her text straight away because we're out at the roller-skating ring but when I do, she wants me to give the children her love and she will drop Andrew's card off when she's feeling better.

There was no mention of me going to collect the card. Something I was waiting for her to say. Carrie wonders why Andrew and Sofie are so adamant about not wanting anything to do with her but her actions justify their feelings. They see her constantly let the little ones down, why would they think they would be any different?! She wants me to help with their relationship but she doesn't give me anything to work on. I can only advise and listen. I can't force them into feeling different towards her.

Ok, Carrie isn't well. I'm not well, I have a chest infection and a sickness bug, which Adam so lovingly shared. Yet, I still forced myself to make sure Andrew has a nice birthday. It's what you do. It's what a parent does!

I know she's selectively forgetful at times but surely, she still knows our address, it couldn't be posted? I find it strange that she hasn't asked me to collect it. I don't believe she's in the area.

Later in the day she mentions the card again-

'There is money inside if he wants it but don't worry if he doesn't, I won't get my hopes up'

Still not asking me to collect it! As a mother, you would want your son to have it, no?! I wanted to test her, to prove myself right. There is no such card! Mentioning money later in the day, I know she knows, that Andrew would never accept it off her. I know that if I said I would come and get it for him, she would tell me she's too ill. I would get to hers and she wouldn't even be there! She ends the text-

'I would like to see the kids Saturday but only for five minutes''

How weird and utterly pointless! Easy to read like a book. In her head she's saying the right things when, in fact, she's being calculating, using the right words to wriggle out of her truth. She had better things to do, she always has. Regardless of being ill, anything to do with the children is not a priority to her. There's even no contact Saturday. She knew I wouldn't drop the little ones off for a measly five minutes and I knew she wouldn't ask for them again. She was never planning on having them! Situations are always worked out in her favour.

chapter twenty-one

Illness vs parenting is quite a challenge. I would love to just leave this duvet over my head and sweat out the germs. With children to look after, a business to get back on track and a cooker that is desperate for a bit of elbow grease attention, I want to shout out "Oh, can you do it" but there's no 'you'. Every parent finds it, energy to push forward. I believe we have a reserve tank especially for these occasions. Unless you're a parent like Carrie. They do have a reserve tank but it's purely for their own needs. Carrie's tank is used for college and socializing.

She has Chelsea and Adam for a few hours but soon calls for their pick up. Chelsea's crying in the background again and I'm told to bring clean clothes for Adam because he's had an accident. Before I get there, she calls again, agitated, wanting me there "right now".

Adam isn't happy and won't use her bathroom. I can't work out if she sounds like she's not coping or she's had enough of them. Or is it both?! When I get there, Adam is wearing a nappy, which I'm not pleased about. He doesn't wear them anymore. He's been doing so well with toilet training in the last two weeks. I settle Chelsea, who seems to have conflicting feelings. She wants to stay but wants to go home. I get given the soiled clothes as I leave, told to wash them.

I think it's a mixture of both. An hour or two of parenting is enough for Carrie. Not only because it's all she can stomach, all she can cope with but it's all she wants. When she wants it, that is. They are a chore to her, a tick off her busy to-do list, with them both always at the bottom of it. University, friends, drinking and partying are higher than them. My to-do list is the complete opposite. The children are always first.

On Chelsea's second parents evening, I make sure Carrie knows not to plan on staying at the house beforehand, that I will meet her at the school. This brings her coldness forward again,

"They should just get used to it"

"I'm going to continue to support what they want. I cannot force them to forgive you. No one can and no one should"

Carrie doesn't sound that bothered about Andrew. Her attention always focuses on Sofie and we talk about when Sofie said she would rather go into care than be with her mum. This statement alone highlights how Sofie feels towards her,

"I cannot show Sofie, or Andrew, that their feelings are unimportant and just tell them to go upstairs!"

Sofie's feelings are nothing, they have no stature where Carrie's concerned. Nor Andrew's. To her, this is nothing more than an obstacle in her way, stopping her from entering the house. She's angry, angry at the older ones' feelings towards her, that are stopping her doing as she likes.,

"Well, maybe Sofie should go into care so she knows what it's like!".

We don't hear from her again for a few days, even though she tells Chelsea she will phone and pick her up from school. Chelsea didn't remember or maybe she's just getting used to Carrie's broken promises. She texts me Saturday asking how they are and will call later. There's no later and it doesn't affect the little ones because I didn't tell them anything about it.

Any communication from Carrie now is nothing more than goodwill gesture. It's hard for me because I know how much Chelsea loves seeing her mum but sometimes, most of the time, she gets a mum she doesn't want or need and all this topsy-turvy contact and temperaments are confusing her. The only routine, the only thing set in stone, is Carrie being Carrie. Like I keep saying, like this story shows. Carrie is all about herself and always will be. Her behaviour is the only thing that is consistent.

She has them one afternoon, eventually. She cooks them dinner and agrees they will be ready for me to collect at 6pm so I can get Adam to bed at his usual time. A few minutes before I leave, she texts-

'I'm still dishing up'

This is added to her 'shouldn't be a big deal' list. There's nothing wrong with it being so late-

'You can just give them a quick bath and put them to bed'

This is how a part time parent speaks because as soon as she's fed them, they leave. She's not the one who has to rush about and get them settled. Simple parenting makes it easy for her to talk utter nonsense. I wonder, when she's a qualified social worker, will she advise parents the same techniques are hers?!

It's a week before we hear from her again, late in the evening. It can't be to talk to the little ones because she knows they'll be in bed-

'How are the kids? I will call tomorrow to arrange to see them. Also, I have a new mobile phone being delivered to yours. Can you let me know when it arrives'

I bet if the phone arrives tomorrow, she will have the kids and it'll be 'oh can you bring the phone too'. Let's see if I'm right.

She calls early evening the following day. To arrange times? No, of course she doesn't. She asks if her mobile phone has arrived, which it hasn't yet, then reminds me to let her know when it does. She does ask how the children are though, she has to. Caring only of the phone will look too obvious otherwise. The call ends because she is "tired" and she will see the little ones tomorrow. Which she does. She's up bright and early and I half expect her to say she's spending the day with them. She wants them at 2pm but I have to collect them at 5pm because she's going out.

"Can't do them dinner because I'm going out"

"Can't have them because I'm busy"

"Can't have them because I'm ill"

"Can't have them because I've got no money"

Can't as opposed to 'don't want too' more like! Why doesn't she just be honest and say she doesn't want to be a parent. I've known it all along, I would hardly faint if I hear it. If anything, I would applaud her for being honest for once in her life. The little ones, however bad this will sound, are better off without her. All she seems to be doing is keeping up appearances. Limited appearances or using contact for other means.

Like when she asks to organise the school holidays. This starts off the conversation. This is her keeping your mood levelled and friendly, then she slowly eases in her true intention. Softly does it, so her attempt doesn't stand out like a sore thumb. If 'I be nice', 'he will be nice'. Choosing her moment, she asks me for more rent money. I have calculated to date that she has had £1800 from tax credits (unlawfully claimed, I might add), £200 for her car, £8000 from her student loan and £5000 from me. That's nearly £15,000! Not to mention she gets another £4000 from her student loan in May. Yet she wants money from me?! Not getting what she wants, she causes a row asking when will I let her see the kids,

"Whenever you're free Carrie, you just let me know"

"I'm always free"

Another word she needs to look up in the dictionary! The kids will always be nothing more than bait to throw. Always resorting back to them, using them, when her true nature is questioned. Her time with them is decreasing rapidly and Chelsea, especially, is noticing it and questioning how ill mummy always is. I struggle mentally with Carrie, so god knows what their little brains are making of it all.

She seems to have them a bit longer than normal when she's been so caught up with herself. She has them 11am-4pm on Thursday and when I get the children home they say they're hungry. I tell them dinner will be soon but Chelsea says they haven't had any lunch, only some chocolate. I ring Carrie and question what they've eaten and she tells me the little ones weren't hungry.

They had breakfast at 8am and they weren't hungry until they arrived home with me?! I don't want to question Chelsea and I don't feel like I need to either. Chelsea would not tell me something that isn't true. Carrie tells them she will see them Saturday but there's no contact when the day arrives.

A tick-list text comes next, relaying how ill she is and she will call the next day to arrange to see them and to give them her love. The next day arrives, a call from Carrie doesn't.

Following one day of contact for four hours, Carrie's then out of the picture for a further nine days. I get short texts about being 'sorry' and that she's 'ill, again'. There's also a text saying she's £400 short for her rent and will contact 'tomorrow'. Tomorrow is any day where Carrie's concerned. She resurfaces and sees the little ones 2pm-5pm because she's 'going out'.

Two weeks go by and its 'radio silence' until a text comes through-

'I haven't been feeling well. Could you drop the kids to me tomorrow?"

She really must think we put our life on hold for her-

'It needs to be a different day. We've already made plans'

"Ok, I will text Monday when I have my university work sheet"

I won't be waiting for the text.

I let Carrie know that the kids have been poorly and Chelsea is on antibiotics. She calls and she sounds very sorry for herself instead,

"I want us to get on better so Sofie and Andrew can see it and it might make them talk to me"

"There's no 'us', I'm not doing anything to halt the process. I don't rant at you out of the blue, I don't cause upset. How can I get on better with you when you have a different personality every day of the week?!"

"Maybe all of us could go out somewhere together?"

"I'm sorry but that isn't something I'm keen on. I don't want to spend time with you. Not in the way I think you're implying"

The little ones see me friendly towards their mother, I'm not the one that needs to work on things. As for the older two, they are at an age of understanding the situation, they are happy with how life is. I've said to them that, if at any point, they decide to want to call or see Carrie, they can. Today is also Sofie's birthday and on hearing Sofie's gifts, motherhood is thrown out of the conversation, with her changing the subject to having no money and that she needs a job. She puts the phone down on me.

Life always brings you the same lessons until you actually learn from them. This happened before. She left for greener grass, soon coming back, but things are different now. Extremely different now. I don't care if the grass she chose turns to a bog infested pit, she will never be back in this house and never have me back.

Seeing the little ones the following day, she agrees to keep them in the warm because they are still a little poorly. Apparently, she is also. She says she will text at 5pm but doesn't, so I ring to see if I should leave to pick them up yet. She answers the phone and is walking back from town. Adam is using an inhaler for his breathing, walking to and from town was a ridiculous thing to make him do and when I get there his breathing sounds worse. It's cold and damp outside. Keep them in the warm, how difficult is it?!

"Chelsea was moaning that she wanted to go out and they both made a lot of mess at mine"

How naive does she think I am?! I believe they were moaning and making a mess and Carrie couldn't cope with it so she took them to the play centre to let them run around. So she didn't have to deal with them. She knew I was unhappy with the little ones looking out of breath and not too well and she agreed she noticed it too but insisted,

"They were ok earlier".

Disappearing again, she has no contact with the little ones for over two weeks but I do get text-

'My phone was stolen. I'll let you know when I'm free'

Carrie is ALWAYS FREE, that's what she said. She really is a joke! Three days later-

"I'm ill again. Will make it up to them"

She does, in her way, they have dinner with her then it's later relayed to me, by social media, that she's been out clubbing for a few days. Clubbing stands for illness. She then gives them a little dose of her time, four hours in fact, then she's a ghost again for ten days but texts-

'I'm too busy. Give them my love'

I don't because words are not want they want or need. Why would I want my children thinking 'this' is what love is?!

A few days later she texts to see them-

'Could you also help me fund my living this month? I've got no money'

She really is a despicable being-

'No I will certainly not fund your living'

'If you don't help and I lose my flat, I will have to move back in with you'

I ring her on her threat and I'm abrupt. I will not cower to her anymore,

"You have had more than enough money to live on and if you've been irresponsible, you've had eight months to find a job"

"I have every right to move back in"

My tone next should assure her that this is not true,

"I WILL NOT and CANNOT let that happen and I WILL NOT allow the children to go through any more pain!! You're selfish Carrie"

"You should help me. You work, get help from tax credits and live in the house"

"Yes, I get government help but that's to help support me and the children. I work to be able to live in this house. The house is being paid by me. You contribute to absolutely nothing"

"Be f****** grateful you have the kids"

It saddens me when she speaks like this, like the children are my possessions. They may be to her. She eventually puts the phone down on me. I later get a text to say she will pick them up tomorrow and that she will never ask for my help ever again. I'm wary of them being with her. I'm wary most of the time but the longer Carrie doesn't get what she wants, the more of a monster she becomes. Giving her want she wants causes mess, not giving her want she wants causes mess.

She firsts changes the time. The little ones are ready to leave but she cancels and makes the time later in the day. When I collect them from her, they're not ready and I have to wait around. Twenty-four days go by and the only contact she makes is one text saying-

'Can you lend me £54'

The answer is an adamant 'no'. The second-

'Can you give me a lift to the doctors? I can't breathe'

'You should ring an emergency doctor or go to A&E'

It is not my problem and I know she's playing me. I'm not falling for it.

Three days later she's miraculously better, 'supposedly' on antibiotics. I know she's trying to gain control of me but each time she tries, I slip out of her fingers. Things are different now, however she is not.

When she next wants to collect Chelsea from school, I tell her she's a tad poorly today but if she's ok tomorrow, she can,

"If she doesn't go to school, I'll come to the house and see her"

How many more times must I tell her! Ok, the older two wouldn't be there but I don't want her in the house anymore!

"You're not helping me with contact with Sofie and Andrew"

"I have spoken to the them! I've made sure I know their feelings on it and the more I ask, the more it upsets them. They don't want me to keep pestering them so I've stopped"

I'm getting the feeling that it has nothing to do with the older ones. She wants to be able to come to the house for me. I inform her, and really hope that she takes it in this time. Regarding me and her, I feel nothing. On hearing this, she ends the call.

chapter twenty two

Carrie's amicable the day before Chelsea's birthday, texting asking what our plans are. Not hearing about any plans Carrie has, we went ahead and made arrangements but, mirroring her friendliness, I ask if she wants me to drop the little ones off to her in the morning for a few hours-

'That would be good. I haven't got a present for her as I have no money, but that would be great'

All the kids are up nice and early and Chelsea is really excited. She opens her presents and I get them ready.

"Daddy, what are we doing today?"

"Well, you and Adam are going to spend a bit of time with mummy first and when I collect you, we will be going out for a surprise"

Chelsea is happy, I'm happy.

Ready to take them to Carrie, I call her and it takes a few tries before I get through, with her eventually answering saying she is still sleeping,

"Can I have them tomorrow instead? I feel sick and I'm really tired. I'd prefer to have them all day tomorrow"

"Oh ok, well, we have a dinner reservation booked for tomorrow but I can bring them to you at 4pm?"

She's wide awake now and certainly doesn't sound ill while she's swearing at me down the phone,

"Carrie, what's your problem?"

"You just play the f****** good guy! What if I wanted to do her dinner?"

"What? Not once have you mentioned any plans for her birthday but, ok, if you really want to do her dinner, I will change my plans"

"I have no money, how am I supposed to do her dinner?"

Causing a problem for no reason then, I think to myself.

"Anyway, I don't want to discuss this now. We will talk about it tomorrow and I'll ring to speak to Chelsea later"

This woman really does makes my head spin!

I'm even more confused when she texts, later in the day-

'Sorry for this morning. I've only just woke up. Don't know what's wrong with me lol. I could sleep again and I feel so sick'

I worry about Carrie's mental state all the time but I find, when I do this, a sound mind action later appears. I just don't know. She's, allegedly, so ill yet social media sites show her out partying so is this her just trying to gain sympathy from me?! Getting me to be there for her like I was there for her before, when she eventually ended up in hospital?

She asks for money again, saying she can't feed herself. I laugh because she's unaware that social media is painting a different picture. She had Chelsea and Adam for a few hours the other day and said she couldn't give them dinner. Not giving her the chance to ask for money, I tell her their dinner will be prepared so it's not a problem. The internet showed she couldn't feed them because she's went to a BBQ.

Carrying on via text-

"If I become homeless, it will leave me no option other than moving back home, which none of us want'

She is full of demands and has conjured up her own high horse,

"I will start the divorce and send someone round to value the house. I don't want things to turn nasty. You've broken the order and as for the £5000 you gave me, it is not legally binding so it doesn't count. The residency order is for the kids, not me and because I'm still your wife, I am legally entitled to move back in. If you've changed the locks, this is illegal for you to do so also"

Someone's been surfing the internet again, I see! Nit-picking at the law, grabbing hold of anything she can find. What works in her favour, totally oblivious to the fact that her behaviour alone, counteracts anything,

"Because I haven't had a sleep over with the kids and it's stated in the order, you have therefore broken it"

She sees things one way and one way only,

"Carrie, Chelsea wanting to come home the time the sleepover was meant to happen, doesn't affect the order or show my disobedience towards it!"

She needs to stop researching ways to dig herself out of her hole and focus on why she's in one in the first place! Everything is a domino effect due to her parenting skills, or lack off,

"Because you didn't personally give me the £5000, that it didn't come out of your pocket, that shows it's not legally binding"

I want to be clever with her and ask for the money back so I can give it back to my mum, then I'll give her it. It should make her feel stupid, but it wouldn't. She would just come out with something even more stupid but in her head, she's making total sense. She has a deluded way of thinking, especially when she then says she will also go for a contact order for Sofie and Andrew!

She wants another £5000 from me and full of audacity,

"If you don't stick to the agreed amount, then I shall go to court and ask for maintenance payments, due to my circumstances and not living in the custom as to what I was, when living with you. I don't want this to end up in court, however, I do have rights and I'm fully aware of them. You should meet me half way for a change. Instead of doing things under your terms"

"Carrie, I shouldn't have to take the kids to you and pick them up, I'm going more over half way!"

"No, this is called - doing what's right by the children so they get to see their mum. You're determined to destroy me but I think You're a reasonable father in my eyes and I only want what is fair"

Wow!! She really is something else. She doesn't want to go to court? Oh, I do! Very much so! I'm done! I do not have to do anything she says. I choose to do sometimes, to keep the peace, in hope that the order we set will work but it clearly means the same as the others. Nothing! She's crazy!

"Carrie, you signed the order, it went through court. A judge stamped it. A judge had to agree to it before allowing us too. You can't get much more legally binding that that!"

This woman has her own law, she is her own judge and jury so there's nothing more for me to say other than tell her, I will speak to my solicitor. This merry-go-round she has us all on is exhausting. Apparently, her solicitor will be contact with me. Good luck with that, I say to myself.

I inform her straight away in the morning that I sought legal advice,

"There need not be any communication between us Carrie, until this is resolved but you're welcome to ring the little ones at any time"

"Ok, I'm going for full residency. Be prepared to spend a lot of your mum's money!"

The thing is, she wants my mum's money. That's her ultimate goal. She knows my mum will do anything to help secure the safety of her grandchildren and crazily believes that money would be given to her because she is cheaper than court proceedings. Yes, I have borrowed a lot of money so far, a ridiculous amount of money, but that was because of how quick the children needed to be brought back home when she took them. Like I said, there was no time for legal aid, filling out forms and sending them off. There is now! My paid solicitor will be soon signing off.

She's obviously read on some internet page about 'wives and their rights'. I find this absolutely absurd. A life they are accustomed to? Someone needs to shut down these pages. Is this type of law prominently carried out? I've heard about it between celebrities. Big high-end earners but really, is it necessary and fair? Spousal maintenance payments. What has marriage come to?! Earn your own way, for Christ sake! If there's a type of living you want, get off your back side and obtain it yourself.

Full of stories, Carrie texts-

'I have evidence that you have emotionally abused the children and I will bring everything to court with me'

I imagine her turning up with internet pages she's printed off, no doubt full of highlighter pen strokes. She is going to be very shocked when she sees what's coming in with me! I don't need to sieve through the internet finding politically correct truths, that I can squeeze myself into. A bit like those toys children play with, where the shapes have to go into their right sections. That's what Carrie's doing. A triangle forcing her way into a circle, causing damage. I am full of my own truths, real truths and honesty, I'm not stiff or tense, recklessly trying to find something I can hold onto and use to my advantage. My shape fits in all the slots.

Most of everything that comes out of her mouth is mirrored. It always has been. Putting onto me who she is. I believe her reality is distorted or she is just a despicable woman.

Her tedious texts continue to come through, about how ill she is, how sorry she is that she hasn't seen the little ones. She texts one day and I'm super busy. Running around after the kids because it's the school holidays and I'm organising clubs for them. I don't want them stuck in all the time. I love that they enjoy coming out in the van, when I'm doing drop offs but I don't want their school holiday diary to be filled with mainly that. Clubs will do them good. As much as I'd love too, I can't stop working. Weekends with no work is easier and keeping them amused then is easier too but work in the week brings in money to make these days happen.

As much as I want to ignore Carrie's contact, I know I can't. Not yet anyway. Not until I know the next step regarding court so text her letting her know I'm busy. She phones, I know she's not going to like it,

"What clubs are you organising then?"

"Gymnastics"

"I'm going to make sure all the schools have my contact information"

Maybe she thinks I'm lying,

"The clubs are private, not run by the school. They have to be paid for. You're more that welcome to help contribute to their fee"

Ignoring my words and having the conversation lead her way,

"I'm busy Wednesday and Thursday"

I really despise talking to her, in fact, the very sound of her voice disturbs the hell out of me. Her patronising tone seeps down the airwaves and into my ears and has the same effect as a sour sweet does on your taste buds,

"Ok, just let me know when you're free"

"Right now,"

She just wants me to jump but I am too busy jumping for my kids.

She phones the following day but Adam won't talk to her. She has a rushed conversation with Chelsea and tells her she will pick her up from school tomorrow. Once their chat is finished, I take over the phone and stress to her, wasting my time really, that she shouldn't tell Chelsea things like that, if she's not certain, because I'm the one that has to pick up the pieces when she doesn't turn up. It's not fair on Chelsea being 'lead up the garden path' all the time and her schooling, especially, is showing signs of her confused mind.

My appointment with my solicitor goes well. We discuss the divorce but Carrie wont hand over the marriage certificate, stating it's with her solicitor and wont hand over their details either to retrieve it. I'm advised that because Carrie hasn't stuck to the order, I can ask her to keep contacts to just the weekends. My diary is showing erratic contact in the week and, though rushed, more contact at the weekends.

True to form, Carrie rings to say she can't pick up Chelsea from school after all. I let her know the changes that will happen in our circumstances and again, true to form, she's rude and powerful,

"I will turn up at her school whenever, regardless. I want any mail addressed to me at yours too"

"Carrie, I strongly advise you not to come to the school and cause trouble, I will ring the police"

I drop her mail off, like a whippet. A quick post through her letter box and I'm out of there but then she texts asking me for it. Using is as an excuse to start, she wants the little ones round hers after school. I stand my ground, she isn't having them in the week anymore. I have a good solid routine in place with them, with all the children. I'm done giving her chances that she doesn't deserve. Her sporadic contact is counteracting our peaceful way of life. She knows this and loves the upheaval she causes, regardless of the negative impact she's having on the little ones.

On another chat with my solicitor, also getting a second opinion from social services, I decide and I'm agreed with, that a contact centre is the best way forward. I want to limit the contact between me and Carrie because I know I'm the reason why she plays up. It's all about me, not the children. She still wants me on that rod of hers and the more times I'm not on it, the worse she behaves. She has contact with the little ones for two reasons. One, to get at me, to use them as her pawns and two, for her show, to feel like she's doing her bit, that she is a 'great mother'.

Hearing of our next steps,

"I will still turn up at her school and I will bring evidence to court, background evidence, on your family!"

She sees no wrong in her doings. I really do believe, that she believes, she sees the children all the time and is the perfect role model. She believes her own lies. Her illness, medical history, in the past, made her forgetful at times. This was due to her B12 deficiency but could this turn someone into a pathological liar? I've seen a change in her mental state again. From when she left to now. Well, not a change, a certain trait surfaces from time to time. She's like a roller coaster. Up and down. Up and down in temperaments. What's clear is, when she doesn't get what she wants, that scary roller coaster keeps on climbing. A contact centre will be safe and secure for the little ones and be safe for me too.

She in full swing tonight, her texting fingers are out-

'I miss the kids. You are not complying to the court order which means you could be held in contempt or even committed to prison'

She's obviously heard from my solicitor because she goes on to say,

'Your concerns regarding my ability to care for the children are unfounded. I urge you to rethink what you're doing'

Her tone, should she had been speaking rather than texting, shouts out authority. She can easily swap between a commoner and someone of high educational intelligence.

'Carrie, the court order has never been stuck to. From the first week, you were due to have them overnight, Friday to Saturday but you never made contact. The school holiday dates are to be agreed no later than the 31st March. Again, you've only decided to mention it recently. The court order was breached a long time ago and as I have now taken advice from my solicitor, the police and social services, this will go back to court and a contact centre is the quickest way of you seeing the kids. Until then, you can call to reassure yourself of their well-being. Again, you are making unnecessary threats. A new court order is needed'

'You are now preventing me from seeing my kids at all, can't you see how unreasonable you are being? I only want what's best for our kids and surely you can see, that stopping me from seeing them is not best for them. Obviously your solicitor is not giving you very good advice cos all that matters here is our kids and I have only eva wanted things to be wot you agreed to in tht order'

'Carrie, by the way, I have not breached the contract from the moment it was in place'

She really does talk a good talk. Text a good talk, I mean,

'Carrie, we are going around in circles. You have never tried to stick to the order. It clearly states, there can be other contact agreed by both parties, which is what I have been doing. I have texts from you, threatening all sorts. I don't need the constant stress you bring to our lives so a contact centre is better for everyone involved. I think it's best that, until a date is set, you only call on the days agreed to speak to the kids. This conversation is getting nowhere'

'I have stuck to the order apart from when things have happened beyond both of our control. To which we have both agreed alternative solutions for. I am doing right by my children. You're the one causing stress to them and me. I would never do this to you if the shoe was on the other foot'

No, she probably wouldn't. She would do a lot worse! She must be in a parallel universe. Where she's living out what she's saying. How can someone speak so truthfully untruthful?

chapter twenty-three

With legal aid in place, I proceed with a new lawyer and it could be three months before the current contact order can be reviewed. I propose to Carrie, through text, that she can have them during the holidays on a Wednesday and Sunday 10am-4pm. That way she only has to supply them lunch, something little. I'm happy to drop off and collect on Sundays but because of work, I can't on the Wednesday. I know she's not at university so it shouldn't be a problem. Should it?

'That is great. All I want is to see my kids, however, what does this mean regarding court? I am more than capable of feeding them lunch and dinner, just to clarify that. That is fine that you can't drop them off due to work but I also will be starting a job on Saturday and I am unsure of my hours so is there any way you could be flexible on these times and days until I know for sure?'

'How would you expect to stick to the order if you don't even know your hours of work, Carrie? This is what I mean, you want to use the order when it suits you, and when it doesn't you expect me to be flexible. If you are due to start a job tomorrow, you would have already agreed the hours you are expected to work. If it's with an agency, you can stipulate, you can't work Wednesdays and Sundays. You have caused a lot of upset and stress, yet again I'm trying to meet you half way. If you can't stick to Wednesdays then just stick to the Sundays. Either way, the kids need a routine and, for them, it needs to be kept too'

'I work at a bar but it's not full time, just as and when they need me. I'm not trying to be awkward. I agree that the little ones do need a routine but you are not their sole parent. A routine should be for both parents to decide and agree upon. It's you that is making this process harder for me'

If I was near a brick wall, I'd head butt it. She makes me fuzzyheaded and frustrated all the time. She just wants the easy route to parenting. The world must evolve around her. She fails to see, she's had the easy route many times before and she still has trouble with it.

She totally contradicts herself. The children need a routine but I have to be flexible. That's not a routine then is it. Certainly, not a routine they need. They need stability. Really, all they need is for their mum to say she's going to do something and she follows it through. How can I let the little ones have a routine of 'see her when they see her'? And why can't I get this through to Carrie? I don't want to work things out with her, I wish she disappeared from the face of the earth and was never able to cause upset ever again but I have too. I know what she's about and I know what she brings to the table. Disorder!-

'I remind you that you've broken the order regarding the overnight stays. The kids haven't got a routine because of your doing'

So again, I have to put her weird way of thinking right-

'The first overnight didn't happen because you didn't want it to happen. If you did, you would have phoned or text to arrange it but no, we heard nothing from you. You then agreed to stop the overnight contact until they were comfortable with staying because the second one didn't go very well did it! Me having to pick them up late at night. You didn't ask again until a few weeks ago and in the past, have only mentioned it in passing but never made contact to see it through'

She needs to stop lying and look back on her text messages. There is no need to keep mentioning the order, it is invalid now. We will await the new one-

'Carrie I suggest you get legal advice and to also be honest with them about the contact you have had with the little ones since you left and to also tell them I offered contact but you can't commit because of an unpredictable work schedule'

'Sorry, I refuse to keep listening to your lies and stories and sorry if you feel my work schedule is unpredictable, before I've even stated it is, so that's rubbish too. I will be in touch, now for the meantime, please leave me alone. I will have the kids on Sunday and, until I have been paid, can you please provide them with a packed lunch'

I'm surprised my fingers aren't bleeding from frustration. Having to be flexible because of her work shows it to be unpredictable. I'm on earth and she's up in cuckoo land! I'm fine with supplying lunch, my children need to eat but this was one of my concerns, that she's unable to feed them. I want the Sunday drop and collect to go as peaceful as possible. I ask her if we cannot discuss anything in front of them anymore. I want it to go smoothly, friendly and their time with her enjoyable-

'I have never said that my work is unpredictable, you're making it up as you go along. I would never not feed my kids, you are just using whatever you can to make me look bad but all your doing is clutching at straws and hurting our kids in the process. So, throw whatever you like at me, it won't hurt me, just our kids and I have never caused a scene when you have picked them up or dropped them off, I never would'

I imagine her getting disarrayed as she writes out her babble. She probably got all finger-tied and drop the handful of straws she was holding! This woman has a very selective memory. The police officer pops into my thoughts. Document everything, he said. He is a huge part of this process even though he's not around. I can be questioned on any chosen date and I'm able to relay EXACTLY what that day consisted of. Texts, phone calls, I am precise and that is why Carrie will never be able to place her dishonesty on to me, as much as she tries.

The Sunday pick and drop goes exactly how I wished it too, other than Carrie putting in a request. She wants to come off the mortgage but wants some money. Expecting her in the morning, Wednesday, but Carrie's a no show. I get a text from her later in the morning-

'It is gone 10am and the children aren't with me. What's going on?'

INHALE. I remind her of what was said about Wednesday-

'Oh I forgot. It's all this messing around with the contact order, it made me forget that part. I've done my back in and it will take an hour to get there because I can't move about fast. Can you drop them off?'

INHALE MORE DEEPLY!

She's soon irate, when I tell her I have made arrangements around this morning's pick up to ensure the children were ready on time and no, I will not drop them off. I'm going nowhere near her's, complete opposite direction, in fact. I should have left already. Three customers have phoned asking my whereabouts. Staying in waiting for her was dumbfounded on my part-

'You're taking the p***! I only forgot that I had to pick them up because it was something you agreed, not me. You're making demands that I must adhere to. I do not agree to see them Wednesdays and Sundays. I'm only doing it so I can see the kids. I won't be controlled by you anymore. I want to see them on the dates and times agreed on the order that was authorised by the judge. I am supposed to have them today and overnight until tomorrow at 6pm and that it what I want. You signed and agreed to it and you have breached it every time! And like I said, until a judge declares that order no longer stands then that is the only way I will back down. You do not decide our children's fate, we both do and it would be great if you could remember that. I will be picking the kids up at 3pm and I expect you to be in. If this doesn't happen, I will bring along a police officer to enforce the order'

'Carrie, please will you listen to what I am saying. That order doesn't mean anything anymore. You have failed to comply with it since day one. I am fed up with repeating myself. You would have been perfectly happy with this arrangement if I would have agreed to drop them to you but because I didn't, you're yet again coming back with threats. All because you haven't got your own way. I have spoken to the police and my solicitor and they both assure me, they will not get involved in any of this as it is a matter my solicitor is already dealing with. You are unable to stick to any regular contact. Last week you wasn't even sure of your hours. You think I'm playing games when I've just simply had enough of your relentless demands and threats'

'Until a judge tells me otherwise, you must have the kids ready for when I turns up'

One last attempt, but really, I'm just sending texts for the sake of it-

'Carrie, the contact you had with the children was mainly on a Sunday, that's why I suggested that day. My diary shows it's more consistent than any others'

I am trying my best to make this dysfunctional headache work. Does she turn up to collect them? Does she heck! She speaks for the sake of speaking and texts for the sake of texting!! She just loves getting her 'lay the law down' fix!

The next Sunday contact day arrives and the little ones go off to hers with their packed lunches. When I arrive to pick them up there is no answer at the door, so I call her. They are still at the beach and I have to drive to where they are. When I get to them, both Chelsea and Adam are upset because they haven't had a drink and are hungry. On the way home,

"Daddy, I'm hungry. Mummy shared our packed lunch"

They had a child sized lunch, obviously. It wouldn't have been enough to share with an adult so no wonder they're hungry!

Wednesday comes and the little ones are ready. We wait. We wait some more but there's no sign of her. A text comes through in the evening-

'Sorry, I had to work. They called me the night before to arrange it'

This, to her, makes reasonable sense. She wants to show that it was out of her hands, that she didn't pick up the kids because she didn't want too.

One tracked mind. This type of excuse happens when you are selfish and lying because any normal parent would had received the call from work, then contacted the other parent to let them know about the change. She should have called or texted. You would want too, wouldn't you? Make contact so your children aren't left standing about waiting for you? but again their shown their mum isn't a certainty. When we're ready to goes to hers on the Sunday morning, she isn't even home-

'Sorry, I stayed at a friend's house out of the area. Could we make the drop off at 12pm?'

The days where she isn't in contact are so blissful and organised. We've get to have a lovely few days Carrie-free. She's like that Monday feeling. I dread her.

I will not alter my plans. I don't mind compromising but I'm not having her dictate how my life should run just so hers runs better. Why would someone make themselves be out of the area knowing they have their children in the morning? I've made plans with family a few days ago, I'm not cancelling. Can you imagine the uproar if I did this? If she was waiting and I said what she said. She would go mental!

Again, no one can say no to Carrie. If you do, you need to be prepared for a lashing-

'You really are pathetic, you know you will be in. Why can't you be reasonable for once? You won't win!'

'Carrie, you knew you had the little ones this morning but you chose to not be home. Perhaps if you could realise this is your doing and accept it, we could all get on with our day'

'You have decided and changed all these times of when I see the kids. This is not what is in the contract we agreed too. Which still stands in place. You have dictated everything to me and if I can't agree to your terms, you punish me with our kids. You do not make the rules. I'm running late by a couple of hours and now I can't see them until Wednesday'

'You can't even stick to two days a week! Let alone what the order states! This is your doing! You knew you had the kids and you are the one who is not home. Do not blame me for your incompetence. I am not here to be a taxi service later in the day, all because you chose to stay at a friend's house and not be home in time. This is entirely your doing! We have somewhere else to be and need to get ready to leave soon'

'Yes, I can stick to two days. We have a legally binding contract which you keep breaking. You can't change the days and times on me like you have so I am not legally doing anything wrong. You have the inability to stick to the contract'

A contract that is in the bin, scrunched up yet she keeps pulling it back out, straightens it out and relays it when she needs a cover up. It's legally binding, it's not. It is, it's not!

I stand my ground and end the conversation asking if she will be phoning the little ones later-

'Yes, I will, like I always do'

Does she really believe what she says, that it happens how she perceives it? When the new order comes through, I will enlarge it to poster size and ask her to stick it up on her wall. Ringing like 'she always does', what garbage! She wouldn't know what truth was if it smacked her in the face.

Adams 3rd birthday falls on the Wednesday and my fingers are crossed that his day goes ok. Low and behold, Carrie arrives at 9.20am to collect them. When they have had time with their mum, we are going out for a birthday meal. Something we always do, as Carrie knows. She doesn't look in the amicable mood so I'll text her later. I want to remind her of our reservation booking and ask that they be back on time. Expecting a miracle, no doubt. I don't fancy having that chat face to face.

I text her, ending it with a 'thankyou' but she just texts back-

'I will do my best'

I knew it wouldn't be easy, there always has to be something. I don't want to annoy her while she's with the little ones so I keep as civil as I can-

'We both want Adam to have a lovely birthday, don't we?'

'I never said I wouldn't get them back on time'

I want to phone her and shout down the phone "YOU SAID YOU WOULD TRY YOUR BEST!" Antagonising, all the god damn time. I don't, obviously. She texts back-

'Though, it is a long way for the kids to walk and they were moaning about it so maybe its best if you pick them up'

I hear her childish giggling jumping from her words. She said to me the other day that I need to let go of the bitterness I have for her. Every single thing she says can be placed in my mouth. This annoys the hell out of me more, her mirrored actions. It's so frustrating, It makes my brain scream.

She calls me at 3.10pm to pick up the little ones,

"They're tired"

"This isn't on Carrie, if you can't stick to two days, picking them up and dropping them back, how on earth are you going to stick to anything"

Her defensive and 'do as your told' tone surfaces and in arm's length of the kids, because I can hear them,

"F*** off and drop dead"

She puts the phone down on me. It's more like she's tired and had enough of parenting today. Someone that stresses so much about seeing her children, now wants to get rid of them early. This shows the difference between me and her. I would enjoy every single minute I had with them. I would make sure I used up those every second of our time together.

I get my shoes on, feeling like I'm still doing as I'm told. Of course, I'm going to go and collect them, I can't not, but it's little things

like this that give Carrie her glory. Marie is here for Adam's birthday meal so we all go to get the little ones. We can then just go straight on to the restaurant. Before we get to head off, I get another call off Carrie but when I answer it it's Chelsea crying,

"Daddy, please come and get me"

I'm now super worried and on edge because she wasn't crying when I heard her in the background. I don't know if she's crying because of what Carrie said to me or she's crying because Carrie's said something to her, took it out on her when she put the phone down. I've never driven so quick!

Chelsea looks very nervous and has been crying hard because her face is read and her eyes are sore and Adam looks lost. I can sense straight away that Carrie is raring to go, so I first swoop the little ones up and put them in the car. I then go back to Carrie, who's standing regal, nose up in the air like some monarch. I want to pin her up against her door and get right up in her face, just like she used to do to me. She scans the street and when she sees Marie,

"AND DON'T BRING YOUR SKANKY SISTER WHEN YOU PICK UP THE KIDS"

"Carrie, you need to take a good hard look at yourself", and I walk away.

Sunday arrives. If it wasn't for a rooftop terrace party, Carrie would have burnt my ear off already but no, she's too busy drinking and making a spectacle of herself. Social media can reveal a lot about a person, especially their whereabouts. Especially if you love attention like Carrie does and have things posted so anyone and everyone can see them. Why hasn't she phoned to see if Chelsea was ok after their last encounter? Why hasn't she phoned, screaming 'contract' at me? This Sunday was never going to happen anyway, not after her behaviour the other day and there's only one reason why she hasn't called to concrete the little ones visit for today. She's too busy indulging in her single, no dependants, lifestyle. Something she so greatly loves over anything and anyone else.

chapter twenty four

The order we put in to place was pointless but I'm not regretting it. It made her leave the house. Social services advice should have enticed her but money was more appealing. Before long, that 'waiting' came back. Our time, our routine way of life is so calm and peaceful until she surfaces. We were back waiting to see what kind of day we were going to have. The only good thing was she wasn't in our faces anymore but the bad thing was, she was in Chelsea and Adam's still. I don't care about myself, my brain is rational and able to set aside her nonsense after a while but young minds like Chelsea's and Adams can't do that. They don't understand, they just feel. I played it safe with the order, extended an olive branch, so to speak, giving Carrie a chance to prove me wrong. For Chelsea's and Adams sake, I wanted her too but Carrie will always have the life she desires. She discards of anyone, including her children, when they are no longer useful to her.

It did cause a lot of stress but I feel I did my best to try and make things orderly but it is just impossible to make life better when you have someone like Carrie you've got to work alongside with. How do you make someone 'parental' when they constantly show you that being a parent isn't their number one priority? It's her way or the highway and if you don't play along to her rules, she will do her upmost until you fall back into line. Exactly how she used Sofie and Andrew, is exactly how she uses Chelsea and Adam. Life with her is like a board game. No matter how ahead you get, you will always end up landing on the snake and going back to where you started.

The only way you get to see if you can win, is if you keep on playing. You keep rolling that dice. I believe we win if we're meant too, if we deserve too but sometimes you've got to play tactical. Small-scale actions that serve a larger purpose. My sole purpose is to secure the well-being of my children and I will keep 'playing', until I accomplish, just so.

Going by her behaviour on that Sunday, until a judge tells me what happens next, I'm allowing Carrie to still see the little ones but I've made alterations to, hopefully, limit any discomfort for Chelsea and Adam. They eat before they see her, I hardly talk to her face to face but if I do it's short and civil. I don't stay around long enough for her to bite. She's now been given notice to leave her flat and must do so in two weeks and, honestly, it couldn't have happened at a better time. Funny though, she had known the situation with her landlord for quite some time yet she still gave me grief about the little ones' sleepovers. She wanted them to be regular? What, until she was homeless?

Her repeating herself to me that she has no money and, soon, no fixed address, gave me just cause to make alterations that she couldn't possibly try and fight me on. I would now, as long as the little ones were comfortable and willing to do so, drop them to her at a park or meet her at the play centre and pay for them to go in. I was comfortable because I knew there was no way Carrie would cause a fuss or be her normal detrimental self, while in the company of so many people. She would play the doting mum to the audience around her.

Amicably, for now, she agrees to ring the little ones three days a week. Mondays, Wednesdays and Fridays. More fitting, the days should be called When I want, If I want and Maybe I won't. She seems to be playing nice and court is on the horizon. Maybe she believes a month of pleasantries will erase her past behaviour.

She asks me if she could take Chelsea and Adam to her mums. WARNING - My parental alarm bell went off straight away! Her voice became muffled and was replaced with a loud buzzing. Not over my dead body! I remember what happened the last time she went there, so there is no way I was going to agree to it. Carrie's mother also had the nerve to ring me one evening. Talking to me like we are best friends, like family. I haven't seen or heard from this woman in over a year yet she spoke to me like we needed a 'jolly good' catch up. Asking how the kids were, when all I could think of was, did she not care how the kids were last week or last month or last year even?! It seemed a bit too coincidental.

Carrie goes AWOL for a week, coming back with toothache as her alibi but she will have the little ones down the park. I feed them first before they leave and no sooner than I drop them off, Carrie asks me for money and gets annoyed when I don't hand any over. She needs cigarettes and still believes I should support her. She thinks her words are solid proof but her online activity is saying differently. She is working, I've seen photos and conversations all about it. She was not impressed getting a telephone call from the C.S.A, who, supposedly, told her, because she is a student, she does not have to pay any child maintenance. Suited her just fine,

"I might as well stay a student for as long as possible then"

Telephone contact with the little ones is still sporadic but she seems very consistent and 'not busy' whenever wants to contact me, and me alone. I get story sized texts yet the little ones get just a five minute chit-chat. One evening she gets annoyed at me for putting Adam into nursery. Something she knew about a while ago. Her memory is so vague. I think she just purposely forgets stuff so she can give me aggravation. She threatens that she will find where he is and take him out of nursery. I informed the police and they advised me to not give her the nursery address and that they would call to have a discussion with her.

I think she just likes disturbing me, she gets a thrill from it, it makes her feel good. She never, ever rings on time either. She's supposed to call before their bath time but I know she calls late just to be finicky. I'm bathing the children, I'm not going to run downstairs to get the phone and I will not take the phone with me upstairs. All this did was give her ammunition to slate me as a parent. I believe she rang late for her own ammunition,

"You're lying! They're not being bathed at all. You're controlling my life through the kids and you have no idea how much you're damaging them. I feel sorry for them. You will have a lot of explaining to do to them when they grow up. Good luck"

Apparently bathing children wasn't plausible. They play out in the garden, they paint and do arts and crafts. Why is it so surprising that they are bathed every night?!

"Carrie, none of this has anything to do with you or control, it's simply a routine they have. When will you realise that! I am not in the slightest bit worried about explaining anything to them because it is very clear, to anyone, who is telling the truth. Just try and stick to the three calls contact, the rest can be resolved in court. Call to speak to Chelsea and Adam and that's it. Don't call me or text me again, just to have a moan because things aren't going your way"

A couple of days later I hear from her again, wanting my tax returns and mortgage statements. My solicitor is having trouble sending her documentation as she isn't being represented by anyone so I can't see why she would need what she's asking for.

"It's not for my solicitor. If you are not able to provide this, then a summons will be placed upon you, which is out of my hands, hence why I am asking you myself instead of you receiving a phone call"

The internet surfboard is out!

"Why would I get a summons and from who? Carrie, this has got to stop. You can't keep threatening me with various actions. I am not financially responsible for you! And I have given every piece of fundamental information to my solicitor to work on the divorce."

"We are still married and I am still your wife, therefore, although you do not like it, my finances are yours and yours are mine, until we divorce"

The divorce. Can you imagine what that is going to bring?! I can! Carrie will want, and believe she is entitled to, the shirt off my back. I wouldn't be surprised if she tries putting a tariff on the very air I breathe. What is spoken about mostly, in turn, is what's more important. She didn't even ask how the kids were. If she did, she would have known Adam was under the weather.

So much so, I had to rush him to hospital a few days later because he was struggling to breathe. Since Adam was born, he experienced breathing problems, especially when poorly. The doctor, back then, said it was too early in age to be diagnosed as Asthma. It was a Friday so when a call comes through from Carrie, I miss it. He is given a nebulizer but it made no change so the doctor proceeded with a steroid inhaler and after a while it his breathing settled. He was ok. My little trooper. The doctor sent him home with the steroid inhalers and advised that if he gets cold or cough symptoms again, to use the inhaler before it's able to turn as severe as it did.

I call Carrie the moment we leave the hospital, apologising for missing her call and explained the reason why. She went straight in on me, shouting that I should have phoned her. I accepted she was right but I was never not going to call. The only person that was on my mind, at that moment, was Adam. Getting him to hospital. Then when I was speaking to the doctors, they were only on my mind because I had to listen to them,

"You should have called me the moment it happened"

"I was more concerned with helping him breathe Carrie!"

Getting Adam home, she calls again,

"You're a liar!! I phoned all the hospitals in the area and none of them have a record of Adam being admitted. You are a disgrace and you are sick"

Even her friend, who she's with, joins in the conversation, saying the same. Both of them shouting the odds. This bad father, making up an illness, what a disgrace.

So, this 'disgraceful father' heads back to the hospital, explains the situation that he has with the mother of his children and obtains proof. I send Carrie a copy of his discharge papers, with an imaginary middle finger stamped to it!!

A mother so shocked and worried at the thought of their son being in hospital, decides…….. not to call for a while. But when she eventually does,

"My phone was broken. And anyway, I would call every night to speak to them if I was allowed too!"

Letting her own comment run up the flagpole,

"You're welcome too Carrie"

Ironically, there are no calls for a while again. Which seem to tie in with university restarting. Has someone received their learning funds and are too occupied?! It looks very likely because when Carrie does get around to phoning, she tells Chelsea,

"Mummy hasn't called for a while because I had an emergency but I will call again later"

Later never arrives, but Chelsea questioning her mummy always lying, does.

I get a random call from one of Carrie's friends, one evening, apologising. It is alleged that Carrie was sofa surfing and causing havoc in their home. When being told about her lack of respect, a row broke out. Carrie did not like being told to pay her way and it escalated into the police being called and Carrie being removed from the property. The friend was saying sorry to me for all the bad things she had said while being under Carrie's illusion. The story sounded too similar, too precise, to not be true. Getting the gist of it, it sounded like Carrie wanted this person removed from their own house. She apparently scratched up her own arms and wanted the police to penalise her friend for it. Carrie never mentioned this, not for a long time anyway, she supposedly lost her phone charger and was unable to call. Bored of hearing lie after lie, I brought it up but her recollection of the event was mirrored.

She wants to arrange having the little ones for Christmas but I don't see how, when she has no fixed address and anyway, Christmas is two months away. If she hasn't got anywhere to live, I'm certainly not going to allow the children to go to any of her friend's houses. If I agree with her, she will just say she will let me know nearer the time and If I don't agree, she will just curse me down the phone for being unreasonable. What can I say other than stating the obvious?! It is pointless making plans right now! She just hurts my head with her conflict for the sake of conflict,

"They need me as much as I need them. Court didn't give you residency of the little ones, I did! There is nothing I want more than to go to court. I will never be out of your lives for as long as my children are still breathing"

"I think it's about time you speak to someone because what your brain relays to you, is not what is happening in reality. It doesn't compute that you go weeks without speaking to them. Carrie, if our roles were reversed, I would move heaven and earth to see my kids. Let's be honest. As long as you continue as you have been, you will be out of their lives"

"You're the one with mental problems! The only thoughts I have, 24/7, is my kids and I pray they don't turn out like you"

Telephone calls are barely happening now, though she does call Christmas Eve and mentions presents to Chelsea and she keeps doing so. Her limited calls, now, are due to her 'working'. She continues to constantly apologise but shows no want in trying to fit them into her life. The longest there isn't contact for, is four weeks, with Chelsea saying mummy isn't very nice, but she does manage to text me back when I ask for her address so Chelsea and Adam can send her a Mother's Day card. At first, she doesn't want to hand it over, she thinks I'm trying to find out where she is, that the card is a ploy. She eventually says,

"Well, it's not like I'm trying to hide my address from you".

Some of what she texts later doesn't make sense and I question her mental state again-

'If I was mad, I wouldn't be able to go into the profession I am. I study law as I am a student social worker, it's part of my profession. I am on the board of nationally recognised social workers. I wouldn't have been allowed on the course and I have had all the relevant checks required. People in glass houses shouldn't throw stones and your house is very thin'.

chapter twenty five

We finally get a hearing in May. Standing up in court, I watch her incognito and I listen with jaded ears. She tells her story, I relay the truth. I don't need to 'word things better' or think about what I'm saying. My words are confident because they have nothing to hide. The judge asks Carrie,

"What it is that you want and how do you feel about things"

"Regarding the house, I would like……"

The judge stops her,

"We are not here to discuss those matters"

"Ok, erm, I want to go back to the original order that has the overnight stays"

"Your honour, I can't go back to that. I don't know where she's living, only that she's out of the area, not to mention her saying so herself, that she has no money and struggling"

I could see how annoyed Carrie was getting. Her mouth was twitching, listening to what I was saying and what the advice from CAFFCASS was. Me and CAFFCASS had identical views. The hatred for us was written all over her face. She really wanted to swear and shout, I could tell. She was trying her hardest to hold in any outbursts.

The hearing was quick and precise.

RE: The hearing

You will recall that the matter was dealt with initially by an interview with both yourself and Carrie, separately with the relevant CAFFCASS officer. Although I do not propose to rehearse exactly what the officer said in her brief written report, it was fairly obvious that she, like you, had concerns about contact continuing out in the community and therefore made the interim recommendation to the Deputy District Judge, that contact should be limited, for the younger two, to a contact centre. As for the older two, the judge indicated that he would not be prepared to make any formal order for them but you agreed, as part of the order, to try and encourage them to go along, if possible with their younger siblings, to the arranged contact periods.

Although Carrie is not represented, it is quite clear that she wants a lot more contact than this and preferably for it to be taken out in the community. Although she is not settled, it seems on a final position with regard to future contact, that she would want contact to increase, particularly, when she has finished her current degree.

When we went into court, the judge had obviously read the recommendations of the CAFFCASS officer and while Carrie indicated that she wanted more contact than was being offered, she was prepared to accept what was being recommended pending a full report.

It therefore follows that contact was set out in the following way and agreed between the parties:-

1. As soon as the referral has been completed to the contact centre, contact will take place almost certainly on alternate Saturdays for three hours at a time for the younger children.
2. Carrie will have the option of ringing your mobile phone every Tuesday and Thursday between 5.30pm-6.30pm so she can speak to the children. In regard to this, can I suggest that you keep a note of any missed telephone calls.
3. Lastly that you will agree such other contact, as may be convenient between the two of you.

The CAFFCASS report that will be prepared will also include a wishes and feelings report in respect to Sofie and Andrew. This is very important once the children become teenagers, as clearly their views are very significant in determining whether the court sets out any further order for contact.

As for Chelsea and Adam, I suspect that while their views will be taken into account, ultimately it is a matter for the court to determine whether it is in their best interest to have contact with their mother. Depending on how the interim contact goes. Clearly the next few weeks will indicate how committed Carrie is to the future contact arrangements.

I did indicate to you that the CAFFCASS officer will almost certainly seek out your views and will wish to see you with the children, at some stage, at your home address.

Once we receive the CAFFCASS report, we will obviously send it on to you so you can do a Position Statement, in advance of the next hearing.

To date, you have been very good at keeping a record of the nature of contact that has occurred between Carrie and the children and also when she has been absent or of any excuses she has provided. Although I have no doubt that you will continue to do this, can you please make sure this is kept up to date as it may ultimately need to be placed in a statement at a later stage.

Signed. My Solicitor.

I'm still apprehensive but at least time with their mum now will be safe and secure, with me paying the centre fees. A month since the hearing, there were thirty calls that could have taken place, yet Carrie only made three and sent an excuse text of 'losing her voice'. On one of those calls, Carrie mentioned that she will see the little ones soon and she would give them their Christmas presents. She also mentioned a birthday present for Chelsea as the first contact session fell on that date but the day before it takes place, Carrie cancels. She is unable to attend because she "can't afford the travel costs". It is then rescheduled for two weeks later.

No cancellation was made this time so I prepared Chelsea and Adam, letting them know we were going to see mummy. Seeing recent photos of Carrie on social media, I phoned the CAFFCASS officer and explained how different Carrie looked, the last time the little ones saw her and on seeing her again, I didn't want her appearance to be a shock. They agreed that Chelsea and Adam would benefit seeing a photo beforehand. When I showed them, they didn't even recognise her, asking who this photo was of.

Chelsea wanted to look 'pretty' so she wore one of her favourite dresses and I did her hair in plaits. Adam didn't seem fussed, he seemed to just follow Chelsea and just wanted to be with her. When we got to the centre, the workers were inviting and friendly but Chelsea was nervous, more so when I told her I would not be there, when they spend time with their mum,

"Daddy, I don't want you to go"

"Don't worry princess, you will be ok. The lady we spoke to is just like your teacher at school. She's daddy's friend. She will be here with you and you can talk to her about anything at any time. I will be back before you know it"

The session time came and went. The workers called Carrie numerous of times but were unable to reach her. Close to an hour we sat there for. Carrie didn't show up or make contact. I was so angry, and hurt for Chelsea and Adam. It was a big thing for them, coming here today, especially for Chelsea. I would have preferred another cancellation, rather than making the kids travel all that way for nothing! It was a total waste of time and energy and emotions. Chelsea was in tears! Even the centre workers were disappointed. I cuddled her,

"It's ok, It's ok. Hey, we have time to go and get an ice cream now before we head home"

I didn't know what else to say. I wanted her to know it wasn't a big deal, that lots of nice things override the bad but of course it was a big deal. How could Carrie do this? Where ever she was, how could she know that her children would be waiting for her, waiting and waiting and not have a shred of decency to lessen their suffering?

Chelsea soon cheered up and got over it. I think she's learnt that these types of days are normal and, yes, they hurt a bit in the moment, but they are soon forgotten about. I believe Chelsea knows the weight of things. Happy moments are more consistent than these horrible mummy incidences.

Due to booking out the room, I still had to pay for the session. I resented handing it over because of how the day unfolded but it wasn't the centres fault. I understood why they had to still charge me. It wasn't their fault, it was Carrie's. They asked if I wanted to book another session. Absolutely not! They understood my answer too. I was not going to chance putting the kids through this again. The first session failed and the second one failed, I wasn't going to go for 'third time lucky'. The first one I let slip, at least she had the heart, a word used loosely, to cancel but this second one?! There was absolutely no need for what happened. As soon as I got home, I phoned my solicitor and asked him to send an update to the judge so he was aware, in advance, of the recent development and change, before the next hearing.

I told Carrie a long time ago that 'it' all looks better on paper. When she would have declared how much of a good mother she is and that it was me who was the problem. Leading up to next hearing, she makes no contact with the little ones. It's been ten weeks and six days. Yet she was more than capable conversing with Citizens Advice, who were sending requests and statements back and forth to my solicitor. She even failed to attend her first appointment with CAFFCASS.

On the next hearing, Carrie turns up at court and has changed drastically in appearance. I knew what she looked like already before seeing her that day because I have a photo album dedicated to her but in person she looks worse. She's extremely thin, thinner than I've ever known her to be and seems to have aged rapidly too. I can't bear to look at her and when holding the door open, to be polite, allowing her to enter the court room first, I had visions of slamming the door in her face. She stands in court and disputes everything I say and is adamant she tried to attend the second contact session.

'I deeply regret not being able to attend the contact session and understand how much of an impact this had on our two youngest children. However, I did do my upmost to attend the appointment. As I did not have the address, I was therefore unable to find the location. This was due to either misplacing the address or not having it in the first place. I arrived at the train station and on the contact centres website, it said that the location was around the corner. However, I was still unable to find it so I then called the centre using a payphone but was unable to get a reply. I left a message asking for someone to return my call immediately as I was trying to find them. I stayed in the area looking for the centre for forty-five minutes and then I left. I did not receive a call from the centre until two days later. This experience really saddened me as, not only was I looking forward to seeing my children again, I also knew they would be looking forward to seeing me. I knew how upset they would be....

... I have not had any recent contact via telephone with Chelsea and Adam. This has been due to my financial circumstances, whereby my mobile phone was cut off. I have not had any funds to be able to continue the telephone contact. I understand this would have been a confusing time for them and regret that I have not been able to speak to them. I am currently homeless and staying on a friend's floor, which is not an ideal situation, however, this friend stated that they will let me borrow their phone, until I am able to buy credit for my own. I am seeking employment in regards to my financial crisis until I return to my studies. I am currently doing everything in my power to ensure that my life and circumstances are more settled, in order to support myself, thus being able to support our children. This has been a very traumatic time for me, not being able to see my children, as indeed, it would have been for them. I believe in order for my youngest two to be content and happy in their lives, they need both parents to be amicable, and to be able to reasonably communicate, to promote their security and well-being. I will do whatever it takes as I only have their best interests at heart and this goes for all four of my children. I understand Sofie and Andrew have stated they do not want contact with me and although this saddens me, I will put their wishes first. Therefore, I hope contact continues with Chelsea and Adam so that I am able to prove that I am, and will always endeavour to be, the best possible mother to my children'.

Oh, bravo, bravo! A round of applause and a standing ovation for Carrie! What you have just read was sent to the judge prior to the court date and she reiterated every single word in front of him. Everything that comes out of her mouth has discrepancies. The contact centre says different. They stated, the main centre that calls are placed, is unoccupied on a Sunday but that no message was left on their answer machine. They were confused as to why Carrie said she had difficulty finding the centre because they are directly opposite the train station, in view, as is their sign.

I refused to pay for any more contact sessions, telling the judge I am done! That there's nothing more I can do, or want to do. I inform him I have evidence that contradicts everything Carrie has said and continues to say. Carrie then states she can prove she's telling the truth. The hearing was adjourned until the beginning of January, with the judge stating he wants everything in front of him. Full CAFFCASS reports, my side, Carrie's side, my evidence, her evidence. Only then will a final ruling be made.

A long time ago a man told me to document everything. A long time ago I was disheartened, and left feeling that I had to prove the words that were coming out of my mouth, even though they were being screamed from my heart. Because of that man, this very story that you are reading right now, exists. I have three months to put my case together. I am telling the truth and I will prove that I am telling the truth.

Leading up to the final hearing, Carrie makes a handful amount of calls to Chelsea and Adam. A child sized handful! Most of the time she is having a conversation totally different to them. She would say "I miss you too" or " I love you too" when a prompt was never giving from the little ones. This showed me, Carrie had spectators around her. Playing out her little act for her flying monkeys. When the conversation ran smoothly, not weird, it seemed Carrie struggled to know what to say sometimes. This happens when your 'heart isn't in it'. There would be pauses and it wasn't a natural sounding conversation, sometimes automated and simple. There was always a reason, as to why she hadn't called. It didn't even seem like the little ones were talking to their mother, sometimes not wanting to talk to her at all, uninterested and getting bored quickly. Most often than not, both Chelsea and Adam would say 'bye' first, ending the conversation mid-way.

Waking up in the morning, Armageddon had arrived. The last battle between good and evil, the day of judgment and I was ready. I had done everything in my power to prove myself as a father, as a parent. The main factor in all of this, Carrie's behaviour is not healthy for my children and if I can't get that through to her, someone needs too, and fast! My evidence folder is seven inches thick and consists of every bit of truth you could possible obtain. Every single text message, phone call, recordings, my diary, school reports and most importantly, what speaks louder than any words I could say, the photo album dedicated to the mother that "will always endeavour to be, the best possible mother to her children".

For every time she said she was too ill to see them, there is a photo of her out partying instead. Every time she said she had no money, there is a photo of her at a festival or event. There's a photo for every single lie that has come out of her mouth. For every lie she has told me, every lie she has told social services and CAFFCASS, the judge and the kids, there is proof. One photograph shows that while Chelsea and Adam waited for her to attend the contact centre, she had better things to do. Something more appealing than seeing her children. A boat party was worthy of her attendance more!

I stayed up for hours!! I learnt her patterns. She, actually, got citizens advice to query how I obtained the photograph that was shown to the children prior to the contact session. A letter was sent to my solicitor-

'Our client is concerned about this in the context of the domestic abuse perpetrated by your client in their relationship'.

Every photograph is shown to be of public viewing, like I said before, ANYONE could see what I was seeing. Evidently, there was one incident where a photo of her was posted by a nightclub itself, then later deleted out of their page's album. Carrie, under the impression that she can sneakily hide, yet I got hold of that photo before she even had a chance to tell them to delete it. Carrie loves attention, she made it easy for me without even knowing so.

How can you tell a CAFFCASS officer you can't even afford 20p for a phone box then be seen at a festival that's £45 to enter?! The reason for her drastic change in appearance was because she was out clubbing way into the next mornings. One club, in particular, opens their doors at 3am and there was Carrie, partying the morning away. Mostly working, handing out flyers, beforehand. My solicitor was told that she isn't technically working, just working to pay off a debt. How can you acquire a debt to a night club? Maybe her bar tab was extremely high? CAFFCASS requested drugs and alcohol tests after a photo surfaced that was untoward. Which I'll add, no such tests ever took place.

Now, at the finale hearing, It was my turn for the judge to read my position statement-

'It is with much hope, yet sadness, that I write this position statement giving reasons as to why I strongly believe Carrie's relationship with her children is detrimental to their well-being. Carrie had displayed for many years now, her lack of care and any form of consideration that her actions have on our children. She has verbally abused them, often using foul language and threatening behaviour. She has continually put her own needs before those of our children. Drinking heavily, abusing drugs, going out and not coming home until early hours or the following day. She has shown over many years, that she is capable of going long periods of time without any form of contact with them, a factor that remains true to this day. Everything I can present, shows that her actions are clearly not of a mother who is desperately trying to be the best mother she can be. She has never contributed towards our children, either emotionally, financially or physically. In the past I have done my absolute best to enable Carrie to be a mother. It was very apparent that when my money would run out, so would her contact with the children and this is how it has stood for the past two years…..

….. There are many reasons why I firmly believe Carrie is incapable of being a mother on any level. We are currently under the 3rd contact order, showing that even the first two were not enough to make her be one. It is obvious to me that she is a compulsive liar and while being so, shows no signs of care that this constant behaviour has on our children. I only want the best for my children and to protect them from what Sofie and Andrew have already gone through. We have a quiet, loving home with stability and encouragement, in which the children thrive on. I wish, whole heartedly, that my children be left to be raised in this way, undisturbed by their mother's fickle actions'.

Speaking to the judge, when asked what I wanted,

"Your honour, I want control of this. If I feel like, in the future, Carrie has bettered herself and it would benefit the children to see her, I want the right to be able to make it happen. At the same time, if I feel she is no good and could damage them further, then I want the right to be able to prevent it from happening. I don't want them to not have a mum, my words are not said in malice. I just know, in my heart, that it is better, in their interests, to not have a mother like her"

I had my moment, I said and presented everything that concreted my plea. The judge heard me and he also heard the recommendation of CAFFCASS. It was final and it was over.

The court orders that:-

1. The children continue to reside with their father until their 18th birthday
2. The applicant father's application, for a prohibited steps order stand dismissed because an order is no longer required.
3. The respondent mother's application for contact stand dismissed

I guess you are wondering what evidence Carrie provided, the proof she said she had. He didn't ask her. He couldn't. The 'best mother' who loves her children 'so much', the mother who wants everyone to know that I am the cause of every piece of hurt, wasn't standing in front of the judge. Carrie did not attend the finale hearing. She is, and will always be, the coldest person I have ever had the displeasure of knowing. I could never put into words how relieved I am now that winter is finally over!

reflection

It felt like I had to stick to a rulebook, that I had to work my way up a parent ladder, where by getting to the top showed I was worthy. I hope, in my lifetime, I get to see father's possessing the same rights that a mother holds.

I'm left with feeling like my parent title, my truth, cost me heartache, misery and stress. Oh, and £40,000. Would I do it all over again? Yes! Should I have had too? Absolutely not! A parent shouldn't have to spend an extortionate amount of money proving themselves.

When will the law understand that things need to change? Men should get automatic rights from their child's birth, like the mother does. It is equal participation, is it not? We both create the life. The only difference between us is the mother has to carry the child. Nine months should NOT give a mother a lifetime of power over us. We deserve automatic rights too! Us not having it gives a certain type of woman the power to put us in the back seat.

It's this kind of double standard, the hurdles I came up against, that made me determined. I was never going to back down. Not only did I become strong willed to secure the welfare of my children but I wanted to prove that mother and father have no difference other than spelling. Different words, exact meaning. Parent! I just wish, mentally, I was able to do it a lot sooner.

It's been a year since the final court hearing and Carrie is non-existent. She's no doubt enjoying her 'no dependents' lifestyle.

She could have quite easily left us alone years ago, without hurting any of us but narcs don't do that, do they?! They stay their course, for their fix but when you take their fix away, you are no longer needed. Carrie knows her reign is over and she's slithered off, possibly finding a new target. I wish them luck, that's for sure.

All of my children look like they are breathing better. Especially Adam, who has now been diagnosed with Asthma. Stress can do so much inside damage, you don't realise. It can make you unable to function on a daily basis. The simplest of things become major factors. I know what stress did to me. I couldn't work, couldn't focus and was always on edge. It was no different for the children.

Chelsea's character retreated, very noticeable at school. Her little head was, no doubt, so confused and at that age they're not able to put things into perspective. She slowly became inwards and withdrawn, like she had her own little corner to sit in. Just like her daddy did. The more contact she had with Carrie, pushed her backwards and the less contact she had with her, pushed her back even further. She would seem to peep her head up at life, still a little nervous and take a look around. When feeling it was safe to come out, she did. I think this goes for me and all the children. Chelsea would get back to her normal self and showed no signs of wanting or needing her mum. She was happy until that one call would come through or drama would start and she was back to the nervous little girl again. At home she was fine, I think, being around people she felt safe with, made her able to shrug her mother's ways off, but at school, when she was on her own, away from us, she was very anxious.

I found Adam maybe understood the situation more than I thought, though Carrie didn't seem to cause as much of an effect on him than the others. For someone so young though, he is quite tough. The only behaviour difference I noticed was when they returned after Carrie took them. He started to spit. I'm not a psychologist either so I don't know if it was due to anxiety or anger towards the situation or it was just something he picked up being in her company or whoever else was around him. He got very close to Chelsea though, sticking close to her.

I often thought about recording their time with their mum. Babysitters are watched sometimes, aren't they? The teddy bears that have hidden cameras in them, parents looking over their children while they can't be with them. I was always too nervous to ever do this, in case I got found out.

Sofie had and still has a lot of anger built up. It came to light that one evening, when Carrie was throwing her verbal cruelty, she said to Sofie, when she found out she was pregnant with her, she contemplated having an abortion and because she decided against it, Sofie should be grateful. Sofie says, out of all of the things her mother said and done to her, this is what hurts her the most. Andrew brushed Carrie off like she was nothing. His take on it all is like 'well, thank god that is over, let's get on with life now, shall we!'

Carrie made me feel that because she held the title 'mother', her and the children were a package. I wish I had the strength I have now, to understand back then that it was just an illusion. A two-way mirror but only Carrie got use of the observation room. She goes, they go, that was her clause, the only reflection I saw. I would never in a million years want my children to go and she knew that. She knew I was weak enough to be controlled by it. We hear about relationships breaking down all the time. The stories mainly end up with the father leaving or the mother leaving with the children in tow. Why is it so hard to comprehend that a mother should leave? That a mother can be the culprit of destruction.

It's hard for me to say I loved Carrie, once upon a time. My hatred towards her doesn't allow me to say those words in the same sentence as her name. Every time she brought me to tears by her actions, every single tear drop took any loving feelings for her with them. I will never forgive her, what she did, how she behaved or how she made us feel. I only have to forgive myself for not having the guts a long time ago, to stand up to her and be accounted for, on behalf of myself and my children. She sewed my mouth shut but I know I handed her the needle.

Why are us males not as open as females? Correct me if I'm wrong but, if you asked me where a man can go for help or advice, I wouldn't know. I didn't. Female guidance is more publicised compared to males. As a man, I never saw it possible to seek advice from someone, to sit and speak openly and honestly about my problems. Not only because I didn't know who would listen but if I did find someone, I'd have to let out all the emotions I was burying. Men don't do that. I was afraid of Carrie's manipulation skills, it made me embarrassed to say anything out in the open.

I'm guessing there's a lot of men out there that feel the same. I want nothing more than to give these men advice, have them learn from me but the only truth of my story, and it being a sad one, is 'money talks'. If I never paid to get the ball rolling, I don't know if my outcome would have been the same. Truth eventually won, not money but money did open the door for me. I just had to be the one that kept that door open. My foot was wedged!! The only advice I would give is exactly what I was told.

DOCUMENT EVERYTHING!! And the most important thing of all, please, please don't give up. Stand strong and know your voice matters. If you are one of those men, reading this right now, I hear you brother, you are not alone. That corner you're in right now, is not healthy. Trust me, I've been there. Stand up! You are only alone because your making yourself lonely. Do not tolerate harmful behaviour of any kind and don't leave yourself in the dark. Whether you have children or not and are in an abusive relationship, please know that staying will not do anyone any good. You think by staying makes life safer. It doesn't! I allowed Carrie to cause harm to me and my children. She had control because I gave it to her. I feed her narcissism appetite. Staying and putting up with it, gave her what she wanted. You have to understand that your life will not get better, living in hope. You have to change things yourself. Talk to somebody! It's ok to cry and it's ok to feel vulnerable. You are still a man if you do. There IS life beyond abuse of any kind but it won't come to you. You have to go out there and grab hold of it yourself. You can do it, you just have to believe you can.

I had such high hopes for my life, all I want now is to get back to the beginning, to start again. The reset button has been hit. The splinter has been removed and it isn't able to cause any more discomfort. My life was carefree, organised and precise but now everything is 'up in air' and needs bringing back down in an orderly manner. I am in such a financial mess and it will no doubt take a while to sort it but I will.

Me and the children will have holidays every year again, eventually, hopefully. This time enjoying them with Chelsea and Adam. I just need to find the balance between running a successful business and being a single parent. It's took a long time but I'm finally happy. Most importantly, my children are happy. That is all I have ever wanted. I don't think I will ever be able to earn what I did in the past but I will find that balance, I will get out of the red and I will do whatever it takes to make life a good one. I have too, I've pinkie-promised Chelsea and Adam that I will take them to Disneyland. We've sat down together looking through the family albums many times and on seeing Sofie and Andrew's memories, I promised the little ones that daddy will take them to great places too. It won't be any time soon. I see laundrette amounts of washing and ironing, school runs with festive performances, parent evenings, mastering girlie hairstyles (plaits I've mastered already), football tournaments and tea parties with teddy bears and you know what………..

I would choose all that over sunbathing any day!

message from the author

Thank-you for purchasing my book. This is my first attempt as an author so I hope I did the subject, in hand, justice. For a long time, he did not have a voice. It has been an absolute pleasure speaking on behalf of him and I hope I spoke for him well.

Your opinion is valued. If you could leave a review, we would be internally grateful. If you use social media, head over to Instagram (@aurora_seraph) We would love to see your posts about our book!

With Love - Aurora xx

DIARY OF A DAD

AURORA SERAPH

Printed in Great Britain
by Amazon